Doing HIS Time

Doing HIS Time

Meditations and Prayers
for Men and Women in Prison

†

James C. Vogelzang
With Lynn Vanderzalm
Foreword by Charles W. Colson

Doing HIS Time Prison Ministry—Santa Barbara, CA

Doing HIS Time: Meditations and Prayers for Men and Women in Prison

Revised, study guide edition

Copyright © 2008, 2014 by James C. Vogelzang. All rights reserved.

Photo of James C. Vogelzang copyright © 2004 by Robert C. Larson. All rights reserved.

Designed by Gerette Braunsdorf and Anna Piro

Edited by Lynn Vanderzalm

Published by Doing HIS Time Prison Ministry
PO Box 91509, Santa Barbara, CA 93190

To protect the privacy of the people who shared their stories with us, we have changed several names.

Unless otherwise indicated, all Scripture quotations are taken from the *Holy Bible,* New Living Translation, copyright © 1996, 2004. Used by permission of Tyndale House Publishers, Inc., Carol Stream, Illinois 60188. All rights reserved.

Scripture quotations marked NIV are taken from the *Holy Bible,* New International Version®, NIV®, Copyright © 1973, 1978, 1984 by International Bible Society®. Used by permission of Zondervan Publishing House. All rights reserved.

Scripture marked "The Message" taken from *THE MESSAGE.* Copyright © 1993, 1994, 1995, 1996, 2000, 2001, 2002. Used by permission of NavPress Publishing Group.

Printed in the United States of America by Cadmus, Port City Press, a Cenveo Company.

ISBN: 978-0-692-25536-0

19 18 17 16 15

11 10 9 8 7

To men and women in prison:

You are not forgotten!

Regard prisoners as if you were in prison with them. Look on victims of abuse as if what happened to them had happened to you.

Hebrews 13:3, THE MESSAGE

An author should never conceive himself [or herself] as bringing into existence beauty or wisdom which did not exist before, but simply and solely as trying to embody in terms of his [her] own art some reflection of eternal Beauty and Wisdom.

C. S. Lewis

Never water down the word of God, preach it in its undiluted sternness; there must be unflinching loyalty to the word of God; but when you come to personal dealing with your fellow men, remember who you are—not a special being made up in heaven, but a sinner saved by grace.

Oswald Chambers
My Utmost for His Highest, June 28

Contents

A Word from Chuck Colson

I have a pretty good idea of what is going through your mind as you pick up this book and flip through the pages. For although I was once Special Counsel to the President of the United States and later went on to found one of the largest Christian ministries in America, I was also prisoner #23227 in the Maxwell Federal Prison Camp. I served seven months, June 1974 to January 1975, not a long time by most inmate standards, but long enough to know the hopelessness and desperation prisoners experience.

The toughest thing for me in prison was not the occasional fights or the racial tensions or the rundown facilities, but the terrible aloneness. I had left a wife and three children on the outside, and not a day went by that I did not anguish for them and worry about them. I was trapped inside a prison; I felt utterly helpless. It was made all the worse by the correctional officer or official who told me, "Mind your own business, and do your time just the way you did your own crime." I had received a three-year sentence (which was later cut short), but it seemed like an eternity.

One cold October day, I was released early from my work detail. In the dormitory dayroom, I found a Bible study book entitled *Design for Discipleship*, published by the Navigators. The topic was based on the second chapter of the book of Hebrews in the New Testament. That day I read Hebrews 2:9–11 from the J. B. Phillips translation of the Bible: "What we actually see is Jesus, after being made temporarily inferior to the angels (and so subject to pain and death), in order that he should, in God's grace, taste death for every man, now crowned with glory and honour. It was right and proper that in bringing many sons to glory, God (from whom and by whom everything exists) should make the leader of their salvation a perfect leader through the fact that he suffered. For the one who makes men holy and the men who are made holy share a common humanity. So that he is not ashamed to call them his brothers."

As I read these words over and over, I had the conviction that God was speaking to me. I was in prison for a purpose. If Jesus could come and live among us, die on the cross for our sins, and not be ashamed to call us His brothers, we could know Him in the most intimate way imaginable, as Jesus our brother. And the men around me were my brothers. The thought staggered me—and also warmed my heart.

I had accepted Christ into my life almost a year before going to prison, but God seemed to use this occasion, sitting one dreary day in prison dayroom, to draw me into the closest possible fellowship. I found peace, yes even joy, inside that prison.

You can find it as well. God gives a free gift—faith. All we have to do is accept that gift and trust Christ completely. I can promise you one thing: If you do that—not overnight in all likelihood but in God's good time—you will sense that Jesus is your friend and your brother, closer to you than anyone you've ever known in your life. He understands our sins and temptations, our fears and our weakness, and He has provided for our salvation.

I don't care what kind of prison you're in; Jesus can knock those walls down. You can be free inside, and you can trust God for your freedom outside.

This book is written by one of my dearest friends. We go back to 1989, when Jim, who was a very successful businessman, started to take an interest in prisoners. I've never seen anybody get more excited about going into a prison and working with the men and women than Jim Vogelzang. When I would come to Colorado and visit Jim, the first thing he would do is whip out pictures of the guys he was meeting with and teaching Scriptures to. He fell head over heels in love with inmates.

Jim may have spent more time in prison that I did because he's been faithfully and consistently going back over the years. He's done it so much, he thinks like a prisoner and writes like a prisoner, and he's determined to bring hope to every prison in America. Jim is an amazing guy. When I was in the White House, Richard Nixon, who was then president, liked me because I was like him, the kind of man who would "walk through doors without opening them." That's why I got the reputation of being the White House hatchet man or the president's tough guy. And that's probably why I have so identified with Jim Vogelzang. He's exactly the same kind of guy—big, tough, walking straight through doors without opening them, if necessary, to bring Jesus to the prisoners.

This is a wonderful work that Jim has done. I have read the meditations and find that he has an uncanny sense for what you need to know day by day, not only to survive in prison but also to find the joy of Jesus in everything you do.

My hope is that this book will help you redeem the time. For me at least, the most painful thing in prison was the helplessness, the realization that I wasn't able to accomplish anything, that I wasn't in control. Some people, as you well know, go crazy just looking at concrete walls and having nothing to do.

Don't let that happen to you; it doesn't have to. Take this book, study it, study the Scriptures, and have the courage to live each day as a Christian. You will find that in the most amazing ways, God will redeem your time behind bars.

I say "have the courage" because being a Christian in prison isn't easy. If people come into prison and tell you that being a Christian will make your life in prison simple, you have my permission to throw your hymnbook at them. Prison culture is tough, cruel, and mean. The leaders are those who can press 350 pounds of iron—or so everybody thinks.

Through my work with Prison Fellowship, I've been in more than 600 prisons. I've met the toughest of the tough inmates. Believe me, pressing 350 pounds of iron is nothing. The really tough inmates are those who say, "I believe in this Jesus. I'm trusting my life to Him. I'm going to live the way He teaches me to live. I'm not going to worry if people mock me or laugh at me. I'm sold out to Christ."

That's being tough.

You can trust Christ. I've known Him since 1973. He is real. He is with you right now. He's not ashamed to call you His brother or His sister. Don't lean on your own understanding, but lean on Him. And know that there are many people on the outside—like Jim Vogelzang and others—who are laboring hard to bring help and hope to you.

Charles W. Colson
Prison Fellowship Ministries
Washington, D.C.
2008

Why I Wrote This Book

During my own personal devotional time one morning, the Holy Spirit spoke to me. The challenge was clear: bring the message of the Gospel to you—incarcerated men and women—using your language, your culture, and your circumstances. *How would I do that?* I wondered. The Holy Spirit told me to use Hebrews 13:3 as a guide—"Regard prisoners as if you were in prison with them. Look on victims of abuse as if what happened to them had happened to you."—and write as if I were in prison too. The command was to bring the living, transforming power of Jesus Christ to you in a way that would be uniquely understood. The Holy Spirit has been faithful to help me do that.

Why is this devotional book necessary? It's needed because, as you are keenly aware, the sky is not blue for those in prison. It may be green or purple, but it is not blue. A blue sky suggests normalcy. And prison life is anything but normal. Normalcy includes making decisions about our lives. Free men and women walk on the grass. They decide what time to get out of bed, how to dress, where to live, where to work, and how to spend their money. That's not the case in prison.

In prison, you are told when to get up, what to wear, when to eat. You are counted several times a day. Your name and identity are replaced with a number. Outgoing phone calls are monitored, the number of books allowed in a cell is limited, and power over your life is surrendered. While this is the expected result of being convicted of a felony, it creates an environment that is abnormal. How does the Gospel of Jesus Christ apply in these circumstances?

The culture inside prison is hostile to the teachings of Jesus. Jesus teaches us to "turn the cheek" and to "bear one another's burdens"; the convict code teaches us to "get the other person first" and to protect ourselves. Jesus preaches submission to authority; the convict code preaches rebellion. While Jesus says, "Love your enemies," the prison code says, "Get revenge" and "Deliver payback." Living the Word of God behind bars takes a special kind of courage that is strengthened by the wisdom of people who understand prison.

While I've never been convicted, I've spent countless hours inside, getting to know you and your culture, slang, rules of engagement, and other particulars of interaction. Many of you have read parts of this book and offered suggestions, helping me shape the meditations. My desire is to put in plain words the transforming power of Jesus in a way that can be clearly understood by anyone living in a world where the color of the sky is anything but blue.

How to Get the Most out of This Book

This book is intended to be a devotional that you spend time in every day. Each meditation includes several elements:

- A passage from the Bible about a certain issue like hope or prayer or fear or anger
- A meditation about that passage and the truth it sheds on our lives
- A question that makes the issue personal, helping us take action or make a commitment
- A prayer that helps us begin to talk with God about the issue
- A suggestion for reading other Bible passages that are related to the issue

I've also included many real-life stories of how God has shown His power through the lives of people. Some of these stories come from the Bible: Rahab, a prostitute; David, who was a murderer; Joseph, who spent years in prison; the apostle Paul, who was also murderer and who spent lots of time in jail; and Jesus, who provides a model for all of us. Other stories are about how God has shown His power in the lives of inmates in prison today, allowing them to serve Him in meaningful ways. I also share my own story of how I came to give my life to Jesus.

I suggest that you find a time every day to read one meditation, letting the passage and your own thoughts about it work their way into your life.

Using the Book in a Group

Some inmates will want to use this book with a group of other inmates. To help with that, I have included some "Study Guide" pages. You will find these sprinkled throughout the book. Look for pages with a black bar that says "Study Guide."

The study guides are intended to help people go deeper,

- to discuss issues and insights and struggles together,
- to explore further passages in God's Word together,
- to pray for each other and encourage each other, and
- to hold each other accountable.

Joining together with a group of other inmates can be a rich time of fellowship and encouragement. To insure that the experience is safe and meaningful, follow these guidelines:

- **Commit to confidentiality.** People will share honestly if they know that what they say in the group, stays in the group.
- **Commit to respecting each other.** Respect where each group member is in his or her faith journey. Never take personal advantage of what you learn in the group time together.
- **Commit to praying for each other.** Each time your group meets, take time to share prayer requests and to pray for each other. Then remember to pray for each other at various times during the week as well. Remember, God hears and answers prayer.

- **Commit to encouraging each other.** Walk with each other and hold each other accountable to stay faithful to what God is calling you to be and do.

At the end of the book, I've also provided an index of Scripture passages covered in the meditations. If you have a favorite passage of Scripture, look it up in the index, and turn to the meditation that discusses that passage.

How the Book Is Organized

The book is organized into different parts, with the meditations in each part focusing on a specific theme. Many of us have been influenced by the work of the late Dr. Bill Bright, who created a straightforward way of understanding the message of the Gospel in his "Four Spiritual Laws":

Law 1—God loves us and offers a wonderful plan for our lives.

Law 2—We are sinful and separated from God. When we acknowledge our sin and accept God's forgiveness, we will fully experience His love and plan for our lives.

Law 3—Jesus Christ is God's only provision for our sin. Through Him we can know and experience God's love and plan for our lives.

Law 4—We must individually receive Jesus Christ as Savior and Lord; then we can know and experience God's love and plan for our lives.[1]

These laws form the basis of the organization of this book.

Part 1: God loves us and offers us forgiveness for our past, peace for our present, and hope for our future. In this section of the devotional, we will look at God's immense love for each of us. Because He made us unique, He has a plan for each of us. We will look at what the plan is. This part focuses on the question, *Who is God?*

Part 2: We are sinful and separated from God. This section looks at our sin and what it does to our relationships. It focuses on the question, *Who am I?* We'll learn about people in the Bible who messed up—big time. We'll study passages about guilt and forgiveness and freedom from the weight of our sin.

Part 3: Jesus Christ is God's provision for our sin. This section teaches us what Jesus did when He took the rap for our sin. These meditations focus on the questions, *Who is Jesus?* and *What is salvation?*

Part 4: We must individually receive Jesus Christ as Savior and Lord. Through Jesus we can experience God's plan for our lives. This final part helps us understand the wonderful plan God has for our lives. These meditations focus on the question, *How can I live for Jesus?* This section of the book is divided into several smaller sections.

Jesus as Savior and Lord looks at what it means to know that Jesus has saved us and explores what it means to allow Jesus to have a place of authority in our lives.

Godly living is an exciting group of meditations that help us grow deep in our relationship to God and help us to show our love for Him by living in ways that please Him.

Godly service reminds us that God wants us to serve Him. The meditations prepare us to serve the Lord wholeheartedly within the walls of the prison. Just because our bodies are incarcerated, that doesn't mean our minds and spirits are imprisoned. We can have full and meaningful lives behind bars. God has a wonderful plan for each of us, a plan that is uniquely designed for how He made us.

Down Thirty-six Years—My Journey to Faith in Jesus

I was in prison for thirty-six years but never spent a day behind bars. My prison had no walls but plenty of anger, cruel abuse, and fear. I didn't have to trade my name for a number, but I gave up my integrity and honor for pride and greed. I was in a maximum-security facility known as "myself" and was enslaved to my own selfishness, self-centeredness, and rebellion against God. I am guilty of everything in my "jacket." I was never paroled—I was pardoned!

God is writing His story in each of our lives. Here's my story of how God loved me, pursued me, forgave me, and offered me real freedom to serve Him and to do *HIS* time.

I was born into a Christian home, but like many families, it had its share of problems. My mother was a female Dr. Jekyl and Mr. Hyde, meaning sometimes she was wonderful and other times she was evil. She was either telling us about the lordship of Jesus Christ and encouraging us to be the best we could be, or she was abusing me and my brothers and sisters verbally, physically, and emotionally. I grew up thinking that anger and hitting were a normal way of expressing one's emotions. Fear and terror visited me at night as I wondered if I would live through it or if my mother would make good on her recurring threat to kill me in my sleep. On those evenings, I went to bed with a chair stuck under the doorknob and a loaded twelve-gauge shotgun as my companion.

When I was growing up, my family prayed before meals and read Bible stories after dinner. I also went to church twice every Sunday and attended Christian schools. I memorized countless Bible verses and learned church doctrine at a very early age. I made a public profession of faith in front of my church when I was fifteen, but it was just routine—a way to please and appease my parents.

I attended a Christian college for four years but left that place without a personal connection with Jesus Christ. I had a ton of knowledge about God, but no personal relationship.

After college, I married and went out to plunder the world of riches to achieve financial independence. I didn't care who I used or what I had to do to milk society for what I desired. Whatever I wanted, I took. And if it required deceitful, sinful behavior to achieve my goals, then that's what I did. Yet, like my family before me, I attended church every Sunday, prayed before meals, and presented myself to the world as a Christian.

I was a fraud.

After fourteen years, my sinful lifestyle led to a serious decline in my marriage, and feeling I would be better off with someone else, I asked for a divorce. I didn't know it at the time, but my wife had been in counseling about our marriage. She told me she'd met Jesus. I mocked her, but as I observed her new behavior, I realized that something had changed in her. She was different. I watched her for several weeks and determined that the change in her life was real. Finally, several months later, in the dead of night, I shouted at God, "If you can change her, I dare you to change me!"

I look back and see the absolute arrogance of that "conversion prayer." I was anything but a humble seeker. I can visualize the archangels Gabriel and Michael standing next to Jesus, scoffing at my prayer and asking permission to send a thunderbolt down on me to get my attention. At that same moment, I can hear Jesus saying in reply, "No, I can save this one. I can clean him up, get the stink off of him, and use him for My kingdom."

And that is what He did. God loved me enough to salvage me. After thirty-six years in my self-centered prison, God pardoned me! I was set free.

Words from Psalm 73 fit my situation: "When my heart was grieved and my spirit embittered, I was senseless and ignorant; I was a brute beast before you. Yet … you hold me by my right hand. You guide me with your counsel, and afterward you will take me into glory" (Psalm 73:21-22, NIV).

God took me, a brute beast of a man, and held me by my right hand, guiding me with His counsel.

After my "conversion prayer," such as it was, I found myself thirsty for God's Word. I started reading the Bible. My wife took me back, and we prayed together. We found a Christ-centered church. Then, three things happened that confirmed my new life in Jesus.

While wiping the kitchen counter one day, I saw my pack of Marlboros lying there. I casually threw them away, thinking, *I don't need these anymore.* Since that day in February 1987, I haven't craved or smoked a cigarette. I never gave this incident much thought until a seasoned Christian man explained it to me. He shared that what happened was a manifestation of the Spirit of God (see 1 Corinthians 12:7). It was a sign that God now lived within me.

Second, I picked up the book *Born Again,* the conversion story of Chuck Colson, former "hatchet man" for President Richard Nixon and founder of Prison Fellowship. When I read the book, I felt God's pull on my heart to serve in prisons. Why? I have no reason, except that I knew God called me there. His right hand was guiding me.

Third, my wife and I wanted to have our daughters educated in Christian schools. There were none where we were living, but I knew of a good one in Denver. Our family had recently moved, and our possessions were still in boxes. I began to pray about the school situation without telling my wife. I didn't want to upset her. Precisely two weeks from that day, my wife entered my office and asked me if I'd consider moving to Denver to get our girls into Christian schools. I was floored at God's direct leading in our lives. Six months later we were in Denver, and they were enrolled.

Our church in Denver was active in prison ministry. We went into Buena Vista Correctional Facility for a weekend Prison Fellowship seminar—and God confirmed His call on my life to work in prisons. For the next eleven years, I worked in our business and went into prisons. Then in June of 1999, on my way to the office, I felt God's hand on my life again. This time I felt Him direct me to do three things: leave my business, start Doing HIS Time Prison Ministry, and begin to write a devotional for men and women inside prison. And that is what happened.

Since 1999, God has done some other profound things. Doing HIS Time Prison Ministry continues to serves incarcerated men and women and their families in Colorado through the Barn-A-Bus transportation ministry. Barn-A-Bus offers low-cost, scheduled, round-trip rides to almost every prison in Colorado on visiting days. More than 25,000 riders have been reunited with their family members in prison. Only God can calculate the impact of these visits.

The 72-Hour Fund was initiated in 2003. Seeking to reach ex-offenders upon their release from Colorado prisons, the 72-Hour Fund is the "face and hands of Jesus" as they experience God's grace in tangible form. The fund provides former inmates—of all faiths—free clothing, shoes, coats, and hygiene items, along with bus tokens and help with identification paperwork such as driver's licenses and birth certificates.

This "cup of cold water" ministry is reducing recidivism in Colorado. The three-year average recidivism rate for men and women released in Colorado is 54 percent. Based on our records and research, for the people who are helped by the 72-Hour Fund, the recidivism rate is only 19.5 percent for men and only 12.5 percent for women.

Additionally, between 2008 and 2014, more than 300,000 copies of this devotional have been distributed in 35 countries in eight languages. It is also available for purchase at www.amazon.com.

Another important thing happened since 1999. As I wrote this devotional, with the invaluable partnership of Lynn Vanderzalm, I found myself changing. The Holy Spirit took me on a journey of discovery concerning my own sins. In 2007, this self-awareness led me to my mother's gravesite, where I stood and spoke, as if to her. It was a conversation of reconciliation and forgiveness since I could now relate to her sin and mine in the forgiving grace of Jesus Christ. It was a healing experience, and I praise God for it.

The same God who pardoned me and lovingly rescued me from destroying myself and those around me will pardon and rescue you. I am confident that the same God who guided me with His right hand will guide you. He is faithful. My prayer is that you will come to be thoroughly convinced that God loves you and offers a wonderful plan for your life. Let Him help you accept forgiveness for the past. Let Him assist you as you make peace with your present situation and, in Him, find hope—real hope—for the future.

In His power and grace alone,

James C. Vogelzang
Doing HIS Time Prison Ministry
Santa Barbara, California
2014

Part 1:
God's Love

God loves us and offers us forgiveness for our past, peace for our present, and hope for our future.

Rescuing Love

You have rescued me from death and have forgiven all my sins. Isaiah 38:17

How had he ended up in jail—again? For ten months Jorge had been sober, the longest time in his twenty-seven years. His head had finally cleared, and he'd even had a job as a cook in the rehab center where he lived.

Then he started to drink again. Soon the alcohol took over, and one night Jorge cornered another resident and raped him. Now Jorge was back in jail—sick of himself and sick of life. Some of the other inmates heard about the rape and threatened Jorge's life. He'd spent four weeks in solitary just for protection.

One night after Jorge was back in his cell, he tied his sheets together and decided he would hang himself. After all, what was the use of living?

However, when he started to tie the sheets to the bars, he heard a voice: "Wait." That's all the voice said, but it was so clear that Jorge untied his sheets and went to sleep.

The next morning a letter arrived from the wife of the director of the rehab center. "God loves you, Jorge, and He wants to rescue you. No matter what you have done, no matter how you feel about yourself, God can transform your life." She asked if Jorge would like a Bible.

When the Bible arrived, Jorge read the entire Gospel of John in one sitting. When he finished, the same voice that told him to wait said to him: "Jorge, I love you so much that I sent My only Son to die for you. If you believe in Me, I will give you life, both for now and for eternity." Jorge willingly surrendered his life to Jesus.

In the months that followed, Jorge did a correspondence Bible study and grew in his love for the Lord. The COs noticed the change and started to trust Jorge. He had become a new person.

†

Making it personal: What would it feel like to believe that God loves you enough to rescue you? Has He ever rescued you?

Prayer: Lord, I'm sick of myself. I give myself to You and trust You to change me. Amen.

Read John 10:1-10 to understand God's love for you.

God Loves You

But God showed his great love for us by sending Christ to die for us while we were still sinners. Romans 5:8

Many of us believe that because of what we have done, God could never love us. The devil whispers to us, "God could never love a child molester, a prostitute, or a murderer." As usual, the devil's got it wrong!

One of the amazing things about God's love is that He loves us *despite* who we are, not *because* of who we are. That is radical grace. We all have spent too many years trying to *be* someone who was worthy of another's love. We've tried to earn love from our parents, our pimps, the people we were sleeping with, drug dealers, and our bosses. We've worked hard to be rich enough, pretty enough, or tough enough to deserve their attention and love.

God's love works differently. God sent His own Son to die for us *while* we were still sinners. Even when we were turning tricks, selling dope, or robbing liquor stores, God loved us. He doesn't say to us, "Straighten yourself up and clean yourself off *and then* I'll take a look at you." No. He loves us as we are—period.

Another amazing thing about God's love is that it's extravagant, over-the-top. God doesn't skimp on love. He shows His love by sending His own Son—not some low-level flunky—to die for us. He sent His own Son—His *only* Son—to die for us. Most of us have never experienced that kind of unconditional love.

That unconditional love is life-changing. It offers forgiveness and gives us value, hope, and peace. When it seems dark in the cellblock, we can hear His voice calling our name, saying, "I love you just the way you are. Come to Me. Accept My love. My Son has covered your sin." Who wouldn't want to say yes to that kind of love?

†

Making it personal: What will it take for you to get over yourself and your crime and accept God's unconditional love for you?

Prayer: Lord, thank You for loving me even while I am a sinner. Amen.

Read Ephesians 3:17-19 to learn of the depth of God's love for you.

God Has a Plan for You

For God so loved the world that he gave his only Son, so that everyone who believes in him will not perish but have eternal life. John 3:16

God has an individual, specific plan for each one of us. From before we were born, God knew who we were going to be and what His plan was for our lives. He made each of us perfectly different for exactly the role He has in mind for us to play.

He also gave us the ability to decide for ourselves what is right. Many of us ignored God's plan and made decisions without consulting His manual—the Bible. We went our own way and dismissed His blueprint for our lives.

Now we sit in prison. *Our* version of *our* plan for *our* lives ran *ourselves* into the ditch. We are away from our spouses and children. We are missing parents' funerals and our kids' graduations. That's definitely *not* God's plan for our lives.

God gives us a set of guidelines to make our lives richer and safer. The Ten Commandments are not God's way to restrict our happiness. They are part of His plan, and they outline the ways we can live safe, abundant lives.

God's plan for our lives involves not only a full life here and now, but also true freedom for eternity. God loves us so much that He wants us to live with Him forever. Imagine living for eternity in the presence of Almighty God Himself. And to make that happen for us, God was willing to sacrifice His only Son to pay the debt for our sin.

God's love is so deep that He offers this gift to us—free. When we believe in Him and accept His gift of salvation, He makes a reservation for us to live with Him forever.

✝

Making it personal: What events in your life made you really aware of the huge sacrifice God paid for you to be able to live with Him forever?

Prayer: Father God, take the blinders off my eyes, and let me really see and know Your plans for me. Amen.

Read Jeremiah 29:11-13 to learn more about God's good plan for you.

Never Separated from God's Love

Does it mean [Christ] no longer loves us if we have trouble or calamity, or are persecuted, or are hungry or cold or in danger or threatened with death? . . . I am convinced that nothing can ever separate us from his love. Death can't, and life can't. The angels can't, and the demons can't. Our fears for today, our worries about tomorrow, and even the powers of hell can't keep God's love away. . . . Nothing in all creation will ever be able to separate us from the love of God that is revealed in Christ Jesus our Lord. Romans 8:35-39

We read about God's love, but sometimes it's hard to feel it. Bad stuff happens. Families fall apart. We get so overwhelmed by fear and pain, plus the difficulty of our own situation, that we begin to doubt that God's love exists. We ask: Where is God? Has He abandoned us like so many others have in our lives? Does it mean He no longer loves us when tough things happen?

Remember the night we got busted and the madness of county jail? Or the shame we felt after turning our first trick? We did more drugs to take the pain of shame away. Do these things make it impossible for God to love us? The apostle Paul asked that same question. We should memorize his response because Paul declares that *nothing* can separate us from God's love. Nothing. Our crimes can't. Our past can't. Our incarceration can't. Our estranged relationships can't. Our cellies can't. Death row can't. Solitary can't. *Nothing* can separate us from God's love.

Think about it. If Jesus didn't come down off that cross, if He didn't leave *us* hanging when He was suffering the most, why would He abandon us now? Jesus' love is solid. We can count on it.

†

Making it personal: Where do you feel separated from God's love? Picture His love as so powerful that it floods that very place right now.

Prayer: Lord, Your love for me is so great that it's hard for me to get my head around it. Thank You, for loving me that much. Amen.

Memorize today's passage, repeating it every morning as a reminder of God's love for you.

Come Near to God's Love

Submit yourselves, then, to God. . . . Come near to God and he will come near to you. . . . Humble yourselves before the Lord, and he will lift you up. James 4:7-10, NIV

Many of us in prison hate ourselves and what we have done. That way of thinking reveals itself in our feelings of unworthiness. Or we conceal our self-loathing by acting out in rebellious ways. Those actions are just ways of hiding the shame and guilt. The bottom line is: We doubt God could love us.

But the Gospel message is just the opposite. No matter how defiant, rebellious, angry, or worthless we feel, when we move toward God, we find that He has already moved toward us. He has already declared His love for us. God does not condemn us. He is seeking a change of heart. He requests a new way of thinking.

When we submit to God, our hearts seek and yearn for His peace. St. Augustine said, "You made us for Yourself, and our hearts find no peace until they rest in You." We find that rest when we draw near to God. That is a message of hope.

With God there is always hope. We must never indulge the notion that we have gone too far, that we have sinned too much, and that God could never love us. The Bible tells us otherwise. The beauty of God's message to us through Jesus Christ is that He loves us, unconditionally and fully. He loves us, renews us, and restores us. That is the amazing power of Christianity. No other religion offers the hope of transformation, renewal, and restoration that God offers through the blood of His Son. When we humble ourselves before this loving God, He lifts us up to new life. We can accept His love and live purposeful and useful lives.

†

Making it personal: What steps will you take to move toward God's love? How will your life change when you accept and embrace His hope for your life?

Prayer: Lord, help me get over my sense of unworthiness. I want to move closer to You. Come into my heart, and work Your transforming changes today. Amen.

Read Psalm 36:5-9 for a message of love and hope.

Jesus Is the Way

Jesus told him, "I am the way, the truth, and the life. No one can come to the Father, except through me." John 14:6

The writer Helen Wodehouse said, "We think we must climb to a certain height of goodness before we can reach God. But He does not say, 'At the end of the way you may find me'; He says, 'I *am* the Way; I am the road under your feet, the road that begins just as low down as you happen to be.' If we are in a hole, the Way begins in the hole. The moment we set our face in the same direction as His, we are walking with God."[2]

Many of us wake up each morning feeling that God could never love us. People we trusted sometimes sexually abused us as children and then afterward angrily told us we were worthless. As adults, we often stayed in abusive relationships, hopelessly searching for love. We misguidedly thought that if we treated our abusers better, we could earn their love.

Many of us view a relationship with a loving God in the same twisted way. We mistakenly feel we must "be good" to *earn* His love. Nothing is further from the truth!

God does not care where we have been; He is concerned only about where we are going. He searches for us and meets us where we are. God comes alongside us at the most depressing moment of our lives and whispers that He loves us, forgives us, and believes in us (see John 3:16; Jeremiah 29:11). We can trust those words!

We can experience God's redeeming love. We can cop to the sin in our lives and turn away (repent) from it (see 1 John 1:9). When we confess and change direction, we will be on the right road. His genuine, authentic love will flood our hearts as we walk in His direction.

✝

Making it personal: What would your life be like if you asked God to rescue you from darkness and bring you redemption and forgiveness?

Prayer: Lord, You are the Way. I want to walk with You. Do Your work in me. Amen.

Read Ephesians 1:7-8 to learn what God in His kindness has done for you.

Doing *HIS* Time

So be careful how you live, not as fools but as those who are wise. Make the most of every opportunity for doing good in these evil days. Ephesians 5:15-16

The title of this book is *Doing HIS Time.* What does that mean? Time moves slowly in prison. One day seems pretty much like the last one. We may not think our future looks all that promising if we are looking at a natural life sentence, but every dawn is another chapter of our future. We have choices about how we do our time.

Are we doing *our* time, or are we doing *HIS* time—God's time? Are we wasting our time, or are we investing it? Are we making the most of every opportunity—"redeeming the time" as the King James Version translates the same words? Our answers to these questions give us insight as to how we are preparing for the future.

We know that what we did when we were kids has had a big impact on our lives today. But our lives are not over. What we do *today* will influence our future—and everyone around us—either for good or for evil. Our future depends on the choices we make on how we spend our lives today.

British author Charles Reade wrote these profound words:

Sow a thought, and you reap an act;
Sow an act, and you reap a habit;
Sow a habit, and you reap a character;
Sow a character, and you reap a destiny.

What thoughts are we sowing? What are we doing today to reap a habit? We can "cash in" the time and make it work for us. We don't have to give up our future to drugged-out time. No matter how much time we have to do, let's do *HIS* time.

✝

Making it personal: What action will you take today to redeem the time, to make a positive impact on people around you?

Prayer: Lord, I want to make every minute count for You. Show me how. Amen.

Read Psalm 31:14-16 to see how our time, our future, is in God's hands; then pray the words back to God as a prayer.

God's Love

These questions relate to the meditations found on pages 2-8:

Discuss together:

1. In "Rescuing Love" (page 2), Jorge contemplates suicide. But God rescues him. Many inmates consider suicide, and more than a few attempt it. Have you tried? How did God's love intervene? Are you considering suicide now? Does the message of God's unconditional make you think twice?

2. Many of you have been close to dying because of other circumstances. What or who saved you from dying? Do you think God is offering you a second chance? God's unconditional love means you don't have to clean up before He loves you. Talk about coming to God just as you are to accept His love. How might this change your life?

3. Before prison, what actions did you take to gain approval, recognition, and love? Share your view of those things now in light of God's unconditional love. How does unconditional love give you value, peace, and hope?

4. Is God's free gift (grace) "too easy" or "too hard"? Discuss how pride and rebelliousness play a role in deciding. Do you ever hide behind your crime as an excuse not to accept God's grace? What events in your life hinder your trusting God's love?

5. What kind of "time" are you doing? What does it mean to you to do HIS time?

Explore God's Word together:

1. **Isaiah 38:17** speaks of bitterness, anguish, and the power of forgiveness. What good came out of Isaiah's bitterness? Are you bitter? What caused your bitterness? The prophet speaks of forgiveness and rescue. Can you remain bitter after such forgiving love?

2. **1 Kings 17:8-24** teaches about trust and deliverance. Do you have trust issues in your life? Share some of those. What things hinder you from totally surrendering to God in faith?

3. **Psalm 103:1-5** speaks about forgiveness and rescue, too. How has lack of forgiveness played a significant role in your current

circumstances? When has forgiveness rescued you? Take time to reflect on how God has worked powerfully in your life. Can you say that God has "filled your life with good things"?

4. **Daniel 6:16-23** is an astounding story. Read this story of rescue, believe it, and share God's rescuing power with others.

Pray together:

1. Begin by praying for all those who are contemplating suicide inside your prison.

2. If God has spared your life in any way, thank Him for that. Lift up each person in the group before God by name, asking for protection and patience and perseverance.

3. Pray a thankful prayer of protection for your study group leader(s).

Commit to **confidentiality** ...

   ... **respect** each other

      ... **pray** for each other

         ... **encourage** one another

            ... **hold** each other **accountable**

Prayer for Acceptance of God's Love

*God, Jesus—whoever You are—I am frightened.
You see, I have never been loved in my life.*

*I cannot remember when I truly felt the warm flannel
blanket of a mother's love around my shoulders.
God, I have trouble with any father figure in my life
because mine raped me for years and
my mother did nothing to stop it.*

*In my heart, I desperately long to have
a loving father and mother in my life, but I am
also desperately afraid of letting someone into
my inner soul. My soul has been pierced and
assaulted so many times. I am struggling with
my desire and need to be loved and
my fear of being wounded again.*

*As I read this book, I ask You to assure me
of the genuineness of Your love. Sow seeds of trust
in my soul so that I will trust Your loving-kindness.*

*May Your love banish my fears and replace them
with a relationship that will fill the hole in my heart.*

Amen.

✝

Part 2: Sin

We are sinful and separated from God.
When we acknowledge our sin and
accept God's forgiveness,
we will fully experience His love
and plan for our lives.

Sin and Death

These desires give birth to sinful actions. And when sin is allowed to grow, it gives birth to death. James 1:15

Jason grew up looking at X-rated DVDs and Internet porn sites. The videos formed his view of women. They became objects—things to be used, not to be valued and honored.

After Jason got married, his buddies at work talked about the women they were sleeping with, bragging about how their wives would never find out about their cheating. He was *a silent witness* to their sinful behavior.

When these men invited Jason to have a drink, he suspected that they were interested in more than a casual beer. Should he join them? He wouldn't do anything, but it'd be fun to watch these guys in action. Jason got a thrill out of seeing his married buddies picking up strange women and leaving the bar with them. By being there, Jason was *a consenting spectator* to sin.

After seven years of marriage, Jason and his wife started having trouble in the bedroom. She was always tired from working and having to care for their two kids. Jason began to wonder what it would be like to "get a little on the side." The next time his buddies went out, he joined them, but this time as *a willing participant.* He complained about his marital trouble to his friends, who assured him that he was on the right track to solving his trouble.

But trouble found Jason. He slept with a woman who cared nothing about him. He caught a sexually transmitted disease (STD) and brought it home to his wife. When she confronted him, he confessed. She eventually left him and filed for divorce. Another broken home. A dead marriage. All of it, the result of sin!

Sin starts with the eyes, moves to the heart, and then into action. Death is always the result.

✝

Making it personal: What will it take for you to admit that you sin? What will make you tough enough to face the truth?

Prayer: Lord God, clean up my heart and erase my sin. Amen.

Read Psalm 38:18, the psalmist's admission, and make it your confession too.

The Wages of Sin

For the wages of sin is death. Romans 6:23

In this section of this book, we will look at the reality that we are sinners and that our sin separates us from God. The meditations will not beat us over the head with our sin but will give us mirrors through the lives of men and women who faced up to who they were—sinners—and found freedom. The goal of these meditations is to show us the truth about who we are.

We all are sinners. No one living in the close-security housing unit of the Ohio Reformatory for Women in Marysville, Ohio, is free from sin. But remember, the yellow shirts in boot camp are just as sinful as the orange-shirted maximum-security inmates. "For *all* have sinned; all fall short of God's glorious standard" (Romans 3:23, emphasis added).

Although God created us to have close fellowship with Him, our willfulness and stubborn rebellion breaks that relationship. Some of us are openly rebellious in the way we act or speak; others of us are passively indifferent to God's love and plan. This is what the Bible calls *sin*. We are unable to bridge the huge canyon between our selfishness and a perfect God who wants what is best for us.

Sin is what got us into trouble with the law and thrown into prison. It is the sin of pride that keeps us from forgiving and apologizing to our victims and families for what we have done to them. If we do not acknowledge our sin, repent, and ask God for forgiveness, our lives will seem like slow death. Separation from God's love is like a death penalty. But Jesus offers us a pardon.

✝

Making it personal: What sin in your life are you nurturing, thinking that it's no big deal? Get rid of it, now!

Prayer: Jesus, I know I have sinned against You. I am sorry and choose to turn away from my sin today. Amen.

Read the full verse of Romans 6:23 to hear the rest of the story.

Knowing Our Sin

If we claim to be without sin, we deceive ourselves and the truth is not in us. 1 John 1:8, NIV

Sin is real. Anyone who truly believes that sin does not exist has not been paying attention! In prison, we look anywhere and see the evidence of sin. We see fighting and angry attitudes. We see inmates being punked out.

But do we know anything about sin? Sin is as common to human beings as sliminess is to a worm. Yet, how many of us understand sin? Why is it important for us to know about sin?

If we choose to ignore our sin and its seriousness, our sinful hearts see it as normal behavior. Sinful deeds will no longer seem wrong to us. We disconnect our behavior from God and live as if our sin does not matter. It's like when we were kids and started stealing. If we didn't get caught, we didn't think it was wrong. But, if we got a whipping, if people found out, we took it much more seriously.

Without knowing our sin, we can never fully know ourselves and the debt of sin we have racked up. Suppose a new fish samples some "yip" (cocaine) a drug runner offers him and is unaware of the debt he is accumulating. If an old con pays it off for him without his knowledge, the new number has absolutely no thought of the price that was laid out on his behalf. The new fish understands his situation only when he learns of the enormity of the gift to him.

When we understand the enormity of the debt that Jesus paid for our sin, we can begin to appreciate God's love for us. Our gratitude breaks down our pride, and we grasp that we have been saved from a terrible fate. This pushes us toward thanksgiving to God. Thanksgiving paves the way to humility. In humility, we can begin to walk with God in a new purpose for our lives.

✝

Making it personal: Be honest with yourself, and take an inventory of your sin. List your most persistent sins.

Prayer: God, grant me insight and courage to face my sins. Amen.

Read Psalm 51:3-4 about acknowledging sin.

The Beginning of Sin

When Adam sinned, sin entered the entire human race. Romans 5:12a

Are we all sinful when we are born? Yes. Did God create sin? No, He gave mankind a choice. God isn't a bully. He doesn't force us to love Him. God knows that forced affection, like coerced confession, is worthless.

God created a perfect, sinless world. Adam and Eve were created perfectly to interact with God on a personal level. God gave them the ability and freedom to choose to obey or disobey His commands (see Genesis 2:16-17). God is not the author of sin, but He did *allow* the possibility of sin.

Before God created Adam and Eve, He offered His angels the same freedom to choose. Satan, Lucifer, was originally one of God's most powerful angels. But Satan wanted to *be* God. He rebelled against God and was thrown out of heaven with many other angels [demons] who supported the rebellion (see Isaiah 14:12 and Revelation 12:7-9).

Adam and Eve chose to listen to Satan instead of God. They ate the fruit of the tree that was forbidden (see Genesis 3:1-7). God did not tempt them; Satan did (see James 1:13-14). God allowed the possibility of evil. God gave Adam and Eve free will and with that, the right to decide. They chose to be disobedient to His command. Because of their decision, sin polluted God's perfect world.

As a result of the choices Adam and Eve made, we are sinful from the day we are conceived in our mother's womb (see Psalm 51:5). Watching a two-year-old grab a toy from another kid and yell "mine!" is all the proof we need. Selfishness and greed come quite naturally to us humans.

We are sinners, and only when we admit that and look for a solution will we find hope. Our hope is in God's grace and forgiveness through His Son, Jesus Christ.

†

Making it personal: Look at the choices you have made over the years. What power have your sins had in your life? What will you do about it?

Prayer: Father God, reveal my sin to me in the light of Your forgiveness. Amen.

Read Genesis 2 and 3 to see how sin came into the world.

Afraid and Ashamed

Adam's sin brought death, so death spread to everyone, for everyone sinned. Romans 5:12b

Does sin make a difference? Does it really matter? Is it that much of a big deal?

We who have committed adultery know the relationships with our spouses changed afterward. They may not have known about our unfaithfulness, but we brought the guilt of our actions home. Our sinful activities killed our peace of mind and self-respect. The shame made us irritable and angry. We were bad-tempered toward our families. They had no clue, but in our hearts, we knew. We *knew!*

Same thing happened to Adam and Eve after they sinned against God. God looked for Adam and Eve in the Garden but couldn't find them. They were hiding, afraid and ashamed—feeling guilty. They were afraid because they *knew* they had disobeyed, and they were ashamed because they *knew* they were naked. They were busted and couldn't face God.

Before they sinned, Adam and Eve and God were homies—they knew each other face-to-face. They had no reason to hide from Him or to be afraid. The Garden was the ultimate safe place.

The serpent told Adam and Eve that if they ate the fruit from the tree, they would know good and evil. And, he was right. Suddenly Adam and Eve knew things they hadn't known before. For the first time they knew fear. They knew guilt. They knew shame. Suddenly, they felt a need to cover up their nakedness.

We're all sons and daughters of Adam and Eve. Things haven't changed. We're born into a world that knows fear and guilt and shame. When we sin, we work hard to cover up. We don't dare look God in the face. We know we've chosen to go our own way instead of trusting God to know what's best for us.

✝

Making it personal: Do you feel you need to hide? What sin are you covering up?

Prayer: God, I'm just like Adam and Eve. You come looking for me, but I hide from You. I'm too afraid to look You in the face. Help me. Amen.

Read Matthew 26:69-75 for the story of how Peter was ashamed after he denied knowing Jesus.

The Blame Game

The Lord God asked, "Have you eaten the fruit I commanded you not to eat?" "Yes," Adam admitted, "but it was the woman you gave me who brought me the fruit, and I ate it." Genesis 3:11-12

It's convenient to have somebody to blame when trouble comes. The joke that nobody in prison admits they're guilty would be funny if it weren't so sad. We blame others when we are busted after doing something wrong: "My girlfriend tempted me." "Drugs got me into trouble." "My parents neglected me." "I'm from a poor home."

Adam would not take responsibility for his disobedience either. When God asked him if he had eaten the forbidden fruit, Adam pointed the finger away from himself. He admitted that he had eaten the fruit, but he wasn't going to take the fall. Rather than making a choice to avoid sin, Adam surrendered to it and then blamed Eve. Adam also blamed God. He accused God of giving him an imperfect woman, falsely thinking that if God knew that Eve was going to tempt him, He should have prevented it. Then Eve blamed the serpent (see Genesis 3:13). Adam and Eve both played the original blame game.

Things haven't changed much. We disobey God's commands. And when God busts us, we make excuses. Sometimes we think as Adam did, saying to ourselves, "If God had wanted me to be a different person, He shouldn't have placed me in the tenements of Houston or South Chicago."

But in the end, God will not be persuaded by such counterfeit arguments. We have choices, and we are responsible for them. Temptation is part of life in a sinful world, but the outcome is not always sin and disobedience. We think the natural result of being tempted is to give in to it. That's not true. We have the power, through the Holy Spirit, to not be persuaded by temptation. The fact that evil exists is no excuse or reason for choosing it.

✝

Making it personal: How will you face your own disobedience?

Prayer: God, I confess that I often blame others for things that I have done. Help me to take responsibility. Amen.

Read Romans 14:12 for God's view on personal responsibility.

It's Not God's Fault

And remember, no one who wants to do wrong should ever say, "God is tempting me." God is never tempted to do wrong, and he never tempts anyone else either. Temptation comes from the lure of our own evil desires. James 1:13-14

Adam blamed God, and we blame God too. In areas where we're weak, we look for any excuse to justify what we have already chosen in our hearts to do. Take sexual sin, for example. We blame God for creating us with strong sexual desire, and we rationalize deviant sexual relations by accusing God for "making us this way." We shout, "Why am I accountable for acting according to the way God made me?"

That position has some logic. Many of life's circumstances are beyond our control. We never chose our parents, the color of our skin, our neighborhoods, or in some cases, our sexual orientation. Many homosexuals feel they were born the way they are. Even if these things are true, do these facts cancel our freedom of choice, and as a result, terminate all personal responsibility? Are we just animated characters following a predetermined script and not accountable for our actions? If that's true, then why are we in prison?

We must never be deceived into believing that because we were born with strong, sexual desires that God tempts us into sexual sin. When we blame God, we're using Him as an excuse for abnormal and sinful behavior that our own sinful natures desire. All things from God are good. If we abuse God's gifts to us, He is not responsible for our sin, just as the maker of matches is not responsible if an arsonist abuses matches and sets a fire.

We all have the freedom to choose. We all are responsible for our choices before God. We cannot pervert good, do evil, and blame God for our sinful actions. We must understand this so we don't make excuses for our behavior by blaming God.

✝

Making it personal: In a quiet moment, consider what sins you're blaming on God. Is He really the one at fault?

Prayer: Father God, forgive me for blaming You for the bad choices I have made. Amen.

Read Psalm 15 for David's description of a blameless life.

The Curse of Sin

Against its will, everything on earth was subjected to God's curse. Romans 8:20

Do we behave as if there are no consequences for our actions? Do we live as if sin doesn't exist and that a day of reckoning will never come? If we do, we're dead wrong. Sin is a big deal to God. When we sin, God doesn't say, "Well, I'll knock down your charges to misdemeanors, and you can walk. I'll ignore your disobedience this time and look the other way." God hates sin and demands that it be punished.

God told Adam and Eve that if they disobeyed Him, they would die. He's a God of His word. He followed through on His punishment. Adam and Eve didn't physically die immediately, but life changed for them. Eve would suffer pain during childbirth and lose the natural equality she shared with Adam in the Garden. God placed a curse on the ground, which meant Adam would struggle and sweat to scratch out a living from it. Work would also frustrate Adam as further evidence of disunity with God. And death became part of their existence. Eventually Adam and Eve would die and return to dust. It was a sad day for Adam and Eve (see Genesis 3:16-19). God banished them from the Garden, the ultimate punishment—separation from God. In all fairness, God punished the serpent too. His offspring would eat dust and forever be enemies with Adam and Eve's offspring.

From the moment Adam and Eve disobeyed, *every* human has gravitated toward sin. Harmony with God and each other was replaced by conflict and discord. God punished Adam and Eve, but in His mercy He provided a way out of this ultimate death and separation. And that's what most of the meditations in this book are about: God's plan to redeem the offspring of Adam and Eve—you and me.

†

Making it personal: Consider your attitude toward sin. Are you serious about it or casual? How does God see your sin?

Prayer: Holy Spirit, convict me of my sin. Make me aware of how serious it really is. Amen.

Read Job 13:20-23, and pray Job's prayer in which he asks God to reveal his sin.

Escaping the Curse of Sin

The sin of this one man, Adam, caused death to rule over us, but all who receive God's wonderful, gracious gift of righteousness will live in triumph over sin and death through this one man, Jesus Christ. Romans 5:17

So, was God too harsh with Adam and Eve? You might think, *Why didn't He just give them another chance?*

In this Scripture passage about how God deals with sin, He shows us a few important things about His character: He is serious about sin, and He is just. His justice means that He couldn't look the other way when Adam and Eve sinned. He had to follow through on the punishment He had told Adam and Eve. It was the only fair thing to do.

The same is true for us. When we steal, when we abuse others, when we are involved in illicit sex, when we curse God, He cannot look the other way. Because He is just, the only fair thing for Him to do is to declare us guilty and punish us.

Even though God sent Adam and Eve out of the Garden, He had a loving plan that would make sure that they would not be separated from Him forever. God offered the death of His own Son so that they—and we—can live forever in His presence and triumph over sin and death. What a gracious gift.

God balances His justice with His grace and mercy. This is really important because one doesn't work in harmony without the other. Mercy *without* justice becomes syrupy sentimentality—all sweetness. Justice *without* mercy becomes harsh, legalistic, and brutal. This is God's beautiful balancing act.

Throughout the pages of this book, we will look at both sides of this situation: our sin and God's plan for helping us to escape the curse of our sin.

†

Making it personal: How have you experienced both sides of God's character, His justice and His mercy?

Prayer: God, I deserve Your wrath, Your judgment. Thank You that You have provided an escape through Your Son, Jesus. Amen.

Read Ephesians 2:4-7 for assurance of God's mercy.

The Power of Sin

I know I am rotten through and through so far as my old sinful nature is concerned. No matter which way I turn, I can't make myself do right. I want to, but I can't. When I want to do good, I don't. And when I try not to do wrong, I do it anyway. . . . Oh, what a miserable person I am! Who will free me from this life that is dominated by sin? Romans 7:18-19, 24

A foundational principle about sin is its *power*. Sin is a strong, dominant force working against our good intentions. Sometimes the driving urge for the gambling table, drugs, or being rebellious pulls on us like a powerful riptide sucking us out to sea. We struggle in our minds and wrestle with the urges, but we are pulled under by the sheer force of sin.

Afterward, in shame and despair, we cry out to God, saying what the apostle Paul said in the verses above, feeling helpless and in despair over his sin.

Paul understood the power of sin. He was a well-educated man, yet his education did not free him from sin. Paul discovered that trying to battle sin with his own strength did not work.

That lesson speaks to us today. If we attempt to overcome sin through willpower alone, we will fail. If we try not to sin by believing we can do what is right in our own power, we will fail. Only the power of the risen Christ has the power to declare victory over sin (see Ephesians 2:4-5). The hymnwriter Charles Wesley summarized it best in his hymn "O for a Thousand Tongues to Sing":

> He breaks the power of canceled sin,
> He sets the prisoner free;
> His blood can make the foulest clean,
> His blood availed for me.

✝

Making it personal: Where does the power of sin grip your life? What will it take for you to confess it to God, surrender it to His power, and be set free?

Prayer: Jesus, thank You for Your power over sin. Come alongside me as I do battle with sin in my life. Amen.

Read Romans 7 to learn about the apostle Paul's struggle with sin.

How Sin Works

Temptation comes from the lure of our own evil desires. These evil desires lead to evil actions, and evil actions lead to death. James 1:14-15

Sinful behavior is frequently the result of many thoughts and actions. Sin isn't a one-shot deal! Life-destroying sin is the result of many little sins feeding on one another until Satan has messed us up.

Satan messed up some of our marriages with adultery. Maybe our spouses were overweight or no longer as romantic as they once were. Our lustful hearts whispered to us that we deserved better than the partner God blessed us with. With that thought, the devil laid a small seed of sin that ultimately resulted in our unfaithfulness.

We may be reading this meditation in the Security Housing Unit (SHU). We may be wondering how we landed here, again. It started with feeling we had no one who understood us. Self-pity set in, along with the desire to be noticed around the living unit. We craved acceptance, and self-centeredness dominated our thinking. To draw attention to ourselves and impress others, we hurt a person in the cellblock. Small, sinful thoughts grew into sinful actions. SHU was the result.

Sin works in very subtle, sneaky, and dangerous ways. To be aware of sin's evil nature and horrendous consequences is just the first step in our war against it. It's like preparing to go off to war in the military. We know it's going to be dangerous. But knowing that fact alone is not enough. Knowing it is dangerous makes us want to prepare for the danger. We train and discipline ourselves for the battles we know are coming.

In our Christian life we must move from *knowing how* sin works to *training for battle* with it. We can start by memorizing Scripture passages, praying for the Holy Spirit's help in our time of need, and surrounding ourselves with Christian friends.

✝

Making it personal: Where does sin have a toehold in your life? What "pet" sins are you protecting?

Prayer: Jesus, my love of sin has left me empty. Come fill me up, and make me the person You want me to be. Amen.

Read James 4:7-8 for hope and encouragement.

Beating the Rap of Sin

The verdict on [Adam's] sin was the death sentence; the verdict on the many sins that followed was this wonderful life sentence. If death got the upper hand through one man's wrongdoing, can you imagine the breathtaking recovery life makes, sovereign life, in those who grasp with both hands this wildly extravagant life-gift . . . that the one man Jesus Christ provides? Romans 5:16-17, THE MESSAGE

God demands payment for sin, but He balances His justice with mercy to insure that Adam and Eve—and you and I—wouldn't be separated from Him forever. A little story will help explain, keeping in mind that God is fully aware of Jesus' sacrifice.

When we were arrested, we hired legal counsel or were assigned a public defender. We needed legal assistance to guide us through the maze of legal rulings and filings. We required a helper—an advocate—who was familiar with the system.

Jesus is our advocate before God the Father. He represents us in God's courtroom, where God demands justice for sin. Jesus comes before God with our rap sheets listing the sins we've committed. He states that we're guilty of the sins in our jackets. But that's not the end of our Advocate's speech.

Jesus reminds the Judge that He Himself has already paid for our sins through His death on the cross. Jesus already bore our death sentence for all our sins—current and future. Jesus reminds the Judge that it isn't fair to punish us for sins that He's already paid for. God accepts Jesus' death on our behalf, and He declares us "not guilty." When He looks at us and our sin, He sees His sinless Son and His sacrifice.

Because Jesus paid the debt for our sin, God pardons us. He sees us as righteous, blameless, honorable, and upright. We can do nothing to earn this pardon. It's grace, a free gift Jesus gives us to pardon us from the death sentence brought on by our sin.

✝

Making it personal: Think about Jesus' sacrifice for your sin. Share with a friend the full meaning of this sacrifice.

Prayer: Jesus, thank You for taking the rap for my sin. Help me to fully understand what that means for my life. Amen.

Memorize the promises in **Matthew 20:28 and Ephesians 1:7**.

God Loves Sinners

This is a true saying, and everyone should believe it: Christ Jesus came into the world to save sinners. 1 Timothy 1:15

The Bible is filled with detailed accounts of many sinners besides Adam and Eve. Some were leaders, some were priests, and others were kings. Some were criminals who might be on death row if they were convicted in today's courtrooms! Jesus made a habit of hangin' with sinners. He chose tax collector Matthew to be a disciple and went to his house for dinner with other tax collectors. Tax collectors were Jewish men who worked for the hated Roman occupiers and were considered traitors by the Jews. They worked for Rome and often swindled their fellow Jews. Another big sinner was Saul (later called Paul). He was the equivalent of a Jewish Gestapo officer. He took families out of their homes in the middle of the night and threw them into prison. These were some of the people Jesus chose to lead His work on earth.

The meditations in this book will look at many of these people's lives to help us see how God works on our lives. In each case we will see that while God hates sin, He loves sinners.

Are we languishing in prison, convinced that God could never love us because of our crimes? Sometimes we flirt with hopelessness and despair, thinking that the world considers us losers. These next few meditations will encourage you.

David, the boy king, the slayer of Goliath, the author of the book of Psalms, and a person called "a man after God's own heart" was a big-time criminal. The next series of meditations will examine David's life and observe how God responded to David's crimes. God didn't gloss over David's sin, but God also didn't reject him.

So too with us. God doesn't gloss over our sin, but he also doesn't toss us aside. God loves sinners. He loves us.

†

Making it personal: In what specific ways are you letting your crime(s) keep you from a relationship with God?

Prayer: Lord Jesus, help me get over my guilt and shame. Help me see that my life can be redeemed through Your love for me. Amen.

Read Matthew 9:9-13 for Jesus' view of sinners.

Sin

These questions relate to the meditations on found on pages 14-26:

Discuss together:

1. Why is not knowing your sin similar to your eyes adjusting to a dark room? Could it be that when you're knee-deep in evil, you cannot see the darkness? Why is knowing your sin like understanding you need a doctor? Why is this knowledge important? How do you come to appreciate and figure out the sin in your life?

2. Before you knew Jesus, was your sin a rebellious habit? How is a rebellious spirit an anti-God state of mind? Has this changed in your life? If so, how? If not, why not? Discuss this, and share some ways Jesus has retooled your heart and your world.

3. What small sins led to larger, more serious ones? Did your crime begin with small sins? Why is sin so difficult to admit? Why do we first blame others rather than ourselves? Why do we blame God? If you could go back to before you came to prison, what would you do differently?

4. As a group, define these concepts: freedom of choice, personal responsibility, and accountability. How are these three things fundamental to acknowledging your sin? How do they help you to live a godly life?

Explore God's Word together:

1. **Romans 7:14-25** reveals that the apostle Paul knew sin and its power. How can you relate to the power of sin? Describe a time when it feels all-powerful in your life. Have you ever felt the battle between good and evil described in verses 21-23? How do you battle this power of sin? What did Paul discover is the only solution?

2. **Romans 3:23-24** puts us all in the same boat as sinners. How is the weight of guilt crushing you? How does God's mercy through Jesus redeem you (pay your debt) and rescue you? How will you let Jesus' love and sacrifice lift the weight of guilt from you? Describe the feelings of peace that His love can give you.

Pray together:

1. Start in silent prayer. Ask God to make your sin plain to you. Confess that sin to Him. Then thank Him for His forgiveness, which wipes the slate clean.

2. Pray as a group for each other, for the facility, the administration, the COs, and for your enemies.

3. Open the prayer time for special concerns and needs. Be patient and wait for the Spirit to move in the hearts of the group members.

Commit to **confidentiality** …

   … **respect** each other

      … **pray** for each other

         … **encourage** one another

            … **hold** each other **accountable**

Small Sins Lead to Big Ones

In the spring, at the time when kings go off to war, David sent Joab out with the king's men and the whole Israelite army. . . . But David remained in Jerusalem. 2 Samuel 11:1

Let's look at lessons from the life of David and see how his sin started and grew. We'll also observe the consequences of his sin.

David was a successful king. He brought security, power, and prosperity to the people of Israel. But he was tired. For fifteen years he had fought Israel's enemies. Before that, he killed Goliath and went on the run from Saul for years. Living and sleeping in caves took its toll on David. When the time came for another war campaign, David decided to stay home. Instead of being a "hands-on" king, he determined that he needed a break. Instead of leading his troops, he sent someone else to do it. He ducked his duty.

In David's defense, being king was an enormous responsibility. He made the tough decisions, dealt with the military egos, comforted families of fallen warriors, and still functioned as king. Maybe David felt he was entitled to perks others wouldn't understand. *He was king! He deserved a break! No one had a clue what a tough thing it was to be king!* These kinds of thoughts set people up for sin.

Do we do the same thing? Taking a break is fine, but shirking our duty is not. As church leaders, do we ever blow off a Sunday, feeling we've done enough for a while? Are we coupling self-pity with laziness? Sin is never an only child. Sins are twins. Small sins of anger in the chow line lead to trash talk in the cellblock. A little attitude jams us up. Then, it's a short hop from God's will to self-will and sin. Beware of small sins that lead to bigger ones.

†

Making it personal: What are the little seeds of sin in your heart? What will you do to keep the devil from nurturing them into even bigger sins?

Prayer: Father God, show me my sin before I fall. Shine Your disinfecting light into the corners of my heart. Amen.

Read James 1:14-15 for a reminder of how sin grows.

How Sin Starts

Late one afternoon David got out of bed after taking a nap and went for a stroll on the roof of the palace. As he looked out over the city, he noticed a woman of unusual beauty taking a bath. 2 Samuel 11:2

So how did David's criminal behavior begin? One day when the king was supposed to be off in battle, he was on his rooftop. He noticed a beautiful woman taking a bath. A spiritually stronger man might have turned his eyes and fled from the roof. But instead of looking away, David looked *into* the temptation, and that look aroused his desires. Sin was born in that simple act. Temptation of the eyes greased the skids to David's failure.

Many of us started down the road to sin this same way. We saw powerful men with big rolls of bills in their pockets. We were attracted to them and how they lived. We basked in the glow of the respect the world gave them. We partied with men and women who had drugs and loads of "bling." We wanted that life for ourselves. Even inside, sometimes we see the drug runners and the OGs (original gangsters) and dream how to be like them. This is sin.

Our eyes are the windows to our souls, and our souls are the core of our being. What we see, read, and think has a direct impact on our walk with God and our usefulness to Him in prison. To combat these evil temptations, we need to stay spiritually strong by keeping our eyes on Jesus. Visualize Jesus standing before you. This works! When our eyes tempt us, we can turn away from the pornography. Morning and evening prayers as well as short "bullet" prayers all day long frustrate the enemy. Reading God's Word gives us armor to stop Satan's arrows, and hanging with Christian inmates lends a hand when we feel weak.

†

Making it personal: What sinful things have your eyes looked at recently? How might that lead you toward deeper sin?

Prayer: God, keep my eyes from looking at things that will lead me into sin. Amen.

Read and memorize Psalm 119:37 as a prayer for strength.

Desires Turn into Sinful Actions

**He noticed a woman of unusual beauty taking a bath. He sent someone to find out who she was, and he was told, "She is Bathsheba . . . the wife of Uriah the Hittite." Then David sent for her; and when she came to the palace, he slept with her.
2 Samuel 11:2-4**

David's sin started with a glance. He walked into the quicksand of sin when his look turned to lust. He sent someone to find out about the woman. His sinful desire turned to action.

The king discovered that the woman was Bathsheba, wife of Uriah, one of David's elite soldiers. Here, Uriah was away doing battle for his king. Yet, without a thought, David took Uriah's wife to bed.

How could David could commit such an unspeakable crime? Never underestimate the power of sin. "All the time [David] was walking with God, . . . writing his holy Psalms, . . . the power of sin was seething and raging in his breast, ready to quench the very inspiration God was giving him, and ruin his religion and his soul for evermore."[3]

David indulged in self-pity. He probably felt his life was so hard that he deserved special privileges. His conscience was so dulled that he blew up his life and didn't even realize it.

Are our consciences blunted in the same way? Do we indulge self-pity and rationalize drug use and immoral sexual behavior because we feel our sentences are unjust? Do we believe we deserve a little forbidden tenderness? We must not deceive ourselves and allow our desires to lead us into sinful action.

The forces of evil that degraded David's life are still active in our lives. We must identify the danger and fight sin's power with God's Word and prayer. We cannot allow sin's power to take root in our lives.

✝

Making it personal: Where does self-pity have a grip in your life? How is it hindering your walk with God and your growth in Christ?

Prayer: Father God, show me my sin, and remove it through the blood of Your Son, Jesus. Amen.

Read Matthew 5:28 to see how seriously God takes the sins of the eyes.

The Path of Sin

When Bathsheba discovered that she was pregnant, she sent a message to inform David. So David sent word to Joab: "Send me Uriah the Hittite." 2 Samuel 11:5-6

Sin follows sin like wet sidewalks follow rain. Human nature is so contaminated with sin that we often try to cover up our sin, often committing even greater sins in the process. Almost certainly there are men in McNeil Island Correctional Center and women in Pulaski State Prison who tried to cover up a felony by committing a worse crime. When held captive inside the prison of our sinful behaviors, we will do anything to avoid being busted.

David found himself in that situation. His adultery with Bathsheba was bad enough. But when he learned she was pregnant, he hatched a cover-up plan. David recalled Bathsheba's husband, Uriah, from the war to get a report. David plotted that while home, Uriah would sleep with his wife, and everyone would think that the baby was Uriah's. David figured he'd be off the hook.

But Uriah had integrity. He refused to sleep with Bathsheba while his comrades were sleeping in fields. David tried to get him drunk, but Uriah's integrity triumphed. He refused (see 2 Samuel 11:5-13).

So a desperate David arranged for Uriah's death. He ordered his commander to place Uriah on the front lines, where he was most likely to be killed (see 2 Samuel 11:14-17). David's cold-blooded action revealed his hardened conscience.

We may shudder at what David did, but we often do the same thing. When faced with the consequences of our sin, instead of confessing it and making it right, we often try to cover it up. And in the process, we often slide further and further into sin. When we sin, we must go before God and confess it immediately. Let's not wait. Let's not make it worse by covering it up or committing more evil to hide it.

†

Making it personal: What cover-up sin is lurking in your heart right now? Confess your sin to God and to another Christian, and avoid making it worse.

Prayer: Lord, grant me the courage to face my sin. Amen.

Read Psalm 32, David's commitment to confess his sin.

Premeditated Sin

David wrote a letter to Joab and gave it to Uriah to deliver. The letter instructed Joab, "Station Uriah on the front lines where the battle is fiercest. Then pull back so that he will be killed." 2 Samuel 11:14-15

Let's examine David's murder of Uriah more closely. It was a calculated sin. We need to appreciate the significance of premeditated sin and apply those lessons to our lives.

As prisoners, we know that a *premeditated* crime is planned. It's not a crime of passion that just happens. It's thought out, designed, and carried out. That's why the punishment for premeditated murder is greater than the sentence for manslaughter.

Premeditated sin is more harmful to our spiritual life too. Why is deliberate sin such a big deal to God? Intentional sin reveals a heart that's in open rebellion against God! Rebellion denies our relationship with God and rejects His place of supremacy in our lives. We become our own god.

When we intentionally sin against God, we're running in the opposite direction from Him. If we're running away, we can't be running toward Him at the same time. The further we sprint away from God, the longer, harder, and tougher it will be for us to return to a right relationship with Him. It's like sliding down a hill. It's easier to stop the slide at the top of the hill than in the middle, after we've picked up speed.

Willful, calculated sin betrays that our hearts are calloused toward sin. Calloused hearts make the next sin much easier to do, since we feel little regret for the previous, intentional sin. When our hands are calloused, we have trouble feeling things. Calloused hearts are the same; they feel very little.

We must avoid *all* sin. But, we must be certain to avoid deliberate, purposeful, and willful sin. Confess every sin quickly. Repent and ask for forgiveness to be able to stay close to God's will for our lives. Avoid traveling the road that leads away from God and toward ultimate separation from Him.

✝

Making it personal: What premeditated sin might be brewing in your heart? What will you do about it?

Prayer: Jesus, keep my heart and mind from rebelling against You. Amen.

Read Psalm 139:23, and use it as a prayer.

Lessons from the Life of David

These questions relate to the meditations found on pages 29-33:

Discuss together:

1. Sin starts with a look or a thought. David looked and thought about sin. What does that mean to you? Does it seem like a small thing or a big deal? Why? Contrast it with *looking away* from sin. In light of James 1:14-15, discuss the two, different outcomes from the choices you make.

2. Can you relate to David's journey from visualizing sin to making it happen? How does this chain of events feel familiar to you? Share how you cultivated the flower of temptation into a sinful bloom. Share the places this path led you. Discuss the alternative choices that you might have made at the point of temptation. How would the outcome have been different?

3. David commits first-degree murder. What did David's premeditated sin reveal about his heart at that moment? Discuss why human pride makes it difficult to confess your sin. Why is pride the root of all sin? (See Chapter 8, *Mere Christianity*, C. S. Lewis.) What does 1 John 1:9 tell us to do when we sin?

Explore God's Word together:

1. **2 Samuel 11 and 12** tell the story of David, Bathsheba, and the prophet Nathan. David intentionally descends the ladder of sin, step by step, into a corrupt abyss. Have you ever willfully climbed down that ladder? Comment on how your decision and David's are the same. How did those actions work out for you?

2. **2 Samuel 11:22-25** tells of David's mild reaction after hearing that Uriah, his good friend, was killed. Was David numb to sin? When have you felt similarly numb to sin? How did sin turn your heart cold? What were the consequences?

3. **Numbers 32:23** is true: your sins will find you out. When did you experience this truth? Explain to the group how this works. Can anyone get away with anything?

Pray together:

1. Pray for any sin that is taking root in your life right now. If you are willing, confess it to the group, and ask for prayer and healing.

2. Lift up all family members in prayer.

3. Pray to Jesus for strength to get through these next days—for whatever may be distressing you.

Commit to **confidentiality** …

… **respect** each other

… **pray** for each other

… **encourage** one another

… **hold** each other **accountable**

God Pursues Us in Our Sin

**So the Lord sent Nathan the prophet to tell David this story. . . .
Then Nathan said to David, "You are that man!" 2 Samuel 12:1, 7**

God could have turned His back on David after he had Uriah murdered. But He didn't. In God's love for sinners, He pursued David. He sent the prophet Nathan to tell David a masterful story about two men: a rich man who had many sheep and a poor man who had only one. The rich man had a guest for dinner. Instead of killing one of his own sheep, he stole the poor man's only sheep, killed it, and served it to his visitor. When David heard the story, he was furious: "Any man who would do such a thing deserves to die!" (2 Samuel 12:5).

At that moment, Nathan busted David. He looked the king in the eye and said, "You are that man!"

Like the rich man in the story, David deserved to die. He had plotted adultery and murder, both punishable by death in Jewish law. But God in His mercy spared David's life. He sent Nathan to confront David about his sin and give him a chance to repent. (David didn't get off scot-free. You can read about his punishment in 2 Samuel 12:7-12.)

God loved the sinner king enough to pursue him and confront him about his sin. Has God done that for us too? Has he sent a "Nathan" to us? Has he placed us in circumstances where we had to come face-to-face with our sin?

We all need "Nathans" because we deceive ourselves about our sin. If we do not have people who are willing to confront us, we can ask a godly woman or man to confront us and speak boldly into our lives. That takes courage, but it is an important step in finding freedom from sin.

†

Making it personal: Find a trustworthy Christian, and ask that person to be honest about the sin he or she may see in your life. Will you listen when/if that person confronts you?

Prayer: Jesus, send me someone to help me see my sin. Help me to listen as You speak through that person. Amen.

Read 2 Samuel 12 for the story Nathan tells David.

Lessons from Nathan

These questions relate to the meditation found on page 36:

Discuss together:

1. God used a fearless but clever Nathan to confront King David about his sin. Why can having a "Nathan" in your life be a critical component for comprehending your sin? Do you want one? Are you willing to give permission to a trusted, loving friend to speak fearlessly into your life?

2. David was blind to his sins of lust, coveting, adultery, murder, and deceit. When have you been in the grip of such a sinful state that you were blind to your actions? Share the story for the benefit of the group. Why is blind sinfulness a common experience? Read Jeremiah 17:9, and consider how his words pour light into your answer?

3. How does being in community, like the study you are in now, contribute to knowing your heart? Why is it hard for you to see yourself clearly? How can regularly attending church services and a small study group help you see yourself more clearly?

4. What would you do if a "Nathan" came to you and spoke words of truth? Would your heart be open, or would you dismiss the words?

5. Are you willing to be a "Nathan" in someone's life? Can you speak the truth in love without gossiping later? What are the burdens of being a "Nathan" to someone? Consider and discuss all the facets of being God's gift to someone—a "Nathan."

Explore God's Word together:

1. **2 Samuel 7:1-17** tells the subtle story of Nathan telling King David that God will not allow him to build the temple. Nathan delivers a message from God that must have disappointed the King. What does this say about Nathan's character? How is God preparing Nathan for what was coming next? How has God prepared your character for something difficult? Share with the group.

2. Now turn to **Proverbs 27:6**. Discuss what this truth meant in the situation with Nathan and David and what it might mean to you and your "Nathan." How will you respond to loving confrontation?

Pray together:

1. Pray as a group that God would open your eyes to your sins.

2. Pray to want a "Nathan" in your life.

3. Pray to *become* a "Nathan."

Commit to **confidentiality** ...

... **respect** each other

... **pray** for each other

... **encourage** one another

... **hold** each other **accountable**

Confession of Sin

Then David confessed to Nathan, "I have sinned against the Lord." 2 Samuel 12:13

Many men and woman are in prison today because of their own words. The Supreme Court's Miranda ruling recognized it was unfair to interrogate suspected criminals who didn't know that what they said could be used against them in a court of law. The first thing we learn inside is to keep our mouths shut; but so many of us don't. Why is that?

Veteran police detectives know that the human heart wants to confess. The human heart *needs* to confess. The old saying "Confession is good for the soul" is accurate. Confession frees the heart of the enormous burden of guilt. It lifts the weight of shame off our consciences and allows us to start fresh with the truth.

Nathan really slammed David with the truth when he surprised the king with the words, "You are that man" (2 Samuel 12:7). David heard the voice of God in those words, and he realized that his sin was found out. The king did what we all must learn to do: He confessed and took responsibility for his actions. He opened his heart to the power of the Holy Spirit and fully understood that he had killed Uriah and hurt Bathsheba. And in the process, a baby also died. David had created victims. He had sinned against them.

But more important, after Nathan confronted him, David recognized that he had sinned against God. David's sin against God was open rebellion against the way God ordered him to live.

When we sin, we also create victims. But we also sin against God. We rebel against His guidelines and go our own way.

When we confess our sin, we are agreeing with God that our sin is rebellion against Him. Our confession keeps us from rationalizing and explaining away our actions. It allows us to begin to repair our relationship with God so that we can walk with Him.

✝

Making it personal: What is stopping you from confessing all your sin to God? What will you do about it?

Prayer: Lord God, I confess that my sin is open rebellion against You. Help me. Please. Amen.

Read and reflect on Psalm 51, David's prayer of confession.

The Stain of Sin

I punish the children for the sins of their parents to the third and fourth generations. Exodus 20:5

David faced consequences for his sin. The baby born to the king and Bathsheba died. David's sin was public. His friends, servants, and enemies knew of his one-night stand with Bathsheba and of Uriah's murder! The baby's death allowed God to make a public announcement that the product of sin was not happiness and harmony. Rather, it was death and destruction.

There's a direct relationship between human sin and the heartbreak of human life. Studies tell us that the most reliable predictor of a child's going to prison is if the father or mother is already inside. We also know that 80–90 percent of inmates' marriages end during the first year of imprisonment.

We must understand the stain of our sin. Our sins are forgiven, but the scar of our sins remains. This is a fact that we cannot avoid or deceive ourselves into dismissing.

Why is it so important to comprehend this fact? Without clear understanding that the tarnish of sin remains, we are prone to depression and loss of hope when life continues to deteriorate after we confess, repent, and accept forgiveness. It's dangerous to assume that once we repent, everything will instantly be all right. It is God alone who can rescue our loved ones from the consequences of our actions. He is in control of our lives and the lives of those who are affected by our sins.

In this fact there is peace and hope that our crimes have not destroyed all the lives they have touched. In this knowledge of God's grace, we can live inside with firm hope and gratitude. Helplessness may send us into depression, but an understanding of God's love conquers despair and can remake us into people *living life* instead of *doing "life without parole."*

✝

Making it personal: What steps will you take right now to let go of despair and let God have His way with your family?

Prayer: Father God, my sin hurts others. I entrust my friends and family into Your care. Help me to trust Your grace. Amen.

Read the rest of Exodus 20:6 to take comfort in God's grace.

Unintended Consequences

Those who live only to satisfy their own sinful desires will harvest the consequences of decay and death. But those who live to please the Spirit will harvest everlasting life from the Spirit. Galatians 6:8

David faced unintended consequences. He had a one-night stand with another man's wife. But David never figured that anyone would find out about his adultery. He ended up with a mess. Bathsheba became pregnant. David had her husband killed. The baby died. All of these were unintended consequences of his sin.

The Law of Unintended Consequences states that actions of people always have effects that are unanticipated or "unintended." For example, when DOC cuts our pay from $1.20 to $.60 a day to save money, we can't afford personal items, stamps, or envelopes. Tensions in the prison rise, and it becomes more dangerous for us and the staff. Those without canteen often bulldog those who have it. Sometimes fights occur, doing physical harm to officers and more costly damage to a facility than the payments of higher wages would've been. The unrest is an unintended consequence.

Many of us men are serving 25-to-life for felony murder because our "homeboy" partner killed the clerk instead of just robbing him as you had intended. Some of us women are doing serious time because although we were only lookouts for our drug-dealing boyfriends, we never thought our actions would carry a conspiracy charge. These are *unintended consequences.*

We need to be aware that our actions have consequences. Bad choices lead to ever-worsening outcomes. Good choices react in the opposite direction. Kindness and encouragement sow seeds of hope and reflect the character of Jesus to others. When we face the consequences of our actions, the decisions we make in dealing with them determine whether we make things worse or better.

✝

Making it personal: What choices are you facing now? Will your decision result in making the situation worse or better?

Prayer: Father God, help me make right, good choices. Amen.

Read Deuteronomy 30:19-20, hearing the words as a challenge from God.

Have Mercy on Me

Have mercy on me, O God, because of your unfailing love. Because of your great compassion, blot out the stain of my sins. Psalm 51:1

We've looked at the story of David's slide into first-degree murder. We've watched Nathan bust him about his sin, and we've heard the king's confession and God's forgiveness. But what was going on inside of David during this time? What emotions tumbled in his heart?

The Bible gives us an intimate look at the raw emotion in David's heart through many of the psalms that he wrote. The next few meditations will work through Psalm 51, which is David's heart cry after Nathan confronted him about his crime.

Today's verse shows that David's response starts in the right place. He didn't begin by defending himself. He didn't play the blame game. He didn't rationalize his crime. Instead, he pleaded for God's mercy. David knew that the only thing that could blot out the stain of his sin was God's mercy.

What are we asking for when we cry out to God for mercy? Mercy is the act of not giving us what we deserve. When we plead for mercy, we are saying to God, "I know I deserve your judgment. You have every right to punish me. But instead, would you give me mercy?"

Why would God give us mercy? First, He extends mercy to us because He is compassionate; it's His nature. But the second reason He gives us mercy is Jesus. Because Jesus willingly took on Himself the cost of our sins, God is free to have mercy on us.

When we are burdened by our sins and the stains they have left—in our lives and the lives of others—we can cry out, "Lord, have mercy on me." He will hear. He will extend mercy.

✝

Making it personal: What prevents you from throwing yourself on God's mercy? Plead with Him to remove the stain of your sin.

Prayer: Have mercy on me, O God. Nothing I can do can take away the stain of my sin. Only Your mercy can cleanse me. Thank You for Your unfailing love. Amen.

Read Psalm 103:1-12 for a look at our compassionate God.

Haunted by Guilt

Wash me clean from my guilt. Purify me from my sin. For I recognize my shameful deeds—they haunt me day and night. Psalm 51:2-3

Like David the psalmist, Maria was haunted by her shameful deeds. She and her boyfriend didn't mean to kill the store owner during the robbery. She didn't mean to get caught and leave her baby daughter without a mother around. How she wished she could undo that October night. For months she couldn't eat. She lost fifty pounds. She couldn't sleep. She tossed and turned in her cell, haunted by her guilt. The nightmares and flashbacks never seemed to end.

King David wrote in another psalm, "I am dying from grief; my years are shortened by sadness. [Sin] has drained my strength; I am wasting away from within" (Psalm 31:10). David's experiences are normal. Guilt and sin can suck the life out of a person.

Do you identify with Maria and David? Do your sin and guilt haunt you? David felt dirty from his sin and guilt. He knew that in order to feel clean, he needed God to cleanse him, purify him.

It's normal for us to *feel* guilt about our crimes and our sin. (We should worry if we don't feel guilt.) But it's not healthy for us to be *crippled* by our guilt.

Maria is doing better these days. She has found a better way. When one of her cellmates invited her to attend church, she begrudgingly went. There she learned about God's mercy and forgiveness. She is learning to face her guilt but not let it crush her. She is learning to allow God to purify her heart and her thoughts. Throughout the day she prays, "Wash me, Lord. Make me clean."

When we feel crushed by our guilt, we can give it to Jesus. We can ask Him to cleanse and purify us.

✝

Making it personal: What sin haunts you today? What can you do to confess that sin and give it to Jesus?

Prayer: God, my guilt is destroying me. Purify me. Help me to accept Your forgiveness and move beyond the crippling guilt. Amen.

Memorize Psalm 51:2, and use it as a daily prayer.

Sinning against God

Against you, and you alone, have I sinned; I have done what is evil in your sight. You will be proved right in what you say, and your judgment against me is just. Psalm 51:4

When Jamal hit his wife, he was blinded by rage. He wouldn't let her get away with talking to him like that. Who did she think she was? So he beat her into unconsciousness. That felt good. He wished the kids hadn't been there to see it, but then, she shouldn't have acted the way she did. Now Jamal sits in his cell with his haunting guilt.

Who did Jamal sin against? Certainly his wife. The brain damage she lives with from that brawl is a constant reminder of his outburst. What about the kids? They live with the stain of his sin too. One of them has already been in trouble with the law.

When David sinned, he sinned against Bathsheba, her husband, the child who died—really the whole kingdom that he ruled. But in the midst of all of that, David realized the real truth about our sin. When we sin, we are really sinning against God, not just our families, not just the owner of the store we robbed, not just the person we beat. We sin against God.

David also realized that God's judgment against him was just. When we sin, we break God's standard. He has told us in His Word to love others as we would love ourselves. He has told us, "Don't hurt others." "Don't steal." When we violate God's commands, we violate *Him*. That's the bottom line of our sin. We violate God.

Have you looked your sin in the face? Have you seen the face of God on the other end of your sin?

But don't be discouraged. Because of Jesus, when God looks our sin in the face, He sees the face of Jesus, who sacrificed His life for us.

✝

Making it personal: Have you recognized that you have offended a holy God? Tell Him what you feel.

Prayer: God, I am so sorry that I have sinned against You. Please forgive me, and give me a new start. Amen.

Read Isaiah 55:6-7 to find direction and pardon.

I Want to Feel Joy Again

Oh, give me back my joy again; you have broken me—now let me rejoice. Psalm 51:8

After David sinned, he lost his joy. He discovered what many of us do: the pleasure and high we sometimes feel after we sin doesn't last. When the initial excitement wears off, we often feel empty, alone, numb.

After David faced the enormity of his sin, he spiraled into despair. We can imagine him saying to himself, "After what I did, how can I ever face my family again? How can I lead other people when I can't even control my own heart? Why would anyone trust me?" Many of us can identify with his anguish.

David was a broken man. But he knew that God could begin to restore him. So what does he ask God for? David longed for joy.

Why joy? Joy is more than happiness. Happiness is based on our current circumstances. Joy is more than feeling optimistic about life. Joy is a spiritual emotion. It's that deep sense of delight and satisfaction that comes from knowing God is in control, that He is good, and that He wants a relationship with us. David knew that his life was not complete without joy.

Reading the other psalms in the Bible shows us that God *did* restore joy to David. In fact, the word *joy* is used seventy times in the book of Psalms. David starts Psalm 32 with these words: "Oh, what joy for those whose rebellion is forgiven, whose sin is put out of sight! Yes, what joy for those whose record the Lord has cleared of sin, whose lives are lived in complete honesty!"

We can have that joy too. We can feel the freedom and release that comes after God takes our brokenness and restores us to full relationship with Him.

✝

Making it personal: Have you lost your joy? What will you do to restore it?

Prayer: God, I long to feel joy again, to be free from the weight of my sin. Please do in my life what You did in David's. Thank You. Amen.

Read Colossians 1:11-14, one of the apostle Paul's prayers for God to fill us with joy.

Clean Me Up

Don't keep looking at my sins. Remove the stain of my guilt. Create in me a clean heart, O God. Renew a right spirit within me. Psalm 51:10

King David was involved in repeated sin. His crime wasn't a one-time slip. His was deliberate sin.

Some of us can identify with him. We, too, were involved with repeated sin. Maybe our drug addiction led us down the slippery slope. Maybe our rage ate away at us and led us into sin. Maybe it was our lust or our greed. We've tried to change, but we can't make it work. We become discouraged and hopeless. We begin to think that maybe *we* are hopeless too. Worthless. And that attitude is not what we need to get beyond the guilt and stain of our sin.

David's pleading prayer points us in the right direction. We need not only forgiveness but also cleansing. We need new hearts.

Only God can give us new hearts—clean hearts—with new attitudes and new values. Through the power of His Holy Spirit, He wants to give us spiritual heart transplants so that His desires will flow through us, directing our emotions and actions. He wants His thoughts to fill our minds.

David also knew he needed a "right" spirit. He needed to have God touch his attitudes.

We need that touch too. Often our spirits are full of negativity, hate, selfishness, greed, and lust. We need God to give us spirits that are full of hope, joy, peace, patience, goodness, and self-control. We need attitudes that help us reach out to each other, help us think the best about each other, and help us trust that God will use our lives to accomplish His good purposes. We need "right" spirits.

✝

Making it personal: What is the state of your heart? Do you need a spiritual heart transplant? What will you do about it?

Prayer: God, I give up. I can't change on my own. I need You to create a clean heart in me. I need You to renew my spirit. Thank You for promising to do that. Amen.

Read Ezekiel 18:30-32 and Ezekiel 36:22-28 to remember God's promises to give sinners a new heart and spirit.

Don't Give Up on Me

Do not banish me from your presence, and don't take your Holy Spirit from me. Restore to me again the joy of your salvation, and make me willing to obey you. Psalm 51:11-12

When Darnell first faced up to his crime—robbery, assault, and rape—and the sin that led to it, he was devastated. He was so ashamed, so regretful about the hurt he had caused. Oh, how he wished he could undo the damage. Every night his dreams took him back to that violent night. And every night he ached to be able to redo the scene, to undo it. But he couldn't get rid of the stain of his sin.

He cried out to God for forgiveness, and he knew that God had heard him. But he wasn't sure what God really thought about him. Had God gotten tired of him? Had God written him off? Darnell sat in his cell, depressed. He couldn't lift himself out of the darkness.

David might have had similar thoughts. He pleaded with God not to banish him, not to give up on him. His joy was gone. He didn't have the will to obey.

The good news is that God doesn't trash us when we sin. He doesn't toss us aside and say, "I've had enough of you. Forget it." No, He restores us. Even after all David had done, the Bible still refers to him as a "man after God's own heart" (see Acts 13:22). God restored David. And He will restore us.

God forgives us, allowing us to hold our heads high again. Through God's Holy Spirit, He restores the joy to our lives, giving us the ability to be productive again. He is so gracious. He shows us His will, and then He gives us the strength to obey it.

†

Making it personal: What keeps you from believing that God graciously accepts you and will restore you from the stain of your sin? How can you change that?

Prayer: God, I'm like David. I plead with You not to look at the stain of my sin. Instead, restore my joy, and make me willing to obey You. Thanks for not writing me off. Amen.

Read Psalm 71:20-21, and use it as a prayer for restoration.

Make Me Useful

Then I will teach your ways to sinners, and they will return to you. Psalm 51:13

Cory is a lot like King David. He took another man's wife and killed her husband. It took getting sent to Massachusetts Correctional Institution before Cory faced the impact of his crimes, the stain of his sin. His "Nathan" was Chaplain Dick, who taught him not only about the destructive force of sin but also about the depth of God's love for him. Cory confessed his sin and pleaded for God's mercy to restore him.

And He has. Cory knows he will serve a life sentence, but he is determined to make that life sentence a life of service to God. He wants to do *HIS* time and make his remaining years count.

Today Cory is one of six men who help Chaplain Dick teach other inmates about who God is and how much He loves sinners. God takes our mistakes and turns them into opportunities. God took Cory's brokenness and is using it to teach His ways to other sinners.

All of us long to have meaning, to make our lives count. Our gracious God does not toss us aside when we fall into sin. He restores us—for a purpose: so that we can serve Him. In the same way that God uses the life of King David to teach millions of people about His forgiveness, grace, and mercy, He will use our lives—the good and the ugly—to teach His ways to other sinners.

We can ask God to take our intelligence—the same intelligence that allowed us to plan a crime—and use it to understand His Word and teach others. We can ask Him to take our power of persuasion—which once was focused only on conning people—and cleanse it and use it to draw others to Christ.

†

Making it personal: How will you take what God has taught you and teach it to others, praying that they will return to God too?

Prayer: God, I thank You that You can take the broken mess of my life and use it to teach others. I want to do Your time. I give You my life. Amen.

Read Psalm 86:11-13, and use it as a prayer.

But I Killed Someone

Forgive me for shedding blood, O God who saves; then I will joyfully sing of your forgiveness. Psalm 51:14

Some of us are serving time because, like David, we killed someone. Maybe we didn't deliberately set out to kill someone, but we took a life. We shed blood. And that reality weighs heavily on our hearts.

We should be grateful that God didn't edit the messy parts out of the Bible. He decided to include stories of people who did awful things. Here was King David, who not only committed a crime, but he committed one of the worst crimes: premeditated murder.

In God's love and wisdom, He left that story in the Bible to comfort and direct those of us who have also taken a life. David's story of sin, confession, forgiveness, and restoration encourages us to see that God can do in our lives what He did in David's.

David's story shows that God can forgive the most self-centered, hateful deeds. And He not only forgives us but also restores us: restores our joy, restores our relationship with Him, restores our purpose, restores our dignity. God didn't say to David after he killed Uriah, "Okay, that's it. You can't be king anymore. I have no more use for you." No, God restored David. And He will restore us too.

The mark of that restoration is the fact that the Scriptures do not remember David as "David, the Murderer." The Bible remembers him as "a man after God's own heart," as the man who wrote the psalms, where he "joyfully sings of forgiveness." The Bible remembers him as the father of Solomon, the wisest king who ever lived. Praise God. If He can forgive and restore David, He can forgive and restore us as well. Even for killing someone.

†

Making it personal: If you have killed someone, what would it feel like to receive God's forgiveness? What steps will you take?

Prayer: God, I did the unthinkable. I killed someone. I am so sorry. I sinned against that person, but more important, I sinned against You. Forgive me. Amen.

Read Exodus 2:11-15 and Hebrews 11:23-28, the story of another murderer whom God used to accomplish His purposes.

Sing a New Song

Forgive me for shedding blood, O God who saves; then I will joyfully sing of your forgiveness. Unseal my lips, O Lord, that I may praise you. Psalm 51:14-15

King David knew where to go to get right about the murder. He asked for God's forgiveness, and God gave it (see 2 Samuel 12:13).

But David realized another profound truth: Forgiveness leads to joy. When we feel the release of forgiveness—that God doesn't hold our sin against us and that He gives us a clean slate and a clean heart—then we are free to be joyful.

When God forgives us and saves us from our sin, we'll want to praise Him and then tell others about who He is and what He has done in our lives so that they will find His forgiveness too.

How can we "sing" of God's forgiveness? How can we praise Him? What does "joyfully singing of God's forgiveness" look like behind bars?

We can adopt a new attitude of praise. We can find psalms of praise, memorize the verses, and use them as personal prayers during the day. Silently say them to God when we're out in the yard.

We must begin to act differently. Our new behavior reflects the new song within us. When our actions "joyfully sing," others are going to notice—and want to join in. Instead of meanness, sing kindness; in place of selfishness, start sharing canteen. People will notice. After people notice our new song, we have to be willing and able to share with them where our new song came from—Jesus' love and forgiveness. We can share that story with anyone who'll listen.

Finally, prison church is a great place to literally "sing" God's praises. If you haven't attended in a while, start going out of gratitude for what God has done in forgiving you. Join with others and sing praises to God.

✝

Making it personal: How will you "joyfully sing" of God's forgiveness this week?

Prayer: God, when I think of what You have done for me in forgiving me, I can't help but tell others. Unseal my lips too, so that I may praise You. Amen.

Read Psalm 103:2-5 as a prayer thanking God for forgiving you.

What God Wants from Us

You would not be pleased with sacrifices, or I would bring them. The sacrifice you want is a broken spirit. A broken and repentant heart, O God, you will not despise. Psalm 51:16-17

When Anita arrived at the Iowa Correctional Institution for Women, she was sorry for her part in the assault that handed her a seven-year sentence. She was bitter when arrested, but a month in county jail changed her heart, and she began to feel sorrow and remorse.

Once inside Iowa Correctional, she dealt with her regret by throwing herself into her work in the laundry. She had no problem grabbing other women's soiled underwear and getting it into the machines. Anita was trying to get clean herself and make good for her crime through her efforts. But Anita can't make up for her sin by working hard or doing good things. Neither can we! We must repent and come to God with our broken hearts and turn in the other direction—away from sin and toward Him.

In King David's day, people expressed their remorse by offering a sacrifice. They brought a lamb or a dove, and offered it to the priests to pay for their sin. But God didn't want David's sacrifice. He wanted David's broken-heartedness. He wanted a repentant heart. God requires that from us today too.

The word *repent* means to have a change of heart. Repentance is doing a "180" and going in the other direction, turning away from sin.

Like Anita, we can work all we want, but we will never remove the stain of our sin by ourselves! If we confess our sin to God, we will find forgiveness for our past. We will be able to make peace with our present and find hope for our future.

✝

Making it personal: How are you trying to do penance to pay off your sin? What will you do about that?

Prayer: God, I can't make up for my sin on my own. I give You what I have—a broken spirit and a heart that is willing to turn from my sin. Help me with the rest. I need You. Amen.

Read Isaiah 57:15 to hear God's desires for repentant hearts.

More Lessons from the Life of David

These questions relate to the meditations found on pages 39-51:

Discuss together:

1. Read Psalm 51, which is David's heart cry after Nathan confronted him. What was David's response to God once he realizes his sin? What has been your reaction when busted by a "Nathan"? Compare your response to David's.

2. Read Genesis 3:12-13, the account of Adam and Eve getting busted by God. How are the responses of David and Adam and Eve different? To which response do you relate most?

3. David pleads to God for mercy. Why do you feel it is such a big thing for David to ask God for mercy? What does mercy mean to you? If you've experienced mercy, what did mercy feel like? Why can we expect God to show us mercy? How does that feel?

4. How does the guilt of being in prison overwhelm you at times? David felt guilt, but he sought forgiveness. Do you feel forgiven— by God, your family, your victims? Do you freely forgive? How does God's forgiveness help you cope with unforgiveness, shame, and guilt?

Explore God's Word together:

1. **2 Corinthians 5:11-21** encapsulates the Good News of Christ. Verse 5 in some translations reads: "Because we understand our fearful responsibility to the Lord, we work hard to persuade others." What do you think Paul meant by the words "fearful responsibility?" Do you follow Jesus because you're afraid or grateful? Paul speaks of being ambassadors. What does an ambassador do? Can you do those things inside the walls?

2. Read **Psalm 51**, the "playbook" for going to God after we fall into sin. Memorize verses 1-2, and repeat them often as you heal after you sin.

3. Read **Psalm 32** out loud, verse by verse, and discuss the joy that is the result of forgiveness. Look at verse 8. How can the Lord guide your life where you are today?

Pray together:

1. Pray silently, asking God to forgive you for your sinful thoughts, attitudes, and actions. If necessary and appropriate, ask people in your group to forgive you.

2. Read Psalm 40:11 as a personal prayer. Thank God for His tender mercies shown to you and your group.

3. Pray as a group for the Holy Spirit to develop in each of you these characteristics: kindness, patience, mercy, and forgiveness. Linger over each one.

4. Lift up the entire population (including the COs) in your facility. Pray for relief from feelings of collective shame, unresolved guilt, and the burden of not being/feeling forgiven.

Commit to **confidentiality** …

… **respect** each other

… **pray** for each other

… **encourage** one another

… **hold** each other **accountable**

The Escalator of Temptation

Temptation comes from our own desires, which entice us and drag us away. These desires give birth to sinful actions. And when sin is allowed to grow, it gives birth to death. James 1:14-15

Most of us have long rap sheets. They are the written history of our brushes with the law and probably don't begin to detail our entire criminal activity. Our rap sheets began with petty stuff. We boosted a car to impress a girl, but soon our crimes got more serious. Take Rachel's story as an example.

Rachel was eleven when her parents split up. She was angry at her parents and angry at herself since she mistakenly blamed herself for her parents' divorce.

The rage got worse when her mom's new boyfriend started making sexual moves on her when she turned thirteen. It boiled over when her mother didn't believe her when she told her about the advances. Rachel decided to run away.

Once on her own, Rachel needed food and began stealing it. Then someone offered her some weed, which took the pain away temporarily. Money was always a problem, so Rachel traded her body for food and drugs. That led to numerous arrests. After getting out, Rachel hooked up with a pimp who was also responsible for a large cook of meth. She started to use and then agreed to sell it. She was busted and sent away for eight years for distribution.

The devil is never satisfied with little temptations. His goal is to lead us up the escalator to bigger and badder sins. Remember: King David's adultery with Bathsheba started with just a peek and ended up in murder-one.

When we realize that each temptation leads to greater sin, we need to stop and think. We must recognize the path that we're on. Never be deceived into thinking temptation is a one-shot deal!

✝

Making it personal: Find a quiet time, and list all the temptations facing you right now. Try to imagine where they might lead.

Prayer: Lord God, I don't really want to let these go, but know I must. Help me release these temptations to Your power. Amen.

Read Psalm 91 to find strength to face temptation.

Jesus Was Also Tempted

Immediately the Holy Spirit compelled Jesus to go into the wilderness. He was there for forty days, being tempted by Satan. Mark 1:12-13

Old numbers know the score. They understand what's going on in the facility. They see someone disrespected on the yard; they recognize someone will even the score. They appreciate the danger. Experienced inmates know the risks facing "short" cons. Cons who are not being released very soon are jealous, and it drives them to jam someone up during the last few days inside. They hope the short-term inmates get written up so their out date is ruined. Knowing how things work is fundamental to handling the dangers inside prison.

We need to understand temptation. We need to know where it comes from, what it looks like, and how it works so that we can identify it, prepare for it, and deal with it. Temptation is ultimately a test. Will we do the right thing, or will we give in to the temptation?

Jesus was tempted too. Jesus did not give in. He did not sin in the face of temptation. He won the battle. We serve a Savior who faced the same temptations we do every day. Jesus went into the wilderness for a showdown with Satan, the enemy of our souls—and Jesus won!

Temptation itself is not sin, but it often leads to sin. Temptations come in all shapes and sizes. Smaller temptations often lead to larger ones. When we were kids, the devil tempted us to steal candy before he tempted us to steal makeup as adults. When someone flirts with us every day—tempting us with sexual sin—it's like water dripping on a rock. The temptation gets more and more difficult to resist, especially after the initial shock of the proposition wears off and it begins to feel normal.

Let's be on our guard. We can be confident of God's strength to give us victory over temptation.

†

Making it personal: Confront the temptations in your life. How can you prepare to fight them?

Prayer: Lord, it gives me comfort to know that You were tempted and did not give in. Amen.

Read Luke 4:1-13, the story of the temptations Jesus faced.

Jesus Understands Our Temptations

Since he himself has gone through suffering and temptation, he is able to help us when we are being tempted. Hebrews 2:18

When we first landed in our cells, some of us felt alone, even helpless. What would it be like? How would we survive? Sometimes, we looked to older numbers, who had spent more time behind bars, hoping they'd help us adjust. They knew the score and they understood what our lives would be like because they'd lived it.

We can take great comfort in the realization that Jesus understands what it's like to be tempted. His Father didn't spare Him that experience. Because Jesus went through the agony of temptation, He can be an understanding friend in our agony too.

The story of Jesus' temptation in Luke 4 tells us that Jesus had been fasting when Satan came to Him. Christ had had no food for forty days. Knowing that Jesus was very hungry, Satan tempted Him at His point of vulnerability. "'If you are the Son of God, change this stone into a loaf of bread.' But Jesus told him, 'No! The Scriptures say, "People need more than bread for their life"'" (Luke 4:3-4).

On the surface the devil's request seems reasonable. After all, Jesus *could* have changed the stones into bread. But Jesus saw beneath Satan's challenge. He saw that the devil really wanted Him to obey him, to do his bidding. But Jesus refused the temptation to be conned by Satan. Jesus passed the test.

Remember that Jesus knows the score. He faced temptation, and He promises to help us face it too. We can trust that God knows our situation and is concerned about our welfare. That is the concrete slab under our lives. It's the firm foundation on which all other defenses against temptation are built.

†

Making it personal: Where is Satan testing you? Where are you the most vulnerable? What steps will you take to resist?

Prayer: Jesus, I'm so glad that You know what it's like to be tempted. Help me to pass the test in my own temptations. Amen.

Read Hebrews 2:16-18 to learn about the God who promises to be our help in temptation.

Know the Enemy

Stay alert! Watch out for your great enemy, the devil. He prowls around like a roaring lion, looking for someone to devour. Stand firm against him, and be strong in your faith. 1 Peter 5:8-9

Satan attacks in many forms. He knows that some of our fathers sexually abused us. He also saw our mothers look the other way when it happened. Satan planted those weeds of worthlessness and anger in our souls to distract us from God's best for us.

If we're going to beat the devil, we need to know what he's like. These verses picture Satan as a roaring lion on the prowl. Our enemy is not some punk. He's a very rough hombre, and he's always on the attack. He's prowling around, eager to rip and tear. His goal is not just to intimidate us. Satan wants to kill us. This is a winner-take-all yard brawl.

How do we defend ourselves against this powerful force? These verses offer us three strategies. First, be careful! That's good advice. If we don't take our enemy seriously, we will become self-satisfied and be an easy mark for the predator. Instead, we must always be on our guard. We must feel the enemy's breath on our backs. John 8:44 reminds that Satan was a murderer from the beginning.

Second, we must take a firm stand. We need to be willing to face down the enemy. That takes courage and strength. Where does that strength come from?

Our courage comes from the third instruction: be strong in our faith. We must understand who Jesus is and that He promises to stand with us when we face the vicious lion. Colossians 2:13-15 tells us that Christ's death on the cross has disarmed the evil rulers of this world and made a laughingstock of them.

✝

Making it personal: What does Satan's breath feel like on your back? What will you do to stay on guard?

Prayer: Thank You, Jesus, that You have already muzzled the lion, Satan. Help me to stand firm. Amen.

Read Colossians 2:13-15 to remember what Christ's death has done to our enemy.

Put on Your Armor

Put on all of God's armor so that you will be able to stand firm against all strategies and tricks of the devil. For we are not fighting against people made of flesh and blood, but against the evil rulers and authorities of the unseen world, against those mighty powers of darkness who rule this world, and against wicked spirits in the heavenly realms. Ephesians 6:11-12

If we're sure something's going to happen, we prepare for it. We get ready. If we knew we were going to be punked during our first ninety days in prison, we'd seek alliances, hit the free weights, and be on guard every day. We prepare for the assault. When it comes to temptation, it's not a question of *if*. It's a question of *when*.

God knows we will face temptation. He also knows that the Tempter is strong and has strategies and tricks. God wants us to be prepared, to know what defensive and offensive weapons are available to us to win over temptation.

God never leaves us alone to fight the devil and the mighty powers of darkness. He has given us what today's verses call "armor." Writing from a prison cell, the apostle Paul gives us a detailed and helpful lesson in how to fight the devil. Using the picture of a soldier and his armor, he tells us how to prepare for battle. We'll look closely at the armor in the next few meditations.

But knowing about the armor is not enough. We have a choice. We need to *put on* the armor. It's not enough for us to know it's there. We must make the choice to put it on. In the same way that it would be foolish for a marine to go into battle without his or her weapons, we cannot expect to win the test of temptation if we do not prepare and arm ourselves.

†

Making it personal: How will you arm yourself for battle with the devil? Prepare to fight.

Prayer: God, some days my temptations are so strong that I can't seem to resist. Teach me how I can fight against temptation. Amen.

Read Ephesians 6:10-20 for the apostle Paul's teaching about fighting temptation.

Put on Truth

Use every piece of God's armor to resist the enemy in the time of evil, so that after the battle you will still be standing firm. Stand your ground, putting on the sturdy belt of truth. Ephesians 6:13-14

While a belt doesn't seem like "armor," it was the first piece of equipment a soldier put on because it would hold the other parts of the armor together. The soldier hung his sword on his belt. The belt also held the soldier's tunic together so that it wouldn't get in his way when he moved. The belt made him feel secure, confident.

Paul tells us that truth is like that belt. When we know the truth, we can feel secure when the devil lies to us. The Bible says that Satan "was a murderer from the beginning and has always hated the truth. There is no truth in him. . . for he is a liar and the father of lies" (John 8:44). When Satan says to us, "You're worthless. After all, you're just a criminal," we can respond with the truth: "God says that He has 'called me by name; I am His. . . . I am precious to Him'" (Isaiah 43:1-4, paraphrase).

When the devil whispers, "No one cares about you. You're alone in the world," we can shout the truth: "God so loved me that He gave His only Son, so that everyone who believes in Him will not perish but have eternal life" (John 3:16, paraphrase). Take that.

Or when the devil taunts us, "You'll never amount to anything," we can stand our ground, look him in the eye, and say, "Jesus said that the truth is, anyone who believes in Him will do the same works He has done, and even greater works" (see John 14:12, paraphrase).

Stand up to the devil. Beat him back with the truth.

✝

Making it personal: What lies has the devil been telling you? What truth can you fire back at him?

Prayer: Lord, that murderous devil has been telling me lies. Remind me of the truth so that I can stand firm against him. Amen.

Read John 14:6 to remember the source of all truth.

Put on Righteousness

Stand firm then, with . . . the breastplate of righteousness in place. Ephesians 6:14, NIV

If you imagine a suit of armor, picture the breastplate as the piece of thick metal that covers the soldier's chest—his heart, one of the most important parts of the body to protect. Today's verse tells us that if we are to stand firm against the devil, we must protect our hearts with the armor of righteousness. What does that mean?

We don't use the words *righteousness* or *righteous* much these days. We might hear someone say that another person is "a righteous dude," meaning he is a good person. But in the Bible, if someone is righteous, that person is morally good, pure, holy, free from guilt or sin. Well, that eliminates us. Only Christ is righteous.

But before we get too bummed, remember that Jesus *gives* us His righteousness. The apostle Paul tells us that "Christ's one act of righteousness makes all people right in God's sight and gives them life" (Romans 5:18). Because of Jesus' death, when God looks at us, He doesn't see our sin. He sees the righteousness of His Son instead. If we confess our sin and accept Christ's death on our behalf, we are protected.

What does that mean for fighting the devil's attacks? When we feel attacks coming, we can protect our hearts by claiming the righteousness of Jesus. We can raise our hands in the air (literally) and speak the name of Jesus out loud. With the name of Jesus, we can declare victory over anger. With the name of Jesus, we can claim triumph over lust. We can rebuke the devil and cast him out of our house by saying, "Christ is my righteousness. In the name of Jesus, I rebuke you, Satan." Evil flees at the mention of Jesus' name. As the bright light of Jesus' name shines into the darkness, wickedness scatters like cockroaches in a filthy kitchen.

†

Making it personal: Where is your heart unprotected? What steps will you take to protect it? Who will you ask to help you?

Prayer: *Lord, thank You for giving me Your righteousness. I claim it in the name of Jesus. Amen.*

Read Romans 4:22-24 and Philippians 3:8-10 to learn more about our righteousness.

Put on Peace

For shoes, put on the peace that comes from the Good News, so that you will be fully prepared. Ephesians 6:15

In our culture, we don't think of shoes as a part of armor. But in many cultures, people didn't normally wear shoes. So, if a person without shoes was attacked and had to fight back, needing to run over rocks or run far, his feet might easily get cut, slowing him down or causing him to stumble. Shoes gave the soldier protection, support, and agility. Shoes were a defensive weapon. If the soldier was to be prepared, he kept his battle shoes on.

The apostle Paul says that the peace that comes from the Good News—the Gospel—is like a pair of protective battle shoes. How is peace a like a defensive weapon?

When we are at peace with God—when we have accepted His grace and forgiveness—we can be at rest. Our hearts are not troubled. That peace is a powerful defense. When Satan tries to tempt us—test us—we can stand firm. We are not vulnerable. We are not distracted. We can call on the inner peace and confidence we have because Christ has paid the price for our sin. We're covered. The apostle Paul reminds us, "Therefore, since we have been made right in God's sight by faith, we have peace with God because of what Jesus Christ our Lord has done for us" (Romans 5:1).

But it's not enough for us to have peace with God. We need to be at peace with each other. When we have peaceful relationships with our cellmates or our family members, Satan has very little room to attack us. Peace is a defensive weapon. It protects us and helps us not to stumble.

†

Making it personal: What does it mean to be at peace with God? Are you at peace with God and others?

Prayer: Jesus, thank You for the peace that Your sacrificial death brings to my life. It fills me up and protects me so that the devil has no chance of getting at my heart. Amen.

Read 2 Peter 3:14, the apostle Peter's wise words about peace.

Put on Faith

In every battle you will need faith as your shield to stop the fiery arrows aimed at you by Satan. Ephesians 6:16

Soldiers relied on a shield to stop fire-tipped arrows. Shields in those days were made of wood and covered in leather that would be soaked in water before battle. That way, when the enemies' flaming arrows struck the shield, the flame would be extinguished. The shield was the first defense. By holding it in front of himself, the soldier's entire body would be protected.

Paul says that faith is like that shield, our first defensive weapon. What is faith? Some people have described it as **F**orsaking **A**ll **I**n **T**rusting **H**im. When Satan sends his fiery darts—temptation to indulge in resentments or exaggerate hurts or score some dope—at us, we can avoid destruction and can boldly face the devil with our shield of faith. That shield is our willingness to place absolute trust in God.

In Paul's day, shields were often decorated with a coat of arms, an emblem of the king or ruler for whom the soldier was fighting. The shield declared the soldier's loyalty. When we trust God for our protection, our shields bear the coat of arms of the cross of Jesus Christ. When we hold the cross in Satan's face, his flaming arrows cannot penetrate.

Picture something else. When a group of soldiers were facing the enemy, they would stand next to each other and hold out their door-like shields. Side-by-side, these shields formed a defensive wall that the enemy was not able to break down.

We can readily see the similarities. When we believers stand together—brother next to brother, sister next to sister—and thrust out our shields of faith, we can withstand any temptation that the enemy would throw at us.

✝

Making it personal: What fire-tipped arrows is Satan hurling at you? How will you trust God to see you through?

Prayer: Jesus, I trust You. Thank You for giving me men and women who will join their faith with mine so that Satan has no power over us. Amen.

Read 1 Peter 1:7-8 for encouragement in standing up to the tests of faith.

God's Helmet Law

Use every piece of God's armor to resist the enemy in the time of evil, . . . Put on salvation as your helmet. Ephesians 6:11, 17

Why do most states have some version of a helmet law for motorcycle riders? Obvious! The helmet protects the head, which is one of the most important parts of the human anatomy. When we dump our Hog on loose gravel, we will suffer some scrapes and maybe a few broken bones, but those are minor injuries compared to bouncing our melons off the asphalt at 75 mph without protection! The helmet is the soldier's second most important defensive weapon. The helmet protects his head, his ability to think and make decisions to insure his safety.

Of all of the places that Satan tries to attack us, the mind is one of his key targets. He knows that if he can get inside our heads and screw up our thinking, he can control everything about us.

The apostle Paul taught us, "If your sinful nature controls your mind, there is death. But if the Holy Spirit controls your mind, there is life and peace" (Romans 6:8). Many of us have felt the "death" caused when our minds are controlled by Satan or our own sinful natures.

We fully understand the effects of being disrespected at a club when we saw our boyfriend kissing another woman or our girlfriend slipping her cell phone number into the pocket of another guy. We know very well how that disrespect churned into anger and rage that resulted in our committing aggravated assault or even attempted murder.

But we can get protection. When we ask Jesus into our hearts, we are saved. After that, He gives us His Holy Spirit. When the Spirit controls our minds through the fruit that the Holy Spirit produces in us, we experience life and peace.

Get saved—get protection from the devil's evil schemes!

✝

Making it personal: How is your mind protected? Will you put on the helmet of salvation?

Prayer: *God, some days my mind is my worst enemy. I desire Your salvation, which will protect me. Amen.*

Read Galatians 5:22-23, and discover the fruit of the Spirit.

Old-school Weapons

Use every piece of God's armor to resist the enemy in the time of evil, . . . take the sword of the Spirit, which is the word of God. Ephesians 6:11, 17

On the street, knives have been replaced by MAC-10s, MAC 11/9s or some other firearm. Knives just don't *cut it* anymore—no pun intended. But, inside it's different. A *shiv* or a *shank* is an old-school weapon—a knife! Today we learn about a spiritual sword, a holy *shiv*—an offensive weapon to do battle with our enemy.

Paul tells us that our shank is God's Word. The Bible can stop the devil, stick him where it hurts, and take him down.

We use the sword by knowing God's Word and keeping it fresh in our minds. When we are tempted by Satan's lies, we can fight back by talking back with the truth from God's Word.

When Satan tempted (tested) Jesus in the wilderness (see Matthew 4:1-11), Jesus beat back the devil's attack by quoting the Bible. When Satan challenged Jesus to prove He was the Son of God by turning stones into bread, Jesus took His Old Testament "sword" and quoted: "People need more than bread for their life; they must feed on every word of God." When the devil took Jesus to the temple and told Him to jump down because God would send angels to protect Him, Jesus shot back, "The Scriptures also say, 'Do not test the Lord your God.'" When Satan took Jesus to a high mountain and said, "I will give it all to you . . . if you will only kneel down and worship me," Jesus said with authority, "Get out of here, Satan, for the Scriptures say, 'You must worship the Lord your God; serve only him.'"

The Bible is the weapon Jesus demonstrates for us, and it's more powerful than any gun or knife. When we say, "Take a hike, Satan," and quote the Bible to him, he runs and hides.

✝

Making it personal: What "sword" words can you use against Satan's temptations?

Prayer: God, I want to memorize Your Word so that I can stand up to Satan's tests. Amen.

Read Matthew 4:1-11 for the whole story of how Jesus used the sword of the Bible.

Prayer Helps Us Fight Temptation

Use every piece of God's armor to resist the enemy. . . . Pray at all times and on every occasion in the power of the Holy Spirit. Stay alert and be persistent in your prayers. Ephesians 6:11, 18

When someone betrays us or makes us angry, our first instinct is to lash back and fight. We need to remember that behind this temptation (test) is the prowling lion (Satan), looking for someone to devour. Satan would love to take us out.

How can we face this test? Today's verses tell us that prayer will help us resist the enemy. Some of us are not comfortable praying. We feel awkward, wondering why God would want to hear from us. However, because of God's great love for us, He wants us to talk with Him. "Don't worry about anything; instead pray about everything. Tell God what you need, and thank him for all he has done" (Philippians 4:6). Rather than act out when someone disrespects us, let's avoid violence, the write-up, and Ad-Seg time by praying and telling God about the situation. God wants to hear everything—our fears, our hopes, and our dreams.

Pray on every occasion. Some of us grew up praying before meals. That's good, but it's only a start. We can pray when we wake up in the morning, when we stand in the chow line, when we have to deal with a knuckleheaded cellmate, when we lie in bed at night. Prayer—talking with God—should become as normal to us as breathing.

Today's verses instruct us to pray in the power of the Holy Spirit. What does that mean? "The Holy Spirit helps us in our distress. For we don't even know what we should pray for, nor how we should pray. But the Holy Spirit prays for us with groanings that cannot be expressed in words" (Romans 8:26). The Holy Spirit prays for us when we can't find the words to express our distress or anxiety or fear.

✝

Making it personal: What steps will you take to begin a practice of praying about everything?

Prayer: *God, thank You that You invite me to talk with You about everything. Amen.*

Read Psalm 138:2-3 for encouragement about the power of prayer.

Run from Temptation

But remember that the temptations that come into your life are no different from what others experience. And God is faithful. He will keep the temptation from becoming so strong that you can't stand up against it. When you are tempted, he will show you a way out so that you will not give in to it. 1 Corinthians 10:13

Backing down from a fight is one of the worst things we can do in prison. We're branded cowards and seen as candidates to be punked everyday from then on. The convict code says that when we are challenged, we cannot back down; we must face our enemy.

But in facing Satan, sometimes it's wise to run from temptation. The power of sin is strong. The Bible teaches that when we are tempted, we should run—not walk—from sin. "Do what is good and run from evil—that you may live!" (Amos 5:14). "Run from anything that stimulates youthful lust. Follow anything that makes you want to do right" (2 Timothy 2:22). "Run away from sexual sin! No other sin so clearly affects the body as this one does" (1 Corinthians 6:18). Sometimes running *is* a good strategy.

In close living environments like prison, literally running away may not be an option. But the Bible offers other helpful ways we can "run from sin." First, we can trust God's power to deliver us from temptation. Second, we can avoid places where we're likely to be tempted. We should not go near the gambling table if we know gambling is a temptation. Third, we can follow Jesus' example when He was tempted by the devil. If we know the Scriptures, we can quote them to Satan when he whispers temptation in our ears. And last, we can find Christian friends who will stand with us when we are being attacked by temptation. Together, with God's help, we can run from temptation.

✝

Making it personal: From what temptations do you need to run? Where will you find the courage to do it?

Prayer: Jesus, walk with me when I feel temptation's pull. Keep me from sin. Amen.

Read and memorize Psalm 18:2 for assurance.

Vulnerable to Temptation

Peter declared, "Even if all fall away, I will not. . . . Even if I have to die for you, I will never disown you." Mark 14:29-31, NIV

A dangerous time in our spiritual walk is right after a great spiritual experience. It could be just after we accepted Jesus as our Savior or repented from some nagging, persistent sin. At that very moment, the temptation to lower our defenses may be strong. And if we do, the devil can strike us and hurt us badly.

Team sports illustrate this point. Sometimes after an upset win over a superior team, the players are emotionally drained from the exciting high of the victory. They get cocky and overconfident. They let down their guard and end up losing to a weaker team the following game.

Several people in the Bible experienced defeat after a great spiritual high. Peter was one of the first disciples Jesus called, and he soon became one of His favorites. Peter walked with Jesus for three years and was chosen to be in the Garden of Gethsemane when Jesus prayed so hard that He sweated drops of blood. Peter attended the Last Supper and bragged about how he would never give Jesus up, even though everyone else could. Peter was proud, arrogant, and ready for a fall. That very evening, Peter denied that he even knew Jesus, cursing strongly that had no relationship to Him.

We don't automatically fall into sin after we experience a time of deep closeness to God. However, as we draw nearer to God in our daily walk, the devil isn't pleased. He's looking for ways to damage our witness, steal our joy, and make us doubt our faith. We must be on guard for his attacks and tricks, especially when we feel confident about our relationship with God. That's a time when self-satisfaction might sneak next to us and set us up for a fall.

†

Making it personal: Be aware of the danger, and let it drive you to your knees to ask God for protection.

Prayer: Lord Jesus, protect me from evil and from the attacks of Satan. Amen.

Read Matthew 26:20-74, the story of Peter's denial.

Temptation Blinds Us

The human heart is the most deceitful and desperately wicked. Who really knows how bad it is? Jeremiah 17:9

While our hearts are capable of love and compassion, they're also full of deceit, dishonesty, and trickery. We must know this and be on guard.

Billy was released after being down four years, but he was still on paper for twenty-three months. In prison his walk with Jesus flourished. He taught Bible studies and was active in the prison church. After he was released, he had a mentor, a job, a place to live, and a church. He was set up for success.

Then he met Lucinda. She was an attractive, single member of his church. They started hanging out. Billy's mentor warned him about the dangers of a relationship so early after his release, but Billy brushed the warnings aside. He unwisely believed his spiritual walk was strong enough. Soon Billy and Lucinda were sleeping together. In their hearts, they knew it was wrong, but instead of confessing and straightening up, they went the other way. They blew off church, started drinking and watching porn. They followed their hearts into sin. Soon, Billy moved in with Lucinda and her two-year-old daughter. When Billy's PO visited, Billy was violated for being in the presence of a child. He was sent back to serve the remaining twenty-three months of his sentence.

Billy's heart wanted the companionship and sexual favors that Lucinda offered. His heart blinded him to the obvious evil that lurked around the corner. He knew he wasn't allowed to be around small children, but his heart tricked him into believing he would never get caught. Now he's back inside.

If we know how the devil will use our hearts against us, we can be prepared. If we humble ourselves and listen to those in authority over us, we can avoid sin.

†

Making it personal: Where is your heart trying to deceive you and lead you into sin? What will you do about it?

Prayer: Father God, help me see the truth, and give me strength to resist temptation. Amen.

Read Psalm 51:10, and make it your prayer for a clean heart that can resist temptation.

Temptation Deludes Us

The temptations that come into your life are no different from what others experience. And God is faithful. He will keep the temptation from becoming so strong that you can't stand up against it. When you are tempted, he will show you a way out so that you will not give in to it. 1 Corinthians 10:13

Enrique's been out of prison five years. He's married and has a baby. He has an active prison ministry and is a man of God.

He arranged lunch with Jesse, a social agency director, and Jesse's assistant, Monica. Enrique and Monica arrived first and were seated while they waited for Jesse. Soon after, Jesse called saying he couldn't come to the meeting. He suggested they cover the agenda without him. A red flag should have gone up in Enrique's mind.

Enrique and Monica discussed the agenda, but the conversation got personal. Monica confided her loneliness and then suggestively placed her hands on Enrique's. When he didn't stop this out-of-bounds behavior, Monica boldly asked for his phone number. Enrique walked further down the road to sin when he gave it to her.

For the next week they flirted with one another through text messages. It thrilled Enrique that someone else found him attractive. When Monica suggested they have dinner together, Enrique agreed. He lied to his wife.

As he drove toward the restaurant, the Holy Spirit nudged him and convicted him of his slide toward sin. This time, instead of ignoring the Lord's voice, Enrique stopped what he was doing. He faced his deceitful heart and cried out to the Lord. With the Holy Spirit's help, he canceled the date and went home to his wife. Because Enrique was willing to submit to the Spirit's leading, the Lord showed him a way out.

When our hearts try to deceive us, we can turn away and focus on Jesus. He will deliver us when temptation strikes.

✝

Making it personal: Where are you resisting God's voice when He is trying to show you a way out of your temptation?

Prayer: Jesus, help me follow when You show me a way out. Amen.

Pray the words from the Lord's Prayer: "Don't let us yield to temptation, but deliver us from the evil one" (Matthew 6:13).

Avoid the Devil's Left Hook

Generous in love—God, give grace! Huge in mercy—wipe out my bad record. Scrub away my guilt. Soak out my sins in your laundry. I know how bad I've been; my sins are staring me down. Psalm 51:1-3, THE MESSAGE

Great fighters have destructive one-two punches—a right cross and a left hook. People who follow boxing know it's the left hook that's usually the knockout punch.

Satan has a deadly left hook too. The reason many of us go back to prison after we're released is because we allow the devil to knock us out. Here's what's going down.

Once on the street, we're scared and bewildered by the world we haven't encountered for years—maybe decades. We're lonely and vulnerable to the attention of predatory women and men or to the allure of drugs—or both! The hard truth is that many of us will fall into sin once released.

The devil tries to convince us that sin is okay. Once we fall to his right cross, he shows us his left hook. He whispers to us that we are worthless because of that sin . . . that God could never love us . . . that we should just keep on sinning. After all, we've already blown it, right? Wrong!

The apostle Peter denied Jesus three times. Judas Iscariot betrayed Christ with a kiss. How the two men *handled* their sin made all the difference. Peter wept and came back to Jesus for forgiveness, avoiding the knockout punch. Judas refused to see his sin, walked into the devil's left hook, and hung himself.

When we get hit by sin (and we all do), don't fall into the devil's trap and keep on sinning. Recognize that God forgives us for Jesus' sake. God accepts us back into full relationship when we confess our sin (see 1 John 1:9). Sin is inevitable—getting knocked out by it is not!

✝

Making it personal: Where is the devil trying to hit you with his left hook? What sinful behavior do you need to confess?

Prayer: Lord God, keep me from sin, but help me seek You when I fall. Amen.

Read Matthew 26:14–27:10, the stories of Peter and Judas.

God's Power against Evil

"Be quiet!" said Jesus sternly. "Come out of him!" The evil spirit shook the man violently and came out of him with a shriek. Mark 1:25–26, NIV

The following true story shows God's power over evil. Limon Correctional Facility in Limon, Colorado, opened in 1991. Soon after men arrived, turf wars broke out between rival gangs who battled for authority over the prison. Murders happened. It was a dark place.

Mel Goebel, Colorado Area Director for Prison Fellowship, sensed evil forces hovering over the facility. He felt led to gather Christian musicians and speakers and a hundred volunteers into the facility for a weekend revival program to retake the prison for Christ. The warden granted permission over the fierce objections of the security chief. The entire weekend was reserved for the program. The event was planned for the open yard, with the entire population invited to attend and mingle with the volunteers. The security chief predicted a hostage situation.

A dark, lightning-spitting cloud surrounded the prison on the Friday afternoon of the event. Wind blew, hail hurled down, and rain pelted the area where all the electronic gear was set up. Mel and some volunteers prayed for the devil's forces to be thwarted. Within minutes the wind, rain, and hail stopped, but the cloud remained. As the first musician stepped to the microphone, the clouds parted, and a beam of sunshine hit the stage. A double rainbow appeared.

That weekend no one was injured or taken hostage. On the contrary, many men came to Christ at the Sunday-morning altar call. Because of the event, the prison was reborn. The evil spirit was driven away. The warden at the time, Robert Furlong, credited that event as the moment Limon Correctional Facility changed course. It became a place where the prison church flourished and spawned many new missionaries to other prisons. We can trust the power of God to fight the evil forces that threaten to overtake us.

†

Making it personal: Where do you feel threatened by Satan's forces? What will you do about it?

Prayer: Lord, thank You that Your power is greater than the enemy's. Shine Your light on this dark place. Amen.

Read Mark 1:21-27 for the story of Jesus' power over evil forces.

Sin and Temptation

These questions relate to the meditations found on pages 54-71:

Discuss together:

1. How many of you have experienced the "escalator of sin"? Share your story. How does understanding that sins are connected touch your walk inside the walls? What temptations are you struggling with? Is it important that Jesus faced temptation too? Why?

2. "If you *know* the enemy and *know* yourself, you need not fear the result of a hundred battles" (Sun Tzu, *The Art of War*, emphasis added). What do you feel the ancient, Chinese warlord meant by his statement? In what ways can you understand the devil? Share what circumstances in your life make you ripe for sin. Knowing yourself means understanding what circumstances make you vulnerable. Describe some of those circumstances.

3. The armor of God protects you from temptation. In your prison, what specific spiritual armor is available to fight the enemy? What is missing? How can you get it? Are you willing to put on the armor? What hinders your readiness? Why?

4. Reread pages 68 and 69 and analyze the real-life stories of Billy and Enrique. What should/could they have done to avoid tumbling into sin? Can you relate to the devil's left hook in their situations, or in any of your circumstances? Discuss how you would have avoided the punch.

Explore God's Word together:

1. **James 1:2-5** says to be joyful when temptations come your way. Does this sound strange? How can temptations be an opportunity for joy? Wouldn't life be easier without the lure of sin? How are temptations similar to lifting free weights on the yard?

2. **Genesis 3:1-7** tells the story of how sin entered our world. Did the serpent (Satan) actually lie to Eve and Adam? Or, did he twist the truth? Does the devil whisper twisted truth into your ear? Give the group an example of it from your experience. How can knowing the devil's techniques help you avoid sin?

3. David writes **Psalm 16** when he is on the run from King Saul, who is out to kill him. Does it describe things that are absent from your life today? Would you like to have them? What is David's recipe for getting refuge, safety, security, and a firm, eternal destiny? How is this psalm a blueprint for dealing with fear, trials, and temptation?

4. **Ecclesiastes 4:12** describes the benefits of joining with your brothers or sisters to stand against the devil and temptation. How can you do this in your group?

Pray together:

1. Practice "pinpoint prayer." Pray precisely for each person's temptation and weak spot.

2. Remember to keep each other's sins confidential. Respect privacy, and honor each other's honesty.

3. Practice "praise prayer." By giving praise to God, it becomes easier and more natural to praise and encourage one another. This builds a strong network of believers.

Commit to **confidentiality** …

… **respect** each other

… **pray** for each other

… **encourage** one another

… **hold** each other **accountable**

The Bridge over Our Sin

You were his enemies, separated from him by your evil thoughts and actions, yet now he has brought you back as his friends. He has done this through his death on the cross in his own human body. As a result, he has brought you into the very presence of God, and you are holy and blameless as you stand before him without a single fault. Colossians 1:21-22

It's very important to view our sin in the warm light of God's grace. Grace is God's *undeserved gift* to us, similar to the occasion when a judge gave us probation when we really deserved jail time. If we focus only on our sin, without consideration of God's grace gift, we risk being preoccupied with our own failures and wrongdoings. When that happens, we can fall into Satan's trap. His finger of accusation (feeling guilty and without hope) can chuck our spirits into a dark hole that offers no promise of transformation.

But even though we all stand guilty before God and can't save ourselves, we are not without hope! God saw that sin created a huge valley between Himself and us. Instead of leaving us wallowing in our sin, He sent Jesus to be our bridge over that valley. God loves us so much that He sent His Son to pay for our sin (see John 3:16). Jesus bridges the gap for us to be reconciled with God.

Look at it this way. Many of us have relationship problems with family members. We have not spoken to our sisters or brothers for years. We ache for someone to act as a go-between to bring us together to patch things up. Jesus does this for us with God (see 1 Timothy 2:5). This new, reunited relationship offers forgiveness and new freedoms. Now, we are free to make right choices. We are free to stop living as a "house mouse." We're liberated to leave destructive relationships and behaviors. Embrace grace!

✝

Making it personal: Why are free gifts hard to accept? How do they disturb our pride? What steps will you take to accept God's grace?

Prayer: Father God, thank You for loving me. Help me acknowledge Your free gift to me. Amen.

Read 2 Corinthians 5:11-21 to learn more about reconciliation.

God's Repair Shop

O Israel, come back! Return to your God! You're down but you're not out. Prepare your confession and come back to God. Pray to him, "Take away our sin, accept our confession. Receive as restitution our repentant prayers." Hosea 14:1-2, THE MESSAGE

Some days we feel broken. Shattered. Useless. We wonder if God could ever find us useful to Him.

We need to remember that even if our lives are completely blown up, they can be repaired. God is a repairman who fixes shattered lives and makes them whole again. His tools are *conviction, confession, repentance,* and *forgiveness of sin.* These are the tools of deep, permanent, personal change in our lives.

One of the dangerous facts about sin is that the more it increases, the more our awareness of it often decreases. We become numb to our own inner rebellion. We need the touch of the Holy Spirit—or friends who are willing to be honest with us—to make us aware of our sins. Conviction is the first great tool in God's repair shop.

Once convicted, we must confess our sins to God. When we confess them, we are agreeing with God that we are not in tune with His plan for our lives. Our confessions to Him tune the radio of our hearts to the exact frequency, bringing clear music into our souls.

When we repent, we turn away from our sinful behavior. We admit that the problem lies in us. When we repent, we give God permission to begin His repair work.

God's forgiveness is like the finish coat of paint on an old toy. It makes it look new again. Forgiveness helps us begin to feel worthwhile again. Our spirits are made whole. We can begin to perceive ourselves as worthy because we *are* worthy in God's eyes.

✝

Making it personal: What are you willing to take to God's repair shop? What are you hesitant to take? Why?

Prayer: Jesus, I am broken. I want to yield to Your tools. Fix me up so that I can serve You. Amen.

Read Jeremiah 15:19-20 for hopeful words about how God will restore you.

Habitual Sins

Let us strip off every weight that slows us down, especially the sin that so easily hinders our progress. And let us run with endurance the race that God has set before us. Hebrews 12:1

All of us have at least one particular sin that poisons our lives and is our weakest point in our walk with God. When the devil attacks us, he loves going for that weak spot. It may be shame, anger, despair, or laziness. We commit this sin repeatedly, even though we try hard to avoid it. We sometimes feel powerless and miserable about it. This is our habitual sin.

Our habitual sin surrounds and harasses us. It makes us feel as if we are being attacked from every angle and every side. How can we walk with Christ and still be so weak in the flesh? We can be encouraged that we are not the only ones who've struggled over this issue. The apostle Paul poured out his heart over his habitual sins (see Romans 7:14-25).

We can do several things to fight our persistent sin. First, we can admit that we really hate this sin that harasses us. Do we feel guilty for just a short time, or do we really want to rid ourselves of it? We must make up our minds to be cleansed of this sin. Second, we must never forget that God loves us in spite of our stubborn sin. We cannot lose faith, hope, or trust in His unconditional love for us. And third, we must constantly remember that we are in a war, a spiritual battle. Wars are not won quickly. Soldiers die one at a time, and so do our persistent, habitual sins. Soldiers operate under the command of a general, and we have the Holy Spirit directing this battle over our sin. Victory may seem slow in coming, but it is inevitable and unstoppable.

✝

Making it personal: What habitual sins assault you repeatedly? What will you do to resist them?

Prayer: Holy Spirit, I confess that I am surrounded by stubborn sin. Lead me to victory over this sin. Amen.

Read Romans 7:14-25 to understand the apostle Paul's struggle with sin.

Confessing Specific Sins

But if we are living in the light of God's presence, just as Christ is, then we have fellowship with each other, and the blood of Jesus, his Son, cleanses us from every sin. 1 John 1:7

Think about really close friends. They're people with whom we've shared our lives. Maybe these friends confided in us when they were feeling hopeless, and we shared something that kept their lives afloat. To be that close to someone, we need to be open and honest about the details of our lives. Generalities about our families, marriages, kids, or crimes don't cut it. If we don't trust our friends with the details of our lives, deep and meaningful friendship isn't going to happen. We can lie to these people to get close to them, but in the end, we're just cheating ourselves out of genuine friendship.

Real relationship with God—living in the light of His presence—takes specific, "keeping-it-real" honesty too. When we confess our sins to God, we cannot glide over them as if we're painting a house with a roller. We need to feel like we're using a fine brush on the windows and get specific about what we have done.

Confessing to God in general ways—that we are "sinners"—is easy. It's harder to admit our specific sins: that we are child molesters, murderers, rapists, drug dealers, prostitutes, gunrunners, racists, or pimps. That takes courage. But we must do it. Only when we are willing to get "real" with God, will we break into "reality" and a relationship with Him that is significant, authentic, and valuable.

We might feel that confession is a sign of weakness, but it's not. Confession is a sign of strength. It is an indication that something greater than ourselves has taken hold of our hearts. It is the first step of walking in the light with God Almighty.

✝

Making it personal: Today, confess your specific sins to God. Lay them all out. Trust Him to cleanse you.

Prayer: Oh, Father God, hear my list of specific sins. Cleanse me. I want to walk in the light with You. Amen.

Memorize 1 John 1:8-10 as an assurance of the cleansing power of the Holy Spirit.

The Root Sin of Pride

Let not the wise man gloat in his wisdom, or the mighty man in his might, or the rich man in his riches. Let them boast in this alone: that they truly know me and understand that I am the Lord who is just and righteous, whose love is unfailing, and that I delight in these things. Jeremiah 9:23-24

Remember the giant Goliath, the one the shepherd-boy David fought (see 1 Samuel 17:1-50)? Goliath thought he was indestructible. He'd never lost a fight. When he'd "raise up" on someone, they'd flinch. He was a nasty piece of work, the shot-caller of the Philistines.

Your story may be similar. You were bulletproof, a successful criminal. You took down scores that impressed your peers. The "heat" was the other person's problem. Your success made you proud.

Pride is the root of all other sin. It was, "through Pride that the devil became the devil: Pride leads to every other vice: it is the complete anti-God state of mind."[4] Through pride Adam and Eve fell out of perfect union with God. Our pride keeps us from God too. We think we are so strong or so powerful or so wise that we don't need God. We shake our fist in rebellion at Him, setting ourselves up as our own gods.

Pride infects us. It parades our accomplishments and convinces us that we are all-important or all-powerful. We are the center of the universe. We look at others around us, and we think we are better than they are. When these thoughts enter our minds, pride has taken root.

The Bible teaches that God hates pride (see Proverbs 16:5). We must learn to hate it as well. The first step in ridding ourselves of pride is to admit that we are proud. This is tough. But a simple test can confirm whether you're infected or not. If you think you are not proud, then you probably are.

✝

Making it personal: Look closely at your life. What things make you proud, vain, and arrogant? Admitting them is the first step toward healing.

Prayer: Father God, purge pride from my life. I surrender everything to You. Amen.

Read Proverbs 8:13, 11:2, 13:10, 16:18, and 29:23 for thoughts about pride.

Freedom from Guilt

As far as the east is from the west, so far has he removed our transgressions from us. Psalm 103:12, NIV

Cynthia is in prison and knows what guilt feels like. She may not admit to someone else that she is guilty of anything, but when the cellblock is dark and no one is listening, her heart betrays her feelings of guilt.

The devil likes to keep us in bondage to guilt. Satan whispers into our ears that we are worthless by reminding us of what we have done. He places us under the finger of accusation. He lies to get us to believe God could never love us because of our crimes and the hurt we have caused during our life. Don't listen to those lies. Remember that Satan is a liar and a murderer.

God does not abandon us in our sin (see Psalm 34:21-22). Jesus never overlooks sin, but He also never allows our sinful actions to become a barrier to His love (see John 8:1-11).

We can't solve our guilt on our own. We can't con ourselves into thinking that if we just go to church enough times or make restitution or take the sexual offender classes, our guilt will go away. We must come face-to-face with Christ, fall to our knees, and accept His loving forgiveness. He will take away our sins and remove our guilt. When we come face-to-face with Christ, we see ourselves in His light. Only then do we see our sin as an obstruction to His purpose for our lives.

Today's verse teaches that He removes our sin from us as far as east is from west—an infinite, unimaginable distance. Through His grace and mercy God declares us both "not guilty" and "righteous." He is getting us ready for service to Him.

✝

Making it personal: With what feelings of guilt are you wrestling? What will you do today to lay your guilt at the feet of Jesus?

Prayer: Jesus, thank You that because You have forgiven me, all my guilt is gone. Hallelujah. Amen.

Read Acts 13:38-39, one of the apostle Paul's early teachings about guilt and forgiveness.

The Positive Power of Failure

For it is by grace you have been saved, through faith—and this not from yourselves, it is the gift of God—not by works, so that no one can boast. Ephesians 2:8-9, NIV

We are all sinners. There is zero chance we can live in this fallen world with our flawed characters without missing the mark. Given that truth, it's a wonder we don't all crawl back to our living units, curl up in the fetal position, and suck our thumbs in despair.

Seriously, we should never fall into to that sort of hopelessness. Failure can play a positive role in our daily lives. As Christians, we try to keep our lives clean, our minds pure, and our actions exemplary. But we must never trust those things to save us. Too often we fall into the "religion trap" of self-justification. Self-justification is just a fancy way of saying that we sometimes try to save ourselves through good living and good works. We still hang on to the notion that if we list all of our good works and the sins we avoided during the week and present that list to God, He will have to love us.

Our sinfulness is a constant reminder that we cannot save ourselves. It performs a positive purpose in our Christian walk. It's the rude, cattle-prod shock to our pride that reinforces the truth that no matter how virtuous our walk with God may be, we're never honorable enough to pay the penalty for our sin.

We work hard to avoid sinful behavior because God teaches us that it's destructive for our lives and damaging to our walk with Him. We avoid sin out of our sense of gratitude to Jesus for taking our death sentence so we could live. The aftermath of sin should remind us of our position before God—sinners saved by grace. It's God's free gift to all of us!

✝

Making it personal: What "religion traps" feed your pride and make you think you are saving yourself?

Prayer: Lord Jesus, You were innocent but took my death sentence so that I, who am guilty, could go free. Thank You! Amen.

Memorize Ephesians 1:7 as a reminder of what God has already done for you.

Resist Evil

Resist the devil, and he will flee from you. James 4:7

Comic actor Dennis Miller said in one famous rant, "Guilt is simply God's way of letting you know that you are having too good a time." There is truth in that statement, but God has higher uses for guilt in our lives. God places the feelings of guilt in our moral consciousness for good purposes.

Many of us sold our bodies on the outside. We were alone, cold, and hungry, and it seemed like the only alternative. For men, it was a degrading yet somewhat pleasurable experience. We loathed ourselves for doing it and even more for liking it a little. For women it sometimes resulted in getting pregnant. Some of us chose abortions. We live with the guilt of those difficult decisions. But God forgives us and can use those experiences to point us in the right direction.

Guilt can act as a deterrent. When we indulge drug use, we feel guilty. Those feelings shame us before God. When we are tempted again, God uses the memories of the shame we felt to restrain us from falling into sin again. Restraint, when exercised repeatedly, turns into discipline. Like muscle that gets stronger from free-weight workouts, our resolve to avoid sin gets stronger as we resist the devil and walk away from temptation.

Pain and guilt are motivators as well as deterrents. When we fully understand that Jesus Christ walked that last mile on death row to pardon us for our sin, we will be motivated to fall to our knees and give thanks to God. We can show our thanks through our words and actions. The realization of God's wonderful gift moves us to a place of accepting God's grace and forgiveness.

†

Making it personal: Think hard: where is God using your guilt as a deterrent to evil? How will you respond and resist evil today?

Prayer: Jesus, keep the devil from using my guilt to kill hope. Use my guilt to point me back to You. Give me strength to resist the devil's power and send him packing. Amen.

Read Proverbs 14:9, 16 for some wisdom about guilt and staying away from evil.

The Dark Alley of Sin

From the time the world was created, people have seen the earth and sky and all that God made. They can clearly see his invisible qualities—his eternal power and divine nature. So they have no excuse whatsoever for not knowing God. . . . When they refused to acknowledge God, he abandoned them to their evil minds and let them do things that should never be done. Romans 1:20, 28

The places we grew up had beautiful things like parks or ponds. They also had ugly and dangerous places. We had choices, and many of us chose dark alleys even when we knew there were better places. Dark alleys were always trouble. Nothing good happened in a dark alley.

We have choices to make about God and evil. We know God exists. We look at creation and know a Creator had a hand in it all. But many of us chose the way of sin and evil, knowing it was bad.

When we choose evil over God, bad things naturally happen. When we choose the dark alleys of life, "we become like the gods we serve. The punishment of sin lies not in any direct intervention by which God disciplines offenders, but in the consequences which naturally follow from a lawless life."[5] The slippery slope of a sinful life leads to chaos—and often prison. Anger, jealousy, and violence are all symptoms of choosing the dark alleys of life. In its final stages, the lawless life is aware of the darkness and God's displeasure, but it has no positive effect on our behavior. We are lost.

This is the reason Christ came into the world. Sin is a serious disease. Sin needs a cure, and the penalty for our sin needs to be paid. We sit in the filth and squalor of our sinful hearts and cry out, "Who will rescue me?" The answer is Jesus.

✝

Making it personal: Are you living on the dark side of life? Is it as great as you think it is, or do you want out?

Prayer: Lord Jesus, lift me out of my sewer and hose me off. Amen.

Read all of Romans 1 to understand the depth of your sin.

God's Shank

For the word of God is full of living power. It is sharper than the sharpest knife, cutting deep into our innermost thoughts and desires. It exposes us for what we really are. Hebrews 4:12

In many prison lobbies there are displays exhibiting different types of shanks. Confiscated during shakedowns, they were fashioned from every imaginable material. A piece of metal bed frame was polished to a razor's edge. A toothbrush was melted and molded into a long shank capable of piercing a kidney or heart. Even a hardcover book was carefully crafted into a deadly shank.

Most convicts caught with a shank argue that it's for self-defense. But that's mostly untrue. Shanks are fashioned to attack someone else. They're made to retaliate and inflict revenge on someone who has disrespected one gang or another. It might be payback to someone for something that happened outside before both of you went to prison. Whatever the reason, shanks cut, expose, and inflict pain on another person.

The Bible is God's shank, but He wields it for our good, not to inflict pain or revenge. His Word cuts deep into our hearts. It tells us fearlessly that we all have sinned and all fall short of God's glorious standard (see Romans 3:23). If we live in defiance about our sinful behavior, God's shank slashes our denial with these words, "If we say we have no sin, we are only fooling ourselves and refusing to accept the truth" (1 John 1:8). God's Word sticks us where we are living in sin. It pulls no punches in exposing our wrong behavior. Look at the list. It includes sexual immorality, eagerness for sexual pleasure, hostility, anger, and jealousy (see Galatians 5:16-21).

God's Word cuts us in order to expose our sin. Just as we go to a doctor when we are aware of an illness, exposing our sin leads us to seek forgiveness. Once we know and own up to our sin, we recognize we need God.

✝

Making it personal: What is hindering you from picking up and reading God's shank? Allow His Word to penetrate your heart.

Prayer: *God, cut me and remove the sin so I can live for You. Amen.*

Read Galatians 5:19-26 to learn how to become free from your specific sins.

God's Operating Room

Healthy people don't need a doctor—sick people do. I have come to call sinners, not those who think they are already good enough. Mark 2:17

During open-heart surgery, a surgeon cuts the chest open from the neck to the navel. The ribs are spread apart, exposing the heart. The physician then uses a scalpel and slices off the clogged arteries and replaces them. The result is a healthy heart pumping blood to the rest of the body.

After God's shank cuts and exposes the sin in our hearts, we need to deal with the sin inside. Each of us in prison, Christian or not, needs open heart surgery. Our arteries are clogged with sin.

What sins clog the spiritual arteries of our hearts? We are proud of our crimes. We victimize weaker members in our living unit by extorting rent or hustling their canteen. We give in to despair and give up on God. God's scalpel must cut away these obstructions that block our spiritual health.

How do we check into God's operating room and submit to His surgery? We first must cop to our sin after it's exposed by God's shank. Let's not hide behind a wall of denial. Let's not look around and deceive ourselves, thinking we are no worse than anyone else. This doesn't fly with God. Other cons aren't the standard by which God judges us. When we get real with our sin, we must confess it immediately to God and ask for His forgiveness (see 1 John 1:9). And, we must simply stop doing it!

When we arrive at these decisions in our lives, we are ready to be prepped for God's operating room. He'll send us brothers and sisters to support our decisions. We'll have a thirst for His Word and feel His peace and assurance. God's scalpel is sharp. His promises are true and can be trusted. Are you ready?

†

Making it personal: What keeps you from facing your sinfulness? What will it take for you to allow God to cut it from your life?

Prayer: God, sometimes I love my sin, but know I need to get rid of it and be healed. Will You be my surgeon? Amen.

Read Psalm 119:33-40, a prayer for the seeker.

Our Immediate Hope

I have hidden your word in my heart that I might not sin against you. Psalm 119:11

Is there any immediate hope for us who struggle with drug addiction every day inside the Men's Colony at Obispo? Where does daily hope come from for us who have violent, angry thoughts at Central California Women's Facility in Chowchilla, California?

Thoughts are critical to our actions. When we indulge bad thoughts, awful actions follow just as clogged roads follow a snowstorm. The opposite is also true. Wholesome feelings produce good actions. Good thoughts drive away bad ones.

To combat and prevent violent thoughts from entering our minds, we can memorize Scripture passages to resist the devil's schemes. Memorizing specific passages that speak to our sinful desires allows us to summon the verses to our minds to defeat the temptation. The writer of Psalm 119 asked the question. "How can a young person stay pure? By obeying your word and following its rules. . . . I have hidden your word in my heart that I might not sin against you" (vs. 9-11). He memorized the Word of God and brought it to mind in the time of need.

This is the immediate hope we are to carry into the pod and our cells. We can memorize Philippians 4:8: "Finally, brothers [and sisters], whatever is true, whatever is noble, whatever is right, whatever is pure, whatever is lovely, whatever is admirable—if anything is excellent or praiseworthy—think about such things." When violent thoughts taunt us, we can ask for the Holy Spirit's power and fill our minds instead with pure things, right things, lovely things, admirable things. We can combat vicious thoughts. With the Holy Spirit's help, we can hold on to the immediate hope God offers us.

✝

Making it personal: What Bible promises can you hold on to and use to resist the devil's temptations?

Prayer: Lord, I confess that I am often ruled by angry, destructive thoughts. I submit them to You. I commit to hiding Your Word in my heart. I want to resist the devil. Thank You, Jesus. Amen.

Read and memorize Psalm 51:10 and Romans 7:21-25 to resist sexual thoughts, and **read James 1:19-20 and Proverbs 29:11** to resist destructive anger.

Sin

These questions relate to the meditations found on pages 74-85:

Discuss together:

1. Why is accepting a gift from another inmate often dangerous? What kinds of strings are attached in most cases? How is God's undeserved gift to us of grace different from an inmate's gift? What keeps you from grabbing hold of His gift? Do you really wish to have the "new freedoms" grace offers (freedom to love ourselves; to stop comparing ourselves to others; to be free from the bondage of other people's opinions of us)? What other "new freedoms" can you list?

2. Unpack the tools God uses to repair our broken lives: conviction, confession, repentance, and forgiveness. What specific tasks do each of these tools perform in repairing your life? How are they also effective against sins that nag at you constantly? Why is patience required to deal with sin that stalks you?

3. Who is the center of your life if you are proud? Why is pride competitive at its core? Why is it difficult to identify pride in your life, yet so easy to see in others? Does pride hinder your kneeling before God and accepting His grace? How and why? What's the antidote for pride?

4. When you sin, is the remorse and regret you feel really wounded "self-love"? Consider and discuss if your shame might really be annoyance with yourself at being weak when you thought you were spiritually strong. How does the tax collector's prayer, "God be merciful to me, a sinner" (Luke 18:13) differ from your regret and shame?

Explore God's Word together:

1. **Luke 22:54-62** tells the story of Peter's denial of Christ. At one point, Jesus turns and looks straight at Peter. When He does, Peter suddenly remembers Christ's earlier words. What was the significance of Jesus' penetrating look? In what ways might Christ be looking straight at you right now? How will you respond?

2. **Galatians 2:20** talks of being crucified with Christ. How can you be crucified with Christ behind the walls? Discuss how being united with Christ must alter your attitude toward service, sacrifice, and selflessness, even if you've been unjustly convicted.

3. **Deuteronomy 8:19-20** is a harsh warning. Share how you relate to this warning. How did your bowing down to other gods almost destroy you? Did it destroy others? How is (could) your life (be) different with the true God at the center?

Pray together:

1. Pray together in silence, confessing your specific sins before God. Avoid platitudes or clichés. Make it real with Jesus.

2. Pray for your enemies—again and again!

3. Create a prayer list, and pray over it now and every session. Keep track of God's answered prayers.

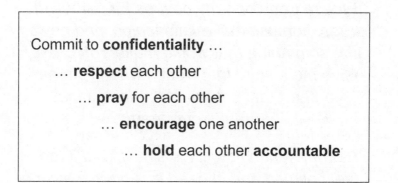

Commit to **confidentiality** …

... **respect** each other

... **pray** for each other

... **encourage** one another

... **hold** each other **accountable**

Prayer for Lovers of Sin

God, I confess that I love sin.
Sometimes my love for sinful desires
overwhelms me like an enormous wave and
pulls on my heart as if it were an oversize magnet.
I love sin because it is the easy way to go—
the path of least resistance.
Yet when I finish doing what my heart
wants me to do, I feel ashamed and angry
that I don't have the will to resist.
But that is merely my anger at my
own weakness—a self-centered emotion.

I really need You and Your transforming power.
Please transform my desires for gambling,
drugs, homosexual relationships, and power
into something that would make You proud.
Give me a spirit that weeps when I sin and
a heart that breaks at the things that
break Your heart!

Lord, as much as I love sin—I hate it too.
I feel polluted and in need of a good washing.
Lord Jesus, I really have no other alternatives left
since everything I have tried fails. Will You wash me?
Will You take me deep into Your soul and
show me that there is a better way?
Take me, Lord—now, before I wimp out.
I surrender my life to You.

Amen.

†

Part 3: Salvation

Jesus Christ is God's provision for our sin.

Set Free from Sin and Death

So if the Son sets you free, you will indeed be free. John 8:36

Miriam Mejabe spent seven years in a women's prison in Kenya, Africa. Her daughter, Precious, was imprisoned with her for five of those years, following the custom that a woman's children live with her until they reach the age of seven.

Rule of law is nonexistent in the area where Miriam lives, so she never had a trial. She was merely pronounced guilty by a local authority and sentenced to death.

On a recent Sunday, Miriam joined three hundred other women inmates who gathered to worship and praise God. That Sunday Miriam shared her testimony. She stood and smoothed out her pink-and-orange uniform. She told the women that in two weeks she would be executed. Execution in that prison is not quick or painless. The women are hung with a rope, left to struggle against the last breath. A frightening death.

But on this day, Miriam was not afraid. In fact, she was radiant with joy. "Two years ago Jesus Christ set me free from sin. God Himself stooped down to care for me. He washed my heart from hatred and evil. How I thank Him. How I praise Him. Today, I am free. I will soon face the rope. It will squeeze the breath from my body, but Jesus has set me free."

As tears fell on Miriam's cheeks, the other women in the chapel rose from their benches, raised their hands to the heavens, and shouted, "We thank You, Jesus. You have set our sister free. We bless Your name, Jesus." They wept and sang praises to God.

Two weeks later Miriam's life on earth ended. But that was not the end of her story. Jesus' death on the cross set her free—free from the punishment of sin while she lived on earth and free to live eternally with Him at her death.

✝

Making it personal: What can you do to have that kind of peace? How has Jesus set you free from sin and death?

Prayer: God, thank You for providing a way to rescue me from sin through Your Son, Jesus. Amen.

Read Romans 6:22 for words about freedom and eternal life.

Jesus: The Only Way to God

For there is only one God and one Mediator who can reconcile God and people. He is the man Christ Jesus. 1 Timothy 2:5-6

On page vi of the introduction, we outlined four "Spiritual Laws" that give a straightforward understanding of the Gospel message. The third Spiritual Law says, "Jesus Christ is God's only provision for our sin. Through Him we can know and experience God's love and plan for our lives." Claiming Jesus is the *only* way to God makes people angry, especially since society makes a god of tolerance and political correctness. People like to say, "If Christ works for you, great. But don't push Him down my throat as the only way to God." How do we defend the view that Jesus is the only way and not appear condescending to other religions?

Exclusivity can be a good thing. Nobody pours water into a car's gas tank and expects it to operate normally. Cars were made to run on gas *only*. No one complains about it.

Here's another perspective: If an old number, with street cred, warned us to avoid an inmate who was a bad dude, we'd listen, trusting his judgment. We'd believe him because he has authority on the subject. The same is true when it comes to the exclusiveness of Jesus. It's not our *interpretation* of the Bible that claims Jesus is the only way to the Father. Jesus Himself declares it. Jesus claims to be one with the Father (see John 14:9-14). He claims to be able to forgive sin—not His sin—everyone's sin (see Matthew 9:1-7). And, He claims to be the *only* way to the Father (see John 14:6).

When we examine Jesus' life, death, and resurrection, we see Him like we see the old con. We believe that Jesus has authority (street cred) to make these assertions. Because we believe in His authority, we believe that what He taught about Himself is true. We didn't make it up. A guy we trust said it, and we believe Him, based on the evidence. That's not arrogance; it's fact.

✝

Making it personal: Study and then decide who Jesus Christ is in history and in your life.

Prayer: Jesus, Your claim of uniqueness sounds arrogant to me. Please show me the right way. Amen.

Read John 14 to hear what Jesus says about Himself.

Salvation Made Simple

We are made right in God's sight when we trust in Jesus Christ to take away our sins. And we all can be saved in this same way, no matter who we are or what we have done. Romans 3:22

On one hand, salvation is a simple matter. When we trust Jesus to take away our sins, we are made right in God's sight. C. S. Lewis said, "The central Christian belief is that Christ's death has somehow put us right with God and given us a fresh start."[6]

On the other hand, salvation is a serious matter—it cost Christ His life in order to free us from our sin. Adam and Eve's sin created a deep valley between a perfect God and imperfect humans. We cannot bridge this gap on our own. We need help, just as a person who's in debt needs someone with money to pay off the debt.

God sent Jesus into the world to pay our debt and to be the only way to be reconciled with Him. Jesus paid the penalty for our sin so that we could again be in a deep relationship with God.

Why didn't God just snap His fingers and make sin go away? God is a just God. The debt for sin in the world had to be paid. Jesus came to earth to pay that price. He died on the cross for our sins. After three days in the tomb, Jesus rose from the dead and appeared before many witnesses. The debt had been paid. "The sense of the infinite worth of the single soul, and the recoverableness of man at his worst are the gifts of Christ. The freedom from guilt and the forgiveness of sins come from Christ's Cross; the hope of immortality springs from Christ's grace."[7]

Salvation changes our lives. It frees us from guilt, remorse, shame, and fear. We've all heard the motto *Change the behavior, and you change the person.* But most of us know that motto is bankrupt. The truth is: *Change the person, and behavior changes.*

†

Making it personal: Have you given your life to Jesus? If not, decide today to give your life to Him and be saved.

Prayer: Jesus, if salvation is true, I want it to be true for me. Amen.

Read Romans 10:8-13 to learn more about salvation.

Rescue and Release

For he has rescued us from the one who rules in the kingdom of darkness, and he has brought us into the Kingdom of his dear Son. God has purchased our freedom with his blood and has forgiven all our sins. Colossians 1:13-14

Jake was serving time for killing a young woman. After twelve years, he surrendered to God, asking for forgiveness and reconciliation. Jake realized his crime had robbed the girl of her life and stripped her family of joy. His burden of guilt was so great that he started attending a Bible study and later an intense Bible-training class. When Jake graduated from the training class, a woman approached him as he left the stage. She told him she was the mother of the girl he had murdered. Through tears, she shared how through the power of Christ, she had forgiven Jake. Her Christ-centered heart desired to be a mentor/mother to Jake during the rest of his life. Jake was overwhelmed. He felt forgiven, and he understood Christ's love. Tears flowed as he and the woman embraced before the astonished audience. Through God's forgiving power, Jake and his new "mother" were pardoned, released, and set free.[8]

To be prisoner to the "kingdom of darkness" is to have the devil be the shot-caller in our lives. To be rescued means to be liberated from that dungeon. To be forgiven is to be granted clemency.

How many of us are in bondage to spiritual pride, condescending attitudes, love of our past, or unforgiving hearts? How many of us really want to be free from fear, hopelessness, and bondage to sin? Freedom begins when we look to Jesus and ask for His power to replace the power of evil. We must drain our hearts of the swamp water of anger and unforgiveness, and replace it with the sweet, pure, living water Jesus offers.

✝

Making it personal: Confront the stink in your heart, and dare to ask God to replace it with sweet, pure, living water.

Prayer: God, I am tired of the smell. Clean me up! Amen.

Read John 4:4-26 to see how Jesus cleans up the woman He met at the well.

Acceptance

Yet now God in his gracious kindness declares us not guilty. He has done this through Christ Jesus, who has freed us by taking away our sins. Romans 3:24

Who are our shot-callers? We have OGs. Maybe it's a woman who protects us in the unit or a guy who trusts us with running his store. We feel safe in their presence and draw identity from being part of their posse. Why give this up and choose Jesus as the One you look up to? Because one system is bogus, and one is genuine.

What happens to our peace and power when we don't do something our shot-callers demand? We're ordered to shank someone. And if we won't do it? How long does the shotcallers' acceptance last? Not long, for their approval is based on our doing what they demand. If we stray from the course, we lose the power and safety of their favor. They accept us only if we obey them, and our motivation for obeying is fear.

Jesus operates an entirely different system. He offers identity, safety, and acceptance—without our having to earn it. Jesus stretches out His hands and accepts us because He loves us. He offers peace and security not because of anything we have done to deserve it. They are His gifts to us. This is called *grace*. When Jesus is our refuge, we don't live in fear that if we screw up, His love will be jerked away from us. We can live with confidence that His acceptance is unshakable. Gratitude, not fear, will be our motivation to serve Him wherever we walk.

Fearing leaders whose acceptance of us is based on what we do for them is like standing near quicksand. Lose our footing, and we sink beneath the surface. Living by the grace that Jesus gives is like standing on firm ground. It is solid and steady. Jesus as OG is a place of real, authentic acceptance.

✝

Making it personal: Who is your shot-caller? Is your loyalty based on fear or gratitude? What would it look like for Christ to be your shot-caller?

Prayer: Lord, I accept Your acceptance of me, by grace. Hug my heart, set me free, and pour Your peace on me. Amen.

Read about peace and joy in **Romans 5:1-11**.

Paul's "First Life": Saul of Tarsus

For you have heard of my previous way of life in Judaism. . . . I was advancing in Judaism beyond many Jews of my own age and was extremely zealous for the traditions of my fathers. Galatians 1:13-14, NIV

Many people live two lives. Chuck Colson was President Nixon's hatchet man in his "first life"; after meeting Christ in prison, Colson started Prison Fellowship—his "second life." St. Francis of Assisi was a rich kid, who, after meeting God, gave his money and life to the poor. Both men had two lives: one without Jesus and one with Him.

Saul of Tarsus (the name of the apostle Paul in his "first life") was on the fast track. He came from a well-to-do family. Saul was young and wise beyond his years. The Jewish religious leaders saw greatness in him.

Saul probably knew he was a star and was perhaps even arrogant. He most likely loved the spotlight and the attention that went with it. He hated Christians and joined forces with the fanatical Jews who were persecuting Christians. In fact he held the coats for the men who dragged Stephen, a Christ-filled believer, into the street and killed him (see Acts 6:8–8:1). Saul's center was himself.

How many of us relate to Saul's life? Some of us were on the fast track too, coming from wealthy families. We have college degrees and were headed for the "bright lights, big city." We were often conceited, living by the motto "Too much is not enough." Yet, in our self-centeredness, we stumbled and landed in prison. Maybe we killed someone while driving drunk or embezzled from our company. Now we sit doing a long stretch. Our center was ourselves. It was always: me, me, *me*. As our center goes, so goes our life.

The next few meditations will study the life of Saul/Paul to see how Jesus saved him and offered him forgiveness, peace, and hope.

✝

Making it personal: What do you value most? The answer will help you identify your center.

Prayer: God, my center is me. I need a new center. Please change my direction to seek You. Amen.

Read Acts 26:4-29, Paul's personal testimony to King Agrippa.

Saul the Executioner

Saul was going everywhere to destroy the church. He went from house to house, dragging out both men and women to throw them into prison. Acts 8:3

Young hotshots love being noticed by their superiors. It's a great way to advance. To capture the attention of the higher-ups, they do something flashy to stand out. Gangbangers who cap a cop or rival gang leader get props. Bikers who cook and deal more meth than anybody else get out front with the gang's leadership.

Saul's attitude was probably no different. He was looking for ways to impress the Jewish leadership. He was on the make. What better way to grab the spotlight than to attack this new Christian movement? Christians were challenging the established order. Saul thought if he could damage or even eliminate these bothersome believers, the Jewish leadership would be impressed with him. Seemed like a first-rate strategy for advancement.

Saul started persecuting the church in Jerusalem. Soon those believers scattered to avoid Saul's punishment and prison. Saul didn't let that stop him. The high priest gave him authority to arrest Christians wherever he found them. His plan was to round them up, jail them, and/or kill them. Saul struck fear in the hearts of Christians everywhere, the same way the Gestapo terrorized Nazi Germany.

How many of us reading these words are applauding the violence and destruction young Saul inflicted? Would we enjoy being in his shoes, terrorizing Christians? If so, we are enemies of Christ. If we approve of Saul, then the center of our hearts is ourselves. Our hearts' compasses are pointed in the direction of our desires. We're on a dangerous road that leads to hell!

Are we afraid of coming to Jesus? Do we fear letting go of our "first lives"? Be honest. Our first lives were dominated by fear and self-centeredness. It's time for a change. Trust Jesus' promises of a better, "second life."

†

Making it personal: How is God calling you to a new life—a second life? What will it take for you to give Him a chance?

Prayer: God, meet me here in my sin, in my fear . . . in my cell. Amen.

Read Acts 6–7, the story of the first martyr, Stephen.

Looking Deep Inside

A simple man believes anything, but a prudent man gives thoughts to his steps. Proverbs 14:15, NIV

Saul squandered his talent and intellectual prowess for a reputation of violence and destruction. He found himself defined by what he was *against* instead of what he was *for.* He was full of potential but used it for destructive purposes and his own gain.

It's easy for us to be a big man on the yard when people are watching, affirming our swagger. We may impress the other women in the cell house with our bravado, but when we're alone with ourselves, the praise of our peers fades away. Real thoughts about our lives come lurking around. Our souls are heavy, and we begin to reflect.

In this silent wilderness our thoughts turn to the true quality of our lives and the talents and opportunities we've squandered. We remember the birthdays missed and the funerals that we could not attend. As we penetrate the darkness of our souls, we conclude that our lives up to this point have been wasted and a mistake. We know we are not as great as the image we show on the yard. Uncovering this truth about ourselves is the first step toward real transformation in our lives.

When we reach this point, our hearts know: We need a center other than ourselves. We hunger for someone to forgive us, to comfort us, and to assure us that a new beginning is possible. We look up at the stars and discern with confidence that there is a God behind them all. In the greatness of creation, God reveals His greatness to our inner being. We realize, perhaps for the first time, that we are small in contrast. We may also recognize that God is out there for us, if we want to meet Him.

We are ripe for a turnaround, for a conversion. Is it time to place Jesus at the center of our lives?

†

Making it personal: As you listen to your inner voice telling you it's time for something better, what steps will you take to implement the change?

Prayer: Jesus, I tear up with longing for something greater than myself. Touch my heart. Reclaim my wasted years. Amen.

Read Ezekiel 36:26-27, and receive a new heart.

Starting Fresh

Those who become Christians become new persons. They are not the same anymore, for the old life is gone. A new life has begun! 2 Corinthians 5:17

One day when Saul was traveling to Damascus to round up Christians and throw them in jail, he was blinded by an intense light. Out of the light, Jesus spoke to the young firebrand: "Saul! Saul! Why are you persecuting me?" When the startled young man asked, "Who are you, sir?" the voice answered, "'I am Jesus, the one you are persecuting!' Now get up and go into the city, and you will be told what you are to do" (Acts 9:4-6).

Saul got up but found that he couldn't see. Three days later God sent a man named Ananias to heal Saul's blindness and give him direction for his life (see Acts 9:7-19). From that moment on, Saul, who later changed his name to Paul, became a zealous advocate for Christ. In fact, he was so bold that soon the Jewish leaders were hunting him down so that they could kill him!

Meeting Christ changed Saul's center. God redeemed Saul's wasted, destructive years. The apostle Paul gave up his self-centered focus and threw himself into the task Jesus had given him. He preached about Jesus. He wrote about Jesus—more than a dozen New Testament books.

Few of us have the kind of dramatic conversion that Saul experienced, but Jesus still pursues us as we walk the road headed toward death. He wants to redeem our wasted years and give us purpose. He still calls out to us, "(*Your name, your name*), why are you running from me?"

We can respond to His call and begin a new life. He will make us into new persons, just as He did for Saul. We will no longer be controlled by filthy talk, pornography, drugs, or boastfulness about our crimes. He will give us new lives, a fresh set of values.

✝

Making it personal: How do you feel about this new identity, this new set of values? How will it impact your life inside?

Prayer: Jesus, help me live for You instead of for myself. I want to be a new person. Amen.

Read Acts 9, the story of Saul's conversion.

Dangerous Choices

After many days had gone by, the Jews conspired to kill him, but Saul learned of their plan. Acts 9:23-24, NIV

When most of us make a decision for Christ, the negative consequences are small. We may lose friends at the poker table and our drug buddies, but that's it. For others who decide for Jesus, the cost is potentially much greater.

The members of the Nazi Low-Riders or the Aryan Brotherhood risk their lives when they renounce their loyalty to the gang. It can amount to a death warrant. Yet, many of these gang members come to Christ and put their lives on the line.

Saul made that same choice. After he met with Ananias and was filled with the Holy Spirit, he immediately stepped out for Jesus. He spoke in the Damascus synagogues and was eloquent in his teaching that Jesus was the Son of God (see Acts 9:20-23). The Jews put out a contract hit on Saul, but he learned of the danger and escaped.

How many of us face the same tough decisions Saul faced? Is the fear of retaliation and revenge stopping us from coming over to the side of Christ in the facility? Is the threat of physical violence keeping us from a saving relationship with God?

No one should minimize the reality of the terrible situation in which we find ourselves. The guys with "88" tattooed on their backs are genuine threats. But God is also genuine. While He doesn't promise to eliminate all our enemies, He does promise to see us through every situation (see 1 John 4:4 and Hebrews 13:5-6).

A life of threats and violence is not a pleasant prospect, but a life without a saving relationship with Jesus Christ is worse—by far! We can seek out other former gang members to strengthen our resolve to follow Jesus. We can ask the Holy Spirit to protect us. But we must break away! God is faithful and will protect us.

†

Making it personal: What will you do to break with the old and come to Jesus? Overcome your fear through prayer and solidarity with your new Christian family.

Prayer: Lord, I am frightened. Give me the strength to decide for You. Amen.

Read Daniel 3, a story of courage, integrity, and deliverance.

Take a Chance on Each Other

When [Paul] came to Jerusalem, he tried to join the disciples, but they were all afraid of him, not believing that he was a disciple. Acts 9:26, NIV

Gang members looking to make a decision for Christ are not the only ones who feel fear. Fear affects even seasoned followers of Jesus.

The disciples experienced the power of the Holy Spirit on Pentecost. The effects of that experience were evident in their speech and the power and boldness of their preaching. Many new converts were baptized (see Acts 2:41). The Jewish leaders were astonished by the authoritative courage of these ordinary, uneducated fishermen (see Acts 4:13). So, why were these bold disciples afraid of Saul?

Did they fear for their own lives? Maybe the vivid memories of Saul holding the coats of the men who murdered their friend Stephen angered them. If so, did that anger cause them to be unforgiving, not *wanting* to accept this hated man as an authentic follower of Jesus? We do not know. We only know they were afraid.

But we *do* know former enemies and rival gang members who have met Christ, repented, and started attending the prison church. Is it the person who flipped on us and sent us to prison? Did this person cut our friend or disrespect us in another facility? Do we react with anger, fear, or disbelief? Maybe we doubt if this person is for real. But isn't it better to take a chance on a person and be disappointed than to lose a relationship because we were afraid to believe in the change that took place?

God never gives up on us. Even though we have lived for ourselves, Jesus takes a chance on us. He loves us and accepts us. We must overcome our fears and anger, and accept new believers into our midst, regardless of our history with them.

†

Making it personal: How would looking at new believers with Jesus' kind and forgiving eyes alter your judgment of them?

Prayer: Holy Spirit, give me the courage to take a chance on these former enemies. Help me love them as You love me. Amen.

Read Romans 5:10-11, and see how God treated us when we were His enemies.

Cautious but Obedient

Then Ananias went to the house and entered it. Placing his hands on Saul, he said, "Brother Saul, the Lord—Jesus, who appeared to you on the road as you were coming here—has sent me so that you may see again and be filled with the Holy Spirit." Acts 9:17, NIV

For three days after Saul's encounter with Jesus, he sat blind, probably wondering what this encounter meant. Then God sent Ananias to Saul. Ananias was wary but never wavered in obeying God's call. He trusted God and went to Saul, even though he was afraid of this man with a reputation of violence. Ananias received Saul as a Christian brother. He touched Saul's eyes (and maybe Saul's heart) as he explained God's purpose. This encounter teaches us several lessons.

Lesson 1: *Ananias was ready for service.* He had a relationship with God and was sensitive to His leading.

Lesson 2: *Ananias was cautious and not afraid to question God's calling.* Ananias tested his impulse to make sure that he was truly hearing from God (Acts 9:13-14). God invites questions, but when He answers, He demands obedience.

Lesson 3: *Ananias acted on the call.* Ananias tested the Spirit, but when he found it genuine, he immediately went to Saul. Ananias trusted God's command and treated Saul as a Christian brother. He laid hands on Saul and restored his sight. More significant, Saul was filled with the Holy Spirit, which created a new center in Saul's life.

Are we near enough to God's heart to hear His voice? Are we courageous enough to engage former enemies of Christ? How about a former racist leader of the Aryan Brotherhood? Would we lay hands on this new brother or sister? Maybe a former child molester has met Christ and needs us to minister to him. Will we go, or will we hide? God calls us to serve all His children.

✝

Making it personal: What would it take for you to be willing to go to former enemies and love them?

Prayer: *Jesus, You loved those who nailed You to a cross. Let me know that kind of love and forgiveness. Amen.*

Read Luke 23:34 to see Jesus' model of forgiveness.

Shot-caller Comes to Christ

I don't deserve to be included in that inner circle [the apostles], as you well know, having spent all those early years trying my best to stamp God's church right out of existence. 1 Corinthians 15:9, THE MESSAGE

What would the prison population's reaction be if the supreme leader of the Texas Syndicate, Neta, or the Black Guerilla Family renounced his gang membership and announced that he had accepted Jesus Christ? The news would rumble through the prison like thunder. Everyone from the warden to the cons in the SHU would hear about it. The effect of the gang leader's flip would be no less dramatic than Saul's conversion was in the first century. Just as the leader of a major gang may be the least likely to come to Christ, Saul was the least likely convert to Christianity. He hated Christians.

The importance of Saul's becoming a follower of Christ cannot be overstated. When other Jewish leaders listened to Peter's sermons or attended John's lectures, they would be impressed. But they would argue that these men loved Jesus before He was crucified, and their testimony would naturally be biased in favor of Jesus. But what were they to do with this former enemy of Jesus? What made Saul change from a killer of Christians to a follower of Christ? Saul was overwhelmed by the argument and evidence of the resurrection of Jesus. Saul met Jesus and believed that He rose from the dead. Saul lived the rest his life preaching about the risen Christ and was in the end killed for his efforts.

What would be your reaction if the meanest, most bitter woman in your facility stood up in the yard and declared herself for Jesus? Wouldn't that courage and faith impress you? Why else would she do it, unless she really believed it to be true?

The next few meditations will look at the evidence for the death and resurrection of Jesus. Did they really happen? Saul was convinced. How about us?

†

Making it personal: Have you declared your faith? Where will you find the courage to do that?

Prayer: Jesus, You changed the heart of a man who hated You. Change my heart as well. Amen.

Read 1 Corinthians 15:30-32 for comment about Paul's pride.

Beyond a Reasonable Doubt

The Jews gathered around Him, saying, "How long will you keep us in suspense? If you are the Christ, tell us plainly."
John 10:24, NIV

Even though Jesus offers us a free gift of salvation, some of us do not believe He lived, died, and rose from the dead. Perhaps, if we consider the evidence of Jesus with an open heart and mind, dramatic changes will result in our lives.

We are personally acquainted with the legal concept of *proof beyond a reasonable doubt.* Lacking eyewitness testimony, some of us were convicted by forensic (DNA) and circumstantial evidence (motive, opportunity—no alibi). Facts piled up by the prosecutor persuaded the jury *beyond a reasonable doubt* that we were guilty. Use this same approach when considering Jesus.

Jesus lived about 2000 years ago in what is now known as Israel. He was born in Bethlehem and was raised as a carpenter's assistant to his father, Joseph. He made tables and produced solid wood furniture, doors, and other things the people needed for their daily lives. Jesus' life is documented in the Bible and other historical records. His life is a matter of historical fact.

But did He really die on that cross? Was He really dead? Or was He just wounded and revived? And did He rise from the dead? When we deal with the facts in a spirit of *proof beyond a reasonable doubt,* they will either rock our world and change our lives forever or leave us cold. Our response to those questions will either drive us to a place of surrender to God or leave us disinterested. There is little choice. In either case, taking time to review the evidence is worthwhile. If we find the evidence unconvincing, then it doesn't matter. However, if we evaluate the facts and find them believable, then nothing else matters! If Jesus Christ is who He claims to be, then our world is about to be turned upside down.

✝

Making it personal: Put away your suspicions of Jesus, and open your mind to the evidence of Christ. How will you judge?

Prayer: Jesus, if You are real, help me to believe it! Amen.

Read the entire Gospel of John for an eyewitness account of the life of Jesus.

Jesus Died That Friday

Pilate was surprised that [Jesus] was already dead. Summoning the centurion, he asked him if Jesus had already died. When he learned from the centurion that it was so, he gave the body to Joseph. Mark 15:44-45, NIV

Some of us suffered all-night interrogations at the hands of police. They were designed to wear us down and make it easier to get a confession. Some of us are in prison because of confessions wrung out of us after long nights of brutal grilling.

After Jesus was arrested, He was subjected to that kind of treatment. The Roman guards beat Him, spit on Him, forced a crown of long thorns on His head, and tortured him. They covered His head, hit Him, and then challenged Him to identify who struck Him. Then they scourged Him with a whip that had pieces of bone sewn into the ends of it. Those jagged pieces ripped the flesh off His back. After that beating, Jesus was forced to carry His wooden cross up the road to the place where Roman soldiers nailed His hands and feet to it.

Roman soldiers were experts in death. They either carried out their duties, or they were killed themselves. The soldiers assigned to the crucifixion detail were trained in the process of carrying out death sentences. In all likelihood, these soldiers were nastier and more sadistic than ordinary Roman warriors. If their officer, the centurion, told Pontius Pilate that Jesus was dead, no slipup was made. Jesus died on that cross at Calvary.

But, if that were not enough, the people who buried Jesus packed seventy-five pounds of spices around the body, weight enough to crush the life out of any severely wounded person (see John 19:39-40). *Beyond a reasonable doubt*, Jesus Christ died that Friday. This is essential truth. For if Jesus did not die, then the Resurrection could not take place.

✝

Making it personal: Think about this chain of events. What is your conclusion? Did Jesus actually die?

Prayer: God, help me see and understand the truth. Amen.

Read Mark 14 and 15 for the account of Jesus' death.

The Locked-down Tomb

So they sealed the tomb and posted guards to protect it. Matthew 27:66

When Jesus died on the cross, the Jews thought they had taken care of their troublemaker. To make sure the body would not be stolen, they locked down the tomb and put Roman guards around it. The goal was to keep Jesus locked in the grave.

Even today, people try to lock down Jesus. After the Christian movement started spreading, Roman emperors persecuted the believers. Throughout history, from Nero to Chairman Mao, powerful forces have attempted to discredit Jesus' death and resurrection. Many Christians died in the process, but Christianity lives on.

We can relate. Society builds prisons to house troublemakers and criminals. Within the prisons, there are Ad-Seg units, Security Housing Units (SHU), and other forms to lock down people who make trouble.

Personally, in many ways we've also tried to seal Jesus in His tomb. On the outside, we used the boulders of money and power to keep Jesus sealed away from our hearts. If that didn't work, we tried sex and drugs. If those failed to keep Jesus locked down, then we attempted bigger and bolder crimes. But nothing was powerful enough to lock down the risen Christ, because no matter how much our minds try to convince us that God doesn't exist and that Jesus is dead, our hearts know the truth.

Jesus is alive. The love of God is shown through the gift of His Son, Jesus. God urgently wants to be in relationship with us. He offers forgiveness for our sins, a new time of hope, purpose, and eternal life. If we are trying to isolate the risen Christ with stones of power, drugs, status, celebrity, or toughness, we will fail. We will fail to recognize the enormity of the gift that God offers to us. It's time to admit in our minds what our hearts already know: Jesus is alive.

And that changes everything.

†

Making it personal: Are you ready to acknowledge that Jesus is alive and wants to capture your heart? If not, what is stopping you?

Prayer: Jesus, my heart knows the truth, but I am afraid of it. Help me get over my fear. Amen.

Read 1 Corinthians 15:1-11 for more thoughts about the Resurrection.

Jesus Kills Our Numbers

But the fact is that Christ has been raised from the dead. He has become the first of a great harvest of those who will be raised to life again. 1 Corinthians 15:20

When Jesus walked out of the tomb, He killed our numbers. This doesn't mean the number of years we have to serve before we're released. It refers to our sin and guilt and the fear of death.

We were sentenced to years in prison. If we serve the entire sentence, we kill our numbers. Our release from prison is proof that we've paid our debt to society.

When Jesus walked out of the tomb, He had served His sentence. He had paid the debt for our sin. That means we are free. We no longer need to cringe about the evil we have done. Jesus frees us from the slavery of racial hatred and the approval of others. He frees us from having to obtain our identity from our crime, power, drugs, or relationships. Jesus kills our numbers in this life. His love and acceptance of us, just as we are, offer genuine freedom.

But His empty grave means even more significant release. The empty tomb means He conquered death! Jesus killed the terror of our dying. He killed the paralyzing fear of what will happen to us when we die. We no longer have to fear the terror of death. Think of the unbelievable freedom that is ours when we no longer fear death. If we do not fear death, we do not have to be afraid of anything.

Why are many of us reluctant to accept this liberation? Have we become so comfortable in our "institution" that anything new frightens us? Or, more likely, is it because the sin in our lives has been with us so long that it no longer pricks our consciences, but feels normal? That comfy feeling is a lie.

✝

Making it personal: What does it mean to you that Jesus Christ rose from the dead to kill your number? What would it feel like to be released?

Prayer: Father God, I've been stuck in my old ways for a long time. Help me let them go so I can be really free. Amen.

Read 1 Corinthians 15:50-57 for Paul's thoughts about death and resurrection.

Eyewitness Testimony

He was buried, and he was raised from the dead on the third day, as the Scriptures said. He was seen by Peter and then by the twelve apostles. After that, he was seen by more than five hundred of his followers at one time, most of whom are still alive, though some have died by now. 1 Corinthians 15:4-6

Many of us were convicted by eyewitness testimony. Eyewitness testimony makes proving something *beyond a reasonable doubt* much easier. When many witnesses agree with certainty that they saw the same event happen with their own eyes, the verdict is almost always guaranteed: Guilty!

The more unbelievable the event, the more people need eyewitness testimony. Fifty years from now, when people are told that terrorists hijacked four commercial airliners and flew two of them into the World Trade Center Towers in New York City, killing more than 3,000 people, some may doubt that this horrifice event occurred. However, if those skeptics could speak to the actual people who escaped the burning towers on that day, they might change their minds. It would be convincing eyewitness testimony.

The same is true with Jesus' resurrection. Many eyewitnesses saw Christ after His resurrection: women, the disciples, and more than five hundred other believers. When the apostle Paul wrote his letter to the Corinthian church twenty-five years after Christ's resurrection, he told them they didn't have to take his word for the resurrection; they could talk to others who had seen the risen Jesus. Many probably did.

Consider the power of eyewitness testimony in our lives. Now relate that to the eyewitness testimony concerning Jesus. We were once convicted by it; are we convicted again now? If Jesus rose from the dead, then He is Lord.

✝

Making it personal: If Jesus really did rise from the dead, what difference does that make for you?

Prayer: Lord Jesus, show my heart that You are real. I want to believe. Amen.

Read Acts 4:33, and ask if that can be said of you.

From Fearful to Fearless

When they saw the courage of Peter and John and realized that they were unschooled, ordinary men, they were astonished and they took note that these men had been with Jesus. Acts 4:13, NIV

As convincing as eyewitness testimony is, nothing tops firsthand experience. It's one thing to hear details of a prison riot from inmates who saw it; it's another thing if we ourselves were in the middle of the riot. To really understand the chaos and feel the fear, we would have to be there.

The disciples had firsthand experience with fear. After Jesus' death, they were terrified that the Jewish leaders would kill them too. They hid behind locked doors in a room on an alley in Jerusalem. Every knock on the door startled them. Then Jesus appeared to them in their hideout. They touched His wounded hands and feet. They ate with Him. Their fear began to retreat.

After Jesus ascended into heaven and the Holy Spirit arrived on Pentecost, the disciples were transformed. The disciples sounded like educated men as they preached effectively to thousands. Their preaching was so successful that they were arrested and brought before the Jewish leaders. The leaders were astonished by the transformation of these uneducated men.

To fully understand the change in the disciples, imagine two uneducated inmates successfully arguing a case before the United States Supreme Court. Or picture two illiterate cons teaching at Harvard University on the finer points of law.

This is another convincing piece of proof that Jesus rose from the dead. And it is important! The disciples were transformed by the power of the resurrected Jesus, manifested through the Holy Spirit. Jesus rose, returned to the Father, and the Holy Spirit of God arrived. Nothing else explained the disciples' dramatic makeover. This transforming power is available today, just as it was for the disciples. Jesus is alive, the Holy Spirit is active, and new life in Christ waits for all who seek it.

†

Making it personal: What evidence will it take for you to let go of your fear and ask Jesus for His strength to change your life?

Prayer: Jesus, transform my life. I need Your help. Amen.

Read Acts 2–4, and see the transformed apostles in action.

The Ultimate Shot-caller

The Son reflects God's own glory, and everything about him represents God exactly. He sustains the universe by the mighty power of his command. After he had provided purification for sin, he sat down at the right hand of the Majesty in heaven. Hebrews 1:3, NIV

Jesus rose from the dead, conquered sin, and now sits at the right hand of God the Father. How does that affect our lives?

What person could most help us in our current situation? Would it be the president, the governor, the head of the parole board, a famous defense attorney? Imagine having direct access to that person 24/7/365! If that person worked tirelessly on our behalf, helping us in ways we couldn't imagine, it would make us feel pretty significant.

We all have that Person available to us. Jesus Christ reflects the exact character of God. Jesus controls the entire universe by the power of His word. To illustrate that vividly, think about this: If the distance between the sun and earth (93 million miles) were the thickness of this page of paper, then the nearest star to Earth would be 70 feet away. The width of our galaxy would be 300 miles wide—and our galaxy is just a flyspeck in the total universe. Jesus controls all of it with just the power of His word![9]

Jesus is not some punk we ignore as a "weak sister." Jesus cannot be dismissed as only an interesting prophet or wise man. He claims to be one with God. He either is who He says He is, or He's a "whack-job." No other options! If we blow Him off, we are *making* the choice to *reject* Him. There are no neutral positions with Christ. We're either in or out! We must come to a decision on Jesus and who He really is. We must make Him the ultimate shot-caller of our lives. He offers forgiveness, salvation, purpose, peace, and freedom. He is worthy of our loyalty.

✝

Making it personal: If Jesus is a fraud, why do people follow Him?

Prayer: Jesus, You're the ultimate shot-caller. I'm open to Your changing power in my life. Amen.

Read Psalm 118 for strength and assurance of God in your life.

Die for a Lie?

Very rarely will anyone die for a righteous man, though for a good man someone might possibly dare to die. Romans 5:7, NIV

None of us would voluntarily go to death row for something we knew was untrue. Suppose another gang member conned the police so that we were charged with a murder she committed. If we had information linking the con to the crime, we would give it up immediately rather than face death row for her lies. This commonsense fact helps prove the resurrection of Christ.

As we read in a recent meditation, the disciples hid after Jesus was crucified. They were frightened of the Jewish leaders. But Jesus appeared to them, even though the doors were locked. They placed their fingers into the holes where the nails had been. They experienced, firsthand, the truth that Jesus was alive. He had risen from the dead. They knew it was true.

Later, after the disciples were anointed with the Holy Spirit on Pentecost, they went out and preached this Resurrection story. They spoke boldly about this amazing experience.

Yet, that is not the end of the story. They all died for their efforts. They all suffered hideous deaths. Church history tells us that all of the disciples except John were martyred. Peter was crucified upside down. Paul had his head cut off, while other disciples were tied to horses and pulled to pieces.

You might be thinking, *So what?* Many people die for their causes. That doesn't prove anything. The fact that the disciples died does not, in itself, prove anything. What is significant is *the beliefs* that led to their deaths. These followers of Jesus had seen and experienced the risen Christ. They were convinced Jesus had risen from the dead. That is why they went willingly to their deaths. People do not willingly die for a lie. They will die for what they know is the truth. Jesus is Truth. He conquered our sin, rose from the dead, and is alive today.

†

Making it personal: If Christ really died and rose again, what does that mean for your life?

Prayer: Jesus, come to me. Let me know the truth. Amen.

Read Hebrews 11:35-40, accounts of people who died for the Truth.

Can the Jury Reach a Verdict?

Look! Here I stand at the door and knock. If you hear me calling and open the door, I will come in, and we will share a meal as friends. Revelation 3:20

We've examined the evidence that demands a decision. We cannot sit on this jury, hear all the evidence for Jesus' life, death, and resurrection, and not render a verdict. Is Jesus really the Son of God—or is He a fraud?

Let's review some of the evidence:

Exhibit A: Jesus was a real-life person, whom history records as being born to Mary and Joseph.

Exhibit B: Jesus claimed to be the Messiah, one with God the Father and able to forgive everyone's sins.

Exhibit C: Jesus was crucified and died at age thirty-three.

Exhibit D: Jesus was buried in the tomb of Joseph of Arimathea.

Exhibit E: The tomb was sealed by a big rock.

Exhibit F: Roman soldiers guarded the tomb to insure the disciples did not steal Jesus' body.

Exhibit G: On the third day after Jesus died, the rock was rolled away, the guards were out cold, and the tomb was empty.

Exhibit H: Jesus appeared in person to Mary and ate with the disciples.

Exhibit I: Jesus appeared again, in person, to more than 500 other believers.

Exhibit J: The disciples were transformed from wimps to warriors.

Exhibit K: The persecutor Saul met Jesus and became the Christian leader Paul.

Exhibit L: Despite numerous, vicious persecutions, the Christian movement has thrived for more than 2000 years.

The evidence says either that Jesus was crazy or that He is who He claimed to be: the Son of God.

✝

Making it personal: What is your verdict?

Prayer: Father God, help me see the evidence clearly. Amen.

Read Mark 15:33-41 to hear the Roman centurion's verdict.

Liar, Lunatic, or Lord?

Jesus [said], "I am the way, the truth, and the life. No one can come to the Father except through me. If you had known who I am, then you would have known who my Father is. From now on you know him and have seen him!" John 14:6-7

How would you react to a guy who stands at chow and shouts that he's god, that he forgives sins, and that he will die and rise from the dead? You'd tell him to shut up and take his meds.

Yet that's what Jesus claimed. Is He a liar? If He's a liar, then He is a hypocrite too, since He preached honesty and integrity.

Perhaps Jesus is "Looney Tunes," you know, nuts. If your bunkmate said she was a polar bear, you would think she's crazy. Jesus claimed to be something greater—God. But if Jesus was crazy, then why are people still following Him after all these years? Plenty of two-bit messiahs attract followers for a few years, but for more than 2000 years? Not likely.

"I am trying here to prevent anyone saying the really foolish thing that people often say about Him: 'I am ready to accept Jesus as a great moral teacher, but I don't accept His claim to be God.' That is the one thing we must not say. A man who was merely a man and said the sort of things Jesus said would not be a great moral teacher. He would either be a lunatic—on a level with the man who says he is a poached egg—or else He would be the Devil of Hell. You must make your choice. Either this man was, and is, the Son of God: or else a madman or something worse. You can shut Him up for a fool, you can spit at Him and kill Him as a demon; or you can fall at His feet and call Him Lord and God. But let us not come with any patronizing nonsense about His being a great teacher. He has not left that open to us. He did not intend to."[10]

✝

Making it personal: What is your decision about Jesus? If you have not yet made a decision, what is stopping you?

Prayer: God, speak to my heart so that I know with certainly that You are real. Amen.

Read what Jesus says about Himself in **John 15:1-17.**

A Living Hope

Praise be to the God and Father of our Lord Jesus Christ! In his great mercy he has given us new birth into a living hope through the resurrection of Jesus Christ from the dead. 1 Peter 1:3, NIV

Eighteen-year-old Johnny is looking at life without parole. He was bright in school, but the other kids picked on him because he was overweight. He was at a drug sale that went bad and where an undercover detective got shot and died. Johnny caught the case, even though he was not the shooter. He will never leave prison to see his daughter go to the prom, graduate from high school, or get married. Is his life over? Can there be any hope in his life?

From Tutwiler Correctional Facility in Alabama to Fairbanks Correctional Center in Alaska, cells are filled with kids who will spend the rest of their lives in prison, asking these questions. Do these lives offer any hope? To have hope in prison is dangerous. To have hope means you believe that God has a plan for your life. Without a meaningful future, life is pointless. So what meaningful future can we hope for serving "life without" in an 8´ x 9´ cell?

The apostle Peter wrote that God, in His great mercy, has given us "a new birth into a living hope" through Christ's resurrection. How does that mean anything to us doing "life without"?

First, we may not be getting out of prison, but we can be confident of an eternal future with Jesus. That reality is sure and secure. More practically, we can live a life of service to others inside the walls and experience the peace and hope in Christ through that compassionate, loving spirit shown toward others. Inside, we can experience life that makes a difference—to God and to others.

Jesus Christ lives! Christ lives for us. His resurrection gives us hope for a future with Him.

†

Making it personal: What would a life of service in Jesus' name look like to you? How would serving others influence your attitude about your future?

Prayer: Lord, sometimes I get pretty discouraged. Today I choose to cling to You as my living hope. In the name of the risen Lord. Amen.

Read Psalm 62 to see how the desperate psalmist finds hope in the midst of despair.

Salvation

These questions relate to the meditations found on pages 90-113:

Discuss together:

1. In John 14:6 Jesus claims to be the only way to salvation. Discuss how this claim of Jesus is not exclusive. Discuss whether Jesus excludes anyone because of color, crime, or class. What are the conditions by which Jesus gives us His grace? What works must we perform to be worthy of His grace? Or, is grace a free gift? Discuss.

2. Have you ever experienced God's grace in a remarkable way? Share your story. What was (is) your response to God's grace? What do God's unconditional love and grace mean to you?

3. Ralph Waldo Emerson wrote, "It is impossible for a man to be cheated by anyone but himself." Discuss what he meant in conjunction with your lives now and on the street. What part did self-deception play in your current circumstances? If you are undecided about Jesus, are you deceiving yourself now?

4. What is your answer to the question, "Who is Jesus?" Does Jesus allow you to label Him simply a "good man"? What are the claims of Jesus about who He is? Do you want a relationship with Him, but only on your terms? Why doesn't that work?

Explore God's Word together:

1. **Psalm 27:11** highlights trust and confidence in God. How does the Lord's light show you the "right paths" in prison? Prison is scary and dangerous. How does this verse speak into your fears and comfort you?

2. **Isaiah 55:1** speaks of "thirst." What kind of thirst is the writer pointing to? On a personal level, what are you thirsty for? Note the inclusiveness of the invitation to drink. Free is a good price. Consider God's grace in light of Isaiah's text. What is the only reality that can satisfy our deep thirsts?

3. In one paraphrase of **Lamentations 3:25-27**, the writer speaks of eagerly waiting, of diligently seeking, of quietly hoping for God's salvation. You've probably had these feelings when you were waiting for a visit from someone you love. How do these feelings apply to your relationship with God? Why does the author of the book of Lamentations say it is a good thing to trust God when you are young? How would that have changed your life?

4. **Philippians 2:12** tells us to "work hard" to show the results of our salvation. What are some of those results in our attitudes, public behaviors, and private moments because of our salvation? Does anything need adjustment? What does Paul mean by "deep reverence"? What would that look like in your life?

Pray together:

1. In the beginning, pray silently, appreciating the quiet communion that time alone with God offers.

2. Then pray together for a true feeling of God's grace and power to come over you and guide you through your time inside.

3. Pray for God's unconditional love to erase any feelings of unforgiveness you feel toward yourself and others.

Commit to **confidentiality** ...

   ... **respect** each other

      ... **pray** for each other

         ... **encourage** one another

            ... **hold** each other **accountable**

Prayer for Seekers of Salvation

Jesus, why would You die for me?
That is the hardest question I ask when
I come close to asking You into my heart
and taking Your free gift of grace.
How could You love me?

Yet, Jesus, I have read how You loved
David even when he committed adultery
and first-degree murder. I have done worse!
You loved Saul when he was terrorizing Christians,
and You turned him into someone valuable.

I long to be of value to someone. I have
abandoned my children, I have let my
parents down, and I have let You down.
But no more! Today, I commit to You and
accept Your free gift—Your grace—for me.
Thank You for loving me so much
that You would die for me.
As I speak these words, my spirit lifts.
I feel Your presence and the
power of the Holy Spirit coming over me.
Thank You, Jesus.

Amen.

✝

Part 4: God's Plan

We must individually receive
Jesus Christ as Savior and Lord;
then we can know and experience
God's love and plan for our lives.

Decide!

For if you confess with your mouth that Jesus is Lord and believe in your heart that God raised him from the dead, you will be saved. For it is by believing in your heart that you are made right with God, and it is by confessing with your mouth that you are saved. Romans 10:9-10

On page vi of the introduction, we outlined four "Spiritual Laws" that give a straightforward understanding of the Gospel message. The fourth Spiritual Law says, "We must individually receive Jesus Christ as Savior and Lord; then we can know and experience God's love and plan for our lives." There are times we must commit. Now is one of those times.

We've studied about God's love for us. We've learned about His plan for our lives and Jesus' sacrifice, which paid for our sins. We understand that Jesus rose from the dead and offers us eternal life. Now, we must decide. Will we follow Jesus?

We can open our hearts to His Word and the Holy Spirit and pray the prayer below and begin a new life in Him. We can be free of self-centeredness and fear. We can leave guilt and shame behind and live for Him and for others. Right now we can accept forgiveness and discover joy as we embrace Jesus' gift of grace.

Father, I know that I have broken Your laws and that my sins have separated me from You. I am truly sorry, and now I want to turn away from my past sinful life toward You. Please forgive me, and help me avoid sinning again. I believe that Your Son Jesus died for my sins, was resurrected from the dead, is alive, and hears my prayer. I invite Jesus to become the Lord of my life, to rule and reign in my heart from this day forward. Please send Your Holy Spirit to help me obey You and to do Your will for the rest of my life. In Jesus' name I pray, amen.

✝

Making it personal: Becoming a new person in prison is tough. The other cons know who you have been and may not believe you are a new person in Christ. Will you take the risk? God is faithful and will not let you down.

Prayer: *Jesus, I commit to You. Don't leave me hanging. Amen.*

Read Psalm 91, a psalm of hope for when you are afraid.

White Funeral

Jesus replied, "I assure you, unless you are born again, you can never see the Kingdom of God." John 3:3

Going to a funeral isn't high on any of our lists. Funerals mean we've lost someone we know or love. We experience pain and sorrow, along with tears and crying. Not a very good time, usually.

Yet for us to get right with God, we've all got to attend what Oswald Chambers would call our own "white funeral"—the burial of our old lives. We call it a white funeral because our old natures—the accepted wisdom that landed us in prison—must die. Most of us who know Jesus Christ as our personal Savior remember the exact time and date when we attended our own white funeral. Our needs changed from craving alcohol, drugs, and sexual encounters to craving a relationship with Jesus. It was as if we became addicted to God. The Holy Spirit pulled at our hearts like a magnet. We became new persons on the inside.

For those of us who do not yet have a relationship with Jesus, we need a white funeral—to be born again. We may scratch our heads, not really knowing what that means. What it means is this: When we come to that place where our hearts cry out to God and we open them to the presence of the Holy Spirit, Jesus Christ enters into our hearts. If we truly appeal to God to change our lives in a transforming way, our old natures die and our new natures are born. We gain freedom from guilt, fear, anger, and an unforgiving heart. In its place is a heart that acknowledges sin and comprehends Jesus' amazing sacrifice on our behalf. We become newborns—new creations in Christ (see 2 Corinthians 5:17). Our sinful selves die, and we begin a new life in Christ, by the power of the Holy Spirit.

✝

Making it personal: Have you had a "white funeral"? Will you trust God enough to give up what you know—the old nature—for His promise of something better?

Prayer: Father God, I want a new heart, a new life—I want to be born again. Come into my heart right now. Amen.

Read John 3, the account of Jesus and Nicodemus.

How Can I Be Saved?

[The jailer] brought them out and asked, "Sirs, what must I do to be saved?" Acts 16:30

After the apostle Paul's conversion, he and Silas traveled and preached in various cities. One day they cast a demon out of a young slave girl, making her owners very upset. The owners dragged Paul and Silas before a judge and lied. As a result, the two missionaries were convicted, stripped, beaten, and sent to prison. Instead of complaining about the injustice done to them, Paul and Silas spent time in jail singing and praying. That night God sent an earthquake, which opened the prison doors and jarred off the prisoners' chains. Thinking that all of the prisoners had escaped, the distraught jailer was about to kill himself. Paul stopped him and told him all of the prisoners were still there. The jailer's life was spared, for if the prisoners had escaped, he would have been put to death.

In Paul and Silas the guard saw something that he wanted for himself. The two men had an obvious confidence and calm. So the jailer asked the question all of us must ask before we die: "What must I do to be saved?"

Paul answered the jailer's question with these words: "Believe on the Lord Jesus, and you will be saved" (Acts 16:31). After Paul and Silas taught the man and his family about salvation through Jesus Christ, the man did believe. Later that night the man and his entire family were baptized. The jailer made the most important decision of his life. He chose to believe in Jesus Christ.

Today, right now, we have that same opportunity. What must we do to be saved? Believe that God loves us so much that He sent Jesus to die for our sins.

✝

Making it personal: Have you made the decision to believe? If yes, what caused you to believe? If not, what is holding you back?

Prayer: Lord Jesus, I choose to believe in You. Thank You for all You have done for me. Amen.

Read Acts 16:16-40 for the full story of the experience of Paul and Silas in jail.

What Do You Believe?

You believe that there is one God. Good! Even the demons believe that—and shudder. James 2:19, NIV

Many people believe in God. They look at the mountains and oceans and confess that a Creator exists. We watch the human body heal itself after being shot three times in a drive-by and marvel. It is a witness to the Creator. If we asked every inmate in our facility if they believed in God, a majority would say yes. But *what* do we believe? What do we mean when we say we believe in God?

When we were kickin' with our biker brotherhood, we would often say that we believed in each other. We looked around the clubhouse and clicked beer bottles in affirmation of the bond we had as kinsmen. Those of us who served in the U.S. Special Forces believed in one another, especially when we needed someone to watch our backs in covert-ops duty. But what did we mean when we said that we believed in our buddies?

We meant more than that we believed our buddies existed. We affirmed that we believed in their loyalty, trustworthiness, and integrity. We believed in their word and love for us.

When we say we believe in God, are we saying the same thing? Do we believe that God promises to forgive our sins? Do we believe that He will give us a new start wherever we are? Do we believe that God will redeem our lives and infuse them with purpose and meaning, even in the SHU at Corcoran? Or, are we just saying that God exists, somewhere?

When we receive Jesus as our Savior, we are saying that we believe He died for us—personally. We are saying that we believe He knows our names and wants a personal relationship with us.

✝

Making it personal: What is keeping you from a personal relationship with Jesus and His life-changing love for you?

Prayer: Jesus, thank You that You loved me enough that even if I were the only person alive, You would have gone to the cross for me. That's love. Thank You. Amen.

Read John 3:31-36 to discover the rich rewards for those who believe in Jesus.

Point Them to Jesus

So don't worry or be afraid of their threats. Instead, you must worship Christ as Lord of your life. And if someone asks about your Christian hope, always be ready to explain it. But do this in a gentle and respectful way. 1 Peter 3:14-16

Taking our faith in Jesus to the yard is an intimidating thing. We are considered wimps for believing in Jesus, and we get confronted with tough questions. People want to know why a "loving" God allows starvation in Africa or massive earthquakes in poor countries or a gunman killing six-year-old kids at school. They consider us arrogant and intolerant for believing that Christianity is the only way to God.

We can validate their questions and exhibit Jesus' sympathetic and understanding heart, but we must avoid the devil's trap. Don't let those questions intimidate us and prevent us from proclaiming the truth. So how do we avoid that ambush and share our faith? Point them to Jesus!

Jesus is not a religion—He's a person. That makes all the difference. He the foundation that must be addressed before any other issues are talked about. As any builder knows, the foundation is the most important thing to get right. It does no good to discuss kitchen cabinets until the foundation is squared away.

People must decide who Jesus is. They must be given the chance to examine His life and ministry so that they can decide if He is a liar, a nut-job, or Lord of the universe. If other cons reject the claims of Jesus, then discussing God with them is a waste of time. If they come to accept Jesus as Lord, then the tough issues are put into context of a loving Lord who gave His life for us.

If the hub of a wheel is true to form, the whole wheel performs correctly. When we take our faith to the yard, we must take our searching sisters and brothers to meet the risen Lord. Everything else will fall into place once they get Jesus right!

✝

Making it personal: Who will you point to Jesus? When? Know Jesus so well that you are prepared to tell others about Him.

Prayer: Holy Spirit, give me the right words to point someone to Jesus. Amen.

Read John 14:6-7, a reminder about who Jesus is.

New Life

Those who become Christians become new persons. They are not the same anymore, for the old life is gone. A new life has begun! 2 Corinthians 5:17

When we accept Jesus as our Savior, we become totally new persons. Our old life of bondage is gone, and a new life of freedom begins.

Many of us know bondage. Some of us were (or still are) in slavery to drugs. We know fear and what it feels like to be really afraid. Many of us were abused and are now held hostage by feelings of abandonment and rejection. We still feel the pinch of the shackles of hopelessness around the wrists and ankles of our lives.

We carry around the chains of pride and self-centeredness that prevent us from asking God to unlock the manacles of hopelessness. Some of us are afraid to trust Christ because we don't really believe He will get our lives right. We fall into the trap of thinking that a life in Christ is all about rules and regulations. It isn't. Anything that stresses rules and regulations as a way to God may be a religion, but it's not a relationship. It is not true Christianity. When Jesus saves us, He saves us for a life of freedom—not freedom to sin, but freedom to do the right things.

Our Savior's keys unlock our chains. Our old lives—with their bondage and negative patterns—are gone. A process of change begins. Our old lives are like polluted fish tanks that smell up a room when the water filter is broken. When we accept Jesus as our Savior, He places a new water filter in the water tanks of our lives. He drops chlorine tablets into the reservoir of our hearts. The result is pure, sweet water that promotes life and health and hope.

✝

Making it personal: What would pure water in your life feel like? Will you trust Jesus to make you a new person?

Prayer: Jesus, thank You for giving me new life, for making me a new person. Clean me up, and use me to build Your kingdom. Amen.

Read Colossians 3:1-10 for a description of new life in Christ.

Belief Is Only the Beginning

Those who obey my commandments are the ones who love me. And because they love me, my Father will love them, and I will love them. And I will reveal myself to each one of them. John 14:21

While God wants our belief, He wants us to move beyond belief to obedience. We who accept Jesus as our Savior and Lord must dig deeper and expand our understanding of who He is and then act on those beliefs.

For example, if we firmly believe that polishing our prison-issue boots to a high-gloss finish everyday will knock a dime off our sentences, we will wear out the buffing brush. If we knew for sure that having neatly ironed clothes, curled hair, and polished fingernails would get us early parole, we would do it.

What about our belief in Jesus? Can it move from simply acknowledging the existence of a supreme being to real faith in a God who knows our names and inmate numbers? Are we willing to study God's Word and see it as the "owner's manual" for our lives? Are we willing to surrender our lives to Christ as our Lord, our Master? Are we willing to desire His will and obey what He wants us to do with our lives? Now we are getting down to it!

What does it mean to receive Christ as the Lord of our lives? It means He is in charge. He's the boss. God says of Himself, "Believe in me and understand that I alone am God. . . . I am the Lord, and there is no other Savior" (Isaiah 43:10-11).

We work in partnership with the Lord, but our role is to joyfully obey. For those of us who have problems with authority figures, we need to remember that Jesus is a loving Lord, not a self-centered, power-hungry Master. We can trust Him with our lives.

†

Making it personal: What step of obedience will you take today?

Prayer: God, I don't want to be contented just to know about You. I want to know You by doing what You say. Amen.

Read Jonah 1–3 to learn what happened to Jonah when he didn't obey God—and then when he did.

Healed by a Touch from the Lord

[Jesus and the disciples] came to Bethsaida, and some people brought a blind man and begged Jesus to touch him. He took the blind man by the hand and led him outside the village. When he had spit on the man's eyes and put his hands on him, Jesus asked, "Do you see anything?" He looked up and said, "I see people; they look like trees walking around." Once more Jesus put his hands on the man's eyes. Then his eyes were opened, his sight was restored, and he saw everything clearly. Mark 8:22-25, NIV

In earlier meditations we said that Jesus is not a domineering, sadistic Master. He is a compassionate, loving Lord. The next few meditations will look at the story in this passage from Mark 8 and see what it tells us about the character of Jesus.

Jesus was a busy man. Once the word got out about the miracles He performed, crowds of people mobbed Him. One would think that after a while He might be irritated by the crowds and want to send the people away. Not our Lord. When people brought a blind man to Him, Jesus moved toward the man and took a personal interest in him. Jesus could have just given the man advice. Or He could have just spoken a word and healed the man. But Jesus is not like that. He took time to *be with* the man. He touched him and led him by the hand.

Jesus then did a surprising thing. He used His own spit to touch the man's eyelids. That's a pretty intimate gesture. Our Lord didn't stand at a distance; He got personally involved in this man's problem.

That's the kind of Lord we serve. He's compassionate. He desires our wholeness. When we have a problem, He doesn't move away from us. He moves toward us and gets personally involved in healing whatever limits or debilitates us.

†

Making it personal: Where do you need a touch from the Lord? Where do you need to be made whole?

Prayer: Lord, please give me Your healing touch. I want to be made whole. Amen.

Read Matthew 8:1-15, stories about how our Lord compassionately touched people who needed to be restored.

Spiritual Blindness

Jesus asked, "Do you see anything?" He looked up and said, "I see people; they look like trees walking around." Once more Jesus put his hands on the man's eyes. Then his eyes were opened, his sight was restored, and he saw everything clearly. Mark 8:23–25, NIV

This is an interesting story in that Jesus did not heal the man all at once. He did it in two stages. Why did He do that? Was Jesus not powerful enough to heal the man the first time?

This story has two levels of meaning: one involves the man's physical blindness, and one involves a deeper message about spiritual blindness. It was not that Jesus was not powerful enough to heal the man in one touch. He wanted to teach the man—and us—about the deeper healing of spiritual blindness.

Many events in our lives have both a physical (visible) level and a spiritual (invisible) level. Our physical eyes allow us to see what is visible—things like people, the sky, rainbows, grass. Our spiritual eyes allow us to see the invisible things—things like love, grace, truth, mercy, holiness. If we are spiritually blind, we see only half of reality, like trying to see through a window that has a film of dirt on it. We don't see the full picture, the full truth.

Spiritual blindness prevents us from seeing God's love for us, His acceptance of us, or His forgiveness. If we are blind to those realities, we end up feeling hopeless and worthless. If we are blind to God's protection of us, we live in fear. If we are blind to His hand reaching out to lead us, we live without direction.

Like the man in the story, we need to come to Jesus and allow Him to touch our spiritual eyes so that they will be opened and we will be able to see everything clearly.

✝

Making it personal: In what ways are you spiritually blind? What would it feel like if Jesus made you whole?

Prayer: Lord Jesus, I ask You today—right now—to start the process that allows me to see You and others clearly. Amen.

Read Matthew 20:30–34 and Mark 10:46–52, stories of blindness that was cured.

What Do We See?

Then his eyes were opened, his sight was restored, and he saw everything clearly. Mark 8:25, NIV

The passage tells us that when the man's sight was restored, he saw everything clearly. But what did he see? The first thing he saw was Jesus.

The same thing happens when we regain our spiritual sight. We begin to see the circumstances in our lives clearly, without shadows. And we see Jesus. We see His face, full of compassion. We see His loving eyes, which look into ours and say, "You are My child." We see His nail-scarred hands, which remind us that He hung on that cross for our sins. We see clearly that it is Jesus who has restored our spiritual vision. He's the One who makes us whole. With our spiritual vision sharpened, we will see Jesus at every turn in our lives, pointing the way, shielding us from harm, carrying our burdens for us, and introducing us to people who need us to tell them about our Savior.

The second thing the man saw when he regained his sight were his friends, the people who brought him to Jesus. If this man had been blind since birth, he had never before seen his friends' faces. He must have been so grateful to them. The same is true for us. Who brought us to Jesus? Who are the friends who recognized that we were blind and who led us to Jesus, knowing that He could make us whole? Think back. Who first told us about Jesus? Who loved us and reflected the Lord's character to us?

Or, think of it this way. What "blind" people do we know? Who needs to have Jesus touch their eyes and give them spiritual vision? Are we willing to be the friends who have enough faith in Jesus' ability to restore vision that we take our friends to Him?

✝

Making it personal: Who are the people who brought you to Jesus? How can you thank them?

Prayer: Oh, Lord, now that You have given me sight, show me the people whom I need to bring to You. Amen.

Read Ephesians 2:1-10, Paul's account of God's grace to us.

Don't Accept Blurred Vision

When he had spit on the man's eyes and put his hands on him, Jesus asked, "Do you see anything?" He looked up and said, "I see people; they look like trees walking around." Mark 8:23-24, NIV

When people help us but don't do a good job, we are reluctant to tell them. In a restaurant most people tell the wait staff the food is "just great" even when it's not.

But look at the man Jesus helped. When He first asked him if he saw anything, the guy replied that he had blurred vision. He was informing Jesus that his sight was better but not completely clear. Wow! How many of us would have the guts to tell Jesus that His healing was "good—not great"? Most of us would have been grateful just to see shadows. But not this man.

Dr. Tim Keller suggests that we have every right, and a responsibility, to feel a "holy dissatisfaction" with our level of sight. Too often we accept a certain depth of relationship with Jesus. We acknowledge that we are sinners and that Jesus died for our sins, but we still don't get the full picture. We sometimes feel that it's okay to have blurred spiritual vision. But it's not! If the man had not been honest with Jesus, he would have walked around, stumbling into things.

It's also not okay with Jesus that we have blurred vision. Maybe He was testing the man, wanting to see if he'd be satisfied with "good enough." Jesus wants 20/20 vision for us. He wants us to see the truth clearly.

Let's not be satisfied with "good enough." Let's keep getting in God's face and demand that He show us where we are clutching to self-love and self-sufficiency that are hindering our sight. We must demand that Jesus will keep touching our eyes so that we will see Him clearly.

†

Making it personal: How is your vision? If it is blurred, what will you do to correct it?

Prayer: Jesus, I'm not satisfied with blurred vision. Touch my eyes again and again and again—until I see You clearly. Amen.

Read Genesis 32:22-30, the story of Jacob wrestling with God.

Friends Help Us to See

When they arrived at Bethsaida, some people brought a blind man to Jesus, and they begged him to touch the man and heal him. Mark 8:22, NIV

If we want to be healed from spiritual blindness, we need other people. It's not enough to privately seek relief from spiritual blindness. We need the help of others who see Jesus clearly. In prison we're taught to "do our own time." But this story shows us the convict code is out of line with God's Word. The blind man's friends brought him to Jesus. They *begged* Jesus to heal him. *They* could see Jesus, and they wanted their friend to see Him too. When we seek out another brother or sister in Christ and ask for help with our blurred spiritual vision, three things happen.

One, we reveal humility by admitting we're spiritually blind. Jesus came down to earth as a human being, humbling Himself so that we could be saved. His example leads the way out of spiritual blindness. When we're humble, we're able to see.

Two, we surrender our problem. When we surrender, we admit defeat and give ourselves over to something greater than ourselves. Only when our rebellious natures are destroyed can we begin to observe the things God wants us to see.

Three, we ask to become accountable. We find a mature Christian who will walk with us. By being accountable, we demonstrate to God and to others that we're willing to submit to the oversight and authority of God.

If those three things make us squirm, then our idol of self-sufficiency is alive and well. Private confession is a good start, but it sometimes allows us to hold on to our idols. Private confession coupled with public humility, declared surrender, and tansparent accountability produce the winning combination that removes spiritual blindness.

Are we, who value privacy so much, willing to open up our hearts to others so that Jesus can open up our eyes to Him?

✝

Making it personal: Ask God to send you a friend you can trust with the intimacy of your heart—and He will.

Prayer: Lord Jesus, I am afraid of exposing my thoughts to someone else. Help me overcome my fear. Amen.

Read Matthew 8:5-13, the story of a soldier who asks for help.

Jesus as Savior and Lord

These questions relate to the meditations found on pages 118-129:

Discuss together:

1. Singer/songwriter Bob Dylan wrote "Gotta Serve Somebody," a song about how we all serve something. What do you worship, and to whom have you given your ultimate devotion? Openly share what things compete for your loyalty to Jesus. What keeps you from committing to Him?

2. Do you believe in Jesus? (The devil does!) What do you believe about Jesus? Have you remade Jesus in your image, or do you accept His claims about Himself? Discuss how belief in Jesus combines intellectual consent and the surrender of your will to God. In what specific ways should your daily life inside the walls reflect your belief?

3. Many of us have heard the comment: "A little knowledge is a dangerous thing." What does this sentence mean? How could this apply to your knowledge of Jesus and your witness to others in the prison? How could a foggy understanding of Jesus be something you hide behind to escape hearing His clear words to you about your life? Why is a clear vision of Jesus so convicting? What does the Bible say is the cure for blurred vision?

4. As you talk with others about God, why is agreeing on who Jesus is so critical? How does focusing on Jesus shield you from being sidetracked by important, but more divisive issues, when talking with unbelievers?

Explore God's Word together:

1. **Habakkuk 2:18-19** asks pointed questions about idols. What form do idols take in prison? Discuss how pardons, commutes, new trials, or better lawyers can become gods. How does making a *good thing* into an *ultimate thing* transform it? What does it become?

2. **Matthew 12:43-45** is a powerful picture. What does Jesus mean when He talks about a house that is swept, in order, and *empty?* How does this sobering message reverberate with you? What changes must you make to be a house that is swept, in order, and *filled?* Filled with what?

3. **Ephesians 4:17-24** describes people who have closed their minds and hardened their hearts toward God. How do these people live? How does a person with a calloused heart interact with others? What happens when a person learns about Jesus? Contrast your "old nature" and your "new nature" in Christ.

4. **Joshua 24:15** offers a challenge to choose! What choice have you made? Will your choice waver when you are on back on the street? How can you take encouragement from Joshua's bold statement? How does making a definitive choice lead to peace of mind?

Pray together:

1. Pray for God to give you a clear vision about any idols you may have built in your life.

2. Pray that you will be generous and gracious, with humble spirits of kindness toward others.

3. Pray for peace of mind in the middle of the night.

Commit to **confidentiality** …

… **respect** each other

… **pray** for each other

… **encourage** one another

… **hold** each other **accountable**

Prayer for the Saved

Lord Jesus, thank You for loving me!
Thank You for becoming a person who was
tempted as I have been tempted.
I praise Your name for not falling into temptation,
as I have so many times. Thank You, Jesus,
for being willing to go to a cross so that
I, who should be crucified for my sin,
do not have to suffer. Thank You, Jesus,
for being obedient to Your Father and
taking away not only my sin but
also the sin of the world.

Thank You, Father God, for sending Your Son
to die for me. How much it must have hurt to watch Him
suffer. What love for me You surely have—
amazing love! Someday I will be free.
Someday my life sentence here on earth will end,
and I will begin my LIFE sentence with You for eternity.
Please accept my praise and thanksgiving to You.

Holy Spirit, have Your way with me as long as
God gives me breath inside this body, inside these walls,
and among these men and women.
Let me feel Your quiet pressure on my spirit,
and give me the will to obey Your every
command on my life.

Amen.

✝

Good News, not Good Advice

This is the Good News about Jesus the Messiah, the Son of God. Mark 1:1

Every prison has its self-help programs, programs to treat violent anger, addiction, and other behavioral abnormalities. Sexual offender classes bump into the 12-Step AA and NA schedules. Inmates discuss Stephen Covey's *Seven Habits of Highly Effective People.* Most of these give good advice and counsel. But let's not mistake good advice for the Good News of Jesus.

Jesus claims that He is the Son of God and the only way to the Father. He is the One who became flesh, was crucified, and rose from the dead. Jesus bridges the gap between sinful humanity and a perfect God. Christ became sin for all of us so that we might be able to live with God for eternity. He paid our debt.

The Good News of Jesus is similar to the *New York Times,* in that the newspaper shares accounts of events that actually happened— fact not fiction. Jesus is not a self-help guru. To see Jesus as an ancient psychiatrist would be to miss His power and life-changing mission.

Many of us prefer the self-help version of Jesus because it allows us to pick and choose which advice to follow. It permits us to keep the rules we like and discard the ones that complicate our lifestyles. It lets us try to save ourselves, rather than surrender to Jesus Christ as Lord of our lives.

Imitating Jesus' commands and life choices is a good thing, but it is not good enough. He wants surrender, not imitation. Bending a knee in total surrender to the living person of Jesus as Savior and accepting His grace is the only way to salvation. This is the cornerstone of lessons from the life of Jesus.

✝

Making it personal: Do you want a personal Lord and Savior or a self-help Jesus?

Prayer: Lord Jesus, I want You to be my Savior, not some advice guru. Take control of my life. Amen.

Read 2 Corinthians 5:21, and compare your current view of Jesus with Paul's view.

A Complete Turnaround

For the kind of sorrow God wants us to experience leads us away from sin and results in salvation. There's no regret for that kind of sorrow. But worldly sorrow, which lacks repentance, results in spiritual death. 2 Corinthians 7:10

Most of us are sorry for our crimes. We are sorry we got busted, convicted, and sentenced to multiple calendars in prison. Some of us truly regret the pain our crimes caused our victims and their families. We may be sorry for the hurt we caused our families, if we have families left. We are penitent.

But do not confuse penitence with repentance. Jesus preached a message of repentance. True repentance is always more than penitence. It calls for a complete turnaround, a 180-degree turn in a new direction. True repentance calls for a new mind. It is like a revolution. Repentance is a hard thing to accomplish, yet it is necessary and fundamental for all real spiritual change.

Genuine repentance leads us away from sin, away from our former mindset. Repentance involves a complete abandonment of pride, self-will, and rebellion. We must be willing to sacrifice our carefully hidden sins. We must do away with deceptive sins like self-righteousness, judgment of others, and arrogance.

Too often our self-important attitudes lead us to look down on others whose crimes are distasteful to us. We see them in the prison church, and we judge them. But remember: Only God can judge the heart. What if the other inmates are in church to find freedom? But what if our cold shoulder makes them feel unwelcome and they miss hearing God's Word? God forbid!

Nothing short of a complete turnaround—repentance—is needed to create radical change in our attitudes, behaviors, and thinking.

✝

Making it personal: Are you sorry for your crime but still walking in the same direction?

Prayer: Father God, I need a new direction. Give me the courage to turn around and walk a new path. Amen.

Read 2 Peter 3:9 for insight into God's desire for our repentance.

Touching Lepers

A man with leprosy came and knelt in front of Jesus, begging to be healed. . . . Moved with compassion, Jesus reached out and touched him. . . . Instantly the leprosy disappeared, and the man was healed. . . . "Go to the priest and let him examine you."
Mark 1:40-45

What if the most despised and disliked inmate in your prison walked up to the most powerful shot-caller on the yard and asked for protection and status?

That is what happened when the leper approached Jesus and asked to be healed. Lepers were shunned socially; no one could talk to them. They were despised physically; no one was allowed to touch them without becoming unclean themselves. They were rejected spiritually; they could not attend worship services.

Jesus violated all the rules of "the yard."

Jesus reached out and touched the leper with compassion and unconditional love. This was a radical action. And the leper was immediately healed. By touching the leper, Jesus was now unclean according to Jewish law. But Jesus did not go to the priest. Why? Because, Jesus is cleanliness. When we come to Him and surrender, we are made spotlessly clean through Him alone. We all are lepers in need of cleansing by the Savior's touch.

Are we willing to go to Jesus and ask to be healed of our anger, discouragement, and bitterness? If we are touched by Jesus' unconditional love, how do we respond?

Are we willing to risk the safety of our anonymous prison life to touch other lepers in Jesus' name? Are we willing to become outcasts ourselves by association with these prison outcasts? This is the call to radical action in response to profound unconditional love.

†

Making it personal: Can you see yourself as a leper in need of cleansing? What are you going to do about it? Does feeling like a leper prick your pride?

Prayer: Lord, a radical response to Your radical love scares me. Give me the strength to follow Your example. Amen.

Read John 4:1-26, another example of the radical love Jesus has for outcasts.

A Delicate Balance

Levi held a banquet in his home with Jesus as the guest of honor. Many of Levi's fellow tax collectors and other guests also ate with them. But the Pharisees and their teachers of religious law complained bitterly to Jesus' disciples, "Why do you eat and drink with such scum?" Jesus answered them, "Healthy people don't need a doctor—sick people do. I have come to call not those who think they are righteous, but those who know they are sinners and need to repent." Luke 5:29-32

This is a familiar passage with the obvious lesson that Jesus loves sinners . . . scum! Society often considers inmates to be scum, and sometimes we feel that way about ourselves. However, this encouraging story says the opposite.

There is another lesson buried in this passage. Jesus teaches in such a loving manner that sinners feel comfortable eating with Him. The "scum" at Levi's dinner do not scurry away for fear of disapproval. They do not cringe under a withering eye of judgment. They sit with Jesus, share dinner, and listen to His whole message of love *and* repentance.

Jesus teaches unconditional love. But, as loving as He is, He also teaches the need for repentance. He does not separate His love for us from our need to turn away from our sin. In Christian communities today that separation seems to be growing. We concentrate on being tolerant and inclusive, but we shrink away from the whole truth by neglecting to preach the Gospel of spiritual revolution! Jesus does not short-change His listeners.

Are we too focused in our church on love and acceptance at the expense of neglecting the need to repent from our sin? Or, are we so focused on sin that sinners do not attend for fear of disapproval and judgment? We must be loving in our approach but firm in the fundamentals. It is a delicate balance.

†

Making it personal: Examine your heart. Are you more inclined toward tolerance or judgment?

Prayer: Lord Jesus, let me find that delicate balance. Amen.

Read: Hosea 6:1, a passage about brokenness and repair.

Feeling Our Pain

Then Jesus was led by the Spirit into the wilderness to be tempted there by the devil. Matthew 4:1

When we miss our mother's funeral, the devil may use our self-loathing and sorrow, may tempt us to score some drugs to numb the pain. We can sidestep that trap if we are willing to share our pain with another inmate or chaplain who has suffered a similar loss. Jesus was also tempted by the devil, and He emerged victorious. His victory is the message of hope for us.

When we accept Jesus, we feel the joy of new freedom and forgiveness. But soon the setbacks of prison life crowd in. The disappointments of confinement batter us. We begin to doubt our faith. The devil whispers to us, "What good is your faith? What good has it done for you?" We wonder if it is all a hoax. The devil adds to our disillusionment by parading our former "good life" before us. He taunts us to see what we're "missing out on" with all this Jesus nonsense.

How do we combat this assault on our faith? First, we take courage because Jesus understands. He faced every kind of temptation. Second, we stay on the alert, losing the illusion that being a follower of Jesus is an easy walk. Jesus never promised a trouble-free life. He said the opposite (see John 16:33). Third, we fill our minds with Scripture verses that defeat our enemy. Fourth, we enlist prayer and fellowship with the body of Christ as powerful weapons. Last, we stay aware that many attacks come when we are lonely and alone. Being accountable to another sister or brother creates a "cord of three strands" that is not easily broken (see Ecclesiastes 4:12). Temptation is inevitable. Giving in to it is not!

✝

Making it personal: If the devil is taunting you, how will you resist him and put him in his place?

Prayer: Lord Jesus, thank You that You stood up to the devil. Give me the strength to do the same. Amen.

Read 1 Peter 4:12-19 to better understand Christian suffering.

Jesus, the Madman

One time Jesus entered a house, and the crowds began to gather again. Soon he and his disciples couldn't even find time to eat. When his family heard what was happening, they tried to take him away. "He's out of his mind," they said. Mark 3:20-21

Abnormal behavior is normal in prison. Nicknames like "Mad Dog" are common. Hearing someone shout, "That bitch is crazy" would not shock anyone at Kentucky Correctional Institution for Women. Many of us landed in prison because someone considered us to be "out of our minds."

Jesus' family had cause to think that He was out of His mind. His claims about Himself were unbelievable. He called Himself the "Son of Man." He claimed to forgive sins and to be the fulfillment of the Scriptures (see Matthew 26:63-64; Mark 2:10-11). If our friends declared they were God, we might call the psych unit ourselves.

So, who is Jesus? His claims about Himself eliminate the "good man, cool prophet" option. He is either a loony-tunes nut, or He is who He claims to be: the Son of God. We must choose sides and declare who Jesus is.

Has anyone ever called us "mad" for Jesus inside the facility? Are we living so radically for Christ that we get called "insane" or "out of our minds"? As we live our faith, our attitudes, actions, and personal choices must reveal a mindset that is radically different from that of the general population. In the presence of aggressive behavior, are we calm? Do we turn away anger with a soft word? Will we share stamps, paper, canteen, or companionship with others? Does our love for God extend to the castoffs in the facility? Are we insane enough to bring them the Gospel as Jesus did with lepers, Samaritans, tax collectors, and prostitutes?

†

Making it personal: Who is Jesus to you? A madman? A Savior? How can you overcome the fear of being called crazy?

Prayer: Jesus, give me Your strength to walk in Your footsteps, even if it means people will think I am out of my mind. Amen.

Read Acts 26 for another story about a person who was called "insane" because of his love for Jesus.

Send Them Away

"Send the people away." Mark 6:36, NIV

When we were sentenced, some of us heard the judge say, "We're going to send you away." Those were cold words. They embodied society's exasperation with our behaviors. It felt as if society was tossing us away like an empty pack of cigarettes.

In today's passage, Jesus' disciples were also exasperated. They resented the huge crowd that followed Jesus. They uttered the same dismissive words, "Send them away."

Do we ever find ourselves uttering those words? There are plenty of things that irritate us in prison. Lousy food, lockdowns, petty administrative regulations, and delayed or returned mail are just a few. After a long day, we get bothered with other inmates asking questions about almost anything. Do we dismiss them and try to "send them away"?

How different was Jesus' reaction to the crowd. He must have been tired too. Yet when He saw the crowd, "He had compassion on them because they were like sheep without a shepherd. So he began teaching them many things" (Mark 6:34).

As followers of Jesus, we must overpower the impulse to "send people away." Remembering how we felt to be sent away and using Jesus as our guide, we can respond with compassion to the new number who is terrified about serving her time. We can help the illiterate con to understand a letter from his wife. We can be easygoing with inmates who need direction.

Whatever the situation, let's not dismiss people and send them away. We must embrace the interruptions and inconveniences as divine opportunities for service.

†

Making it personal: How many times have you rejected (or embraced) a divine opportunity in the past few days? Who needs your compassion and attention today?

Prayer: Lord Jesus, give me the vision to see Your interruptions and embrace them as You did—with compassion and patience. Amen.

Read Mark 5:25-34 to learn of another time Jesus turned an interruption into a time of healing.

Overlooked Resources

"How many loaves do you have?" He asked. "Go and see." When they found out, they said, "Five loaves—and two fish." Mark 6:38, NIV

Prison strips away most everything—our names, our choices, and our freedom. We often feel as if we have nothing left. When we are asked to give, we often resist. When Jesus asks us to care for others, we say back to Him, "With what? I have nothing."

When Jesus said to His disciples, "You feed them," they responded similarly, "With what?" Jesus responded calmly to His disciples' annoyance. He asked them one simple question: "What do you have?"

Then He showed them (and us) that we have forgotten two very critical things—our own resources and the power of God. We all have spiritual gifts (see 1 Corinthians 12:4-11). There are five loaves and two fish in every prison church! Some of us are gifted to understand and teach the Bible. Others are natural leaders able to attract other inmates to church or Bible study. The bottom line is, when we place what we have—even if it feels as if it is nothing—into Jesus' hands, He blesses it and makes it more than adequate for the task He calls us to do.

We must also remember that "Nothing is impossible with God" (Luke 1:37). This is the *truly* overlooked resource. We lean on ourselves and forget who is working through us. We leave the power of the living God on the sidelines.

We must accept and embrace our calling to use whatever resources we have to feed the hungry sheep inside our facilities. We have a ravenous population starving for the Word of salvation, though they may not realize it, yet! We may never again be in a place where we can have such a tremendous impact for God. Let's commit to give everything we have to Jesus, relying on His power, and see what happens.

✝

Making it personal: What do you have? Take inventory of your gifts. Bring them to Jesus.

Prayer: "Take my life and let it be, consecrated Lord to Thee." Amen.

Read Romans 12:3-21 as a blueprint for spiritual service.

The Anger of Jesus

[Jesus] looked around at [the religious leaders] angrily and was deeply saddened by their hard hearts. Then he said to the man [with the deformed hand], "Hold out your hand." So the man held out his hand, and it was restored!" Mark 3:5

Anger and prison time are dance partners. On the street, anger waltzed us into our crimes. Inside, our anger-fueled, hip-hop dance gets us bustin' moves toward our former accomplices, lying witnesses, incompetent lawyers, maybe even ourselves. Our anger dance is usually sinful, destructive, and bent on revenge. But not all anger is destructive.

Jesus became angry. This fact alone should get our attention. We understandably focus on His unconditional love, but we should also note the things that angered our Savior. Jesus' anger was directed at injustice, lack of mercy, unfruitfulness, harm to children, and hard hearts. In today's passage, Jesus expressed His anger toward self-righteous, hard-hearted religious leaders. These leaders were bound to tradition and to preserving their own power. Their stubborn self-importance blinded them to real human need.

Today's lessons from Jesus center not only on what made Him furious but also on how to avoid being the target of His anger. Our lives must be guided by kindness, mercy, and compassion. Are we so fussy and focused on the form of Sunday worship that we forget the genuine needs on the prison yard? Any self-satisfaction in our walk with God or any concern about our status in the prison church or among others must be brought low in humility to avoid the angry look of Jesus.

There is a place for "angry men and women." It must be righteous anger, fueled by our hearts being broken and angered by the same things that broke and angered the heart of Jesus.

†

Making it personal: What makes you angry? Is your anger healthy or destructive? What can you learn from Jesus' anger?

Prayer: Lord, God, my anger often leads me to sin. Through Your Holy Spirit keep me from destructive anger. Amen.

Read Mark 10:13-16 to learn why Jesus got angry with his own disciples.

What We Need, Not What We Want

While [Jesus] was preaching God's word to them, four men arrived carrying a paralyzed man on a mat. They couldn't bring him to Jesus because of the crowd, so they dug a hole through the roof above his head. Then they lowered the man on his mat, right down in front of Jesus. Seeing their faith, Jesus said to the paralyzed man, "My child, your sins are forgiven." Mark 2:2-5

Isn't it strange that instead of immediately reaching out and healing the paralyzed man, Jesus says, "Your sins are forgiven"? Didn't He see the man's obvious need, the need for which his friends brought him to Jesus?

Of course Jesus recognized that the man was paralyzed. But He also saw the man's deeper need: to have his sins forgiven. Jesus healed the need, which was not what the man's friends had wanted.

In a way, we are all paralyzed—by guilt, anger, greed, despair, loneliness. We tell ourselves, "What I need is a commute, a pardon, a better lawyer, or more money. Then my life would be perfect." We trust those things to save us. In a sense they are our "gods." We pray and ask Him to give us what we want, not what we need.

But Jesus loves us so much that He will not simply give us what we want. He knows that many of the things we want will not satisfy. They might even ruin us. Lotto winners, for example, have a history of bankruptcy, wasting their wealth on drugs and gambling.

In Jesus' wisdom and love, He gives us what we need, not necessarily what we want. He gives us spiritual restoration through the One who satisfies and who forgives when we fail Him.

This biblical story has a happy ending. Mark 2:10-11 tells us, "Then Jesus turned to the paralyzed man and said, 'Stand up, pick up your mat, and go home!'"

†

Making it personal: How is God giving you what you need? How does that compare with what you want?

Prayer: Lord, forgive me for simply trying to use You for what I want. Please give me what I need. Amen.

Read Isaiah 1:18 for assurance of pardon.

A House Divided

The religion scholars from Jerusalem came down spreading rumors that he was working black magic, using devil tricks to impress them with spiritual power. Jesus confronted their slander with a story: "Does it make sense to send a devil to catch a devil, to use Satan to get rid of Satan? A constantly squabbling family disintegrates. If Satan were fighting Satan, there soon wouldn't be any Satan left." Mark 3:23-26, THE MESSAGE

Would prison gang Mara Salvatrucha (MS-13) survive as a criminal enterprise if its shot-callers were warring against each other? No way! Many of us come from homes broken apart by family members plotting against each other. Without a focused and unified purpose, organizations and families disintegrate.

The religious leaders were looking for a way to discredit Jesus' authority over demons. His power to cast out devils was impressive, making Him very popular. The church leadership was threatened, so they labeled Jesus' power "black magic" and "devil tricks."

Jesus reveals their foolishness by stating the obvious. If Satan is throwing out Satan, then Satan will not be around long. A house divided cannot stand.

There are lessons here for the prison church and for us personally. Church leadership that is not unified in Christ and that is not preaching the Gospel with one voice will doom the church. Unity is critical for a vibrant prison congregation. The focus must be on the message of the cross and the victory of the empty tomb.

Similarly, if our lives are compromised by a gambling addiction, pornography, anger, envy, jealousy, or lust, our personal walk with Jesus will come to a standstill. Dwight L. Moody wrote in a new believer's Bible, "The Bible will keep you from sin, or sin will keep you from the Bible." Exactly! We must identify and remove those things that frost our spirits and chill our intimacy with God.

✝

Making it personal: Deny denial! Get real. Make a list of the sins that are camping out in your life. Show them the door!

Prayer: *Lord, let me fully grasp that freedom in You gives me the power to reject sin, make right decisions, and live for You. Amen.*

Read Colossians 3:12-17 as a benediction for daily living.

The Family of Jesus

Jesus replied, "Who is my mother? Who are my brothers?" Then he looked at those around him and said, "Look, these are my mother and brothers. Anyone who does God's will is my brother and sister and mother." Mark 3:33-35

Most of us love our families and cherish visiting with them. Jesus' seemingly dismissive comments toward His family make us wonder if He felt the same. However, there is no doubt that Jesus valued His family. He dearly loved His mother. When Jesus was dying on the cross, He made sure that the disciple John would look after her.

Jesus' comments in this passage are not so much a reflection of how He viewed His mother and His biological brothers; the verses tell us what Jesus says about priorities, about doing His will, and about who He considers His true family.

While families are important, they are not to be our top priority. Jesus teaches that the most important thing is doing God's will.

How do we know God's will? We can pray, asking for guidance, committing our path to God. We can search the Scriptures for direction. We can list the things we love to do; God created our work specifically for our talents (see Ephesians 2:10). We can seek advice from wise counselors to insure our goals are biblical and centered on Christ. After that, we can take small implementation steps, walking out the plan, conscious that small successes breed larger ones. Finally, when we are at a decision point, we can have the courage to do what we believe is God's will in the matter.

When we do God's will, we become brothers and sisters with Jesus. We become heirs to all His goodness and purity. This is our ultimate identity and source of comfort and gladness. We are part of God's eternal family.

✝

Making it personal: What does it means to you to be considered a brother or sister of Jesus—a part of the eternal family of God?

Prayer: Lord, thank You for welcoming me into Your heavenly family. Help me to be responsible to the challenge of that calling. Amen.

Read 1 Peter 1:3-9 to learn about your inheritance as a member of Jesus' family.

Is Bigger Better?

Jesus said, "How can I describe the Kingdom of God? . . . It is like a mustard seed planted in the ground. It is the smallest of all seeds, but it becomes the largest of all garden plants. Mark 4:30-32

"Bigger is better" is the world's slogan. Cities compete to claim the world's tallest buildings. Sporting events and stadiums boast about being the biggest and most expensive in history. We relate to that in prison. Cons with certain crimes are often considered heroes and get respected. We label them Original Gangsters, Shot-callers, or The Man.

But that's not how Jesus rolls. He compared the Kingdom of God to an insignificant mustard seed, the smallest of all the seeds. Jesus never confused size with importance.

Jesus entrusted His world-changing mission to a group of largely unskilled men. When Jesus rose from the dead, He appeared first to the least significant people on the planet at the time: women. Today, Jesus is still using small seeds—us!

As inmates, we often feel powerless, isolated, and worthless. We are usually not eloquent. Many of us speak with fractured grammar. We are afraid and uneducated. We feel we have no value to society and cannot help anyone.

We must throw off that mindset. Jesus certainly does. When we have "the mind of Christ" (see 1 Corinthians 2:16), we will see significant results from our work. But we need credibility. The growth of the mustard seed depends on an authentic walk with Jesus and on a witness that has integrity. If we have that, planting a kind word or being a help to someone in His name will produce a harvest of eternal consequences. When we bring a brother or sister to church or when we share a favorite Scripture verse, we cannot calculate the size of the result that may come from that seed. Our responsibility is to sow the seeds. We leave the results up to God.

✝

Making it personal: Take a look around. Where could you plant a mustard seed? Do it today!

Prayer: Lord, help me to sow a seed in someone's life today. I will trust You for the results. Amen.

Read 2 Corinthians 9:6 to see the results of planting seeds.

Harmony Out of Chaos

With a shriek, [the demon] screamed, "Why are you interfering with me, Jesus, Son of the Most High God?" Mark 5:7

Many of us inside like to excuse or rationalize inappropriate behavior by saying we "all have our personal demons." As if somehow that justifies our rebellion. It's really just a way of giving us cover to act out in a way we've already decided to do.

In this account, Jesus confronts a man who is filled with *actual* demons. These demons recognize Jesus and ask Him a question we often ask, "Why are you interfering with me, Jesus?" When Jesus asks the demons for their names, they reply cleverly with a fake name to conceal their identity. But Jesus is never fooled. He throws out the demons.

Our smoke screens never fool Jesus either. He sees our real identities. Our smoke screens take the form of paralyzing fear, inner insecurity, restlessness, self-loathing, anger, sexual immorality, drugs, and unsettled minds. We are consumed by racial hatred and love of power, and we are tormented by conflicted spirits. We deny and cling to these demons because we believe we cannot live without them. Yet, Jesus looks into our lives, "interferes" with them, and brings harmony out of our chaos.

How?

He delivers genuine peace by assuring us that we can trust His will for our lives. How many of us would welcome the peace of knowing that a powerful God has our backs? Jesus gives us true sleep-through-the-night rest by demonstrating love that is relentless and unconditional. We can rest in a love that died for us! He anoints our hearts with joy when we serve others in His name.

✝

Making it personal: Name your "demons." Surrender them to Jesus, and ask Him to throw the scoundrels out!

Prayer: My Father, give me courage, and help me let these familiar demons go. Amen.

Read 1 Corinthians 10:21, and choose your path.

Hard Soil

"When you hear what I say, you will not understand. When you see what I do, you will not comprehend. For the hearts of these people are hardened, and their ears cannot hear, and they have closed their eyes—so their eyes cannot see, and their ears cannot hear, and their hearts cannot understand, and they cannot turn to me and let me heal them." Matthew 13:14-15

In the next few meditations, we will look at what is called the "Parable of the Soil" (see Mark 4:3-9, 13-20). Jesus tells the story of a farmer who sowed seeds that landed on four different surfaces. The first was hard-packed soil. Because of its hardness, it was difficult for the seed to take root. The seed represents the Word of God, the birds represent the devil, and the soil represents the human heart.

In the Bible, the heart is depicted as the center of all human personality. It is the nerve center of emotions, thoughts, words, and actions.

What causes a heart to harden? Many of us experienced tough living environments, where abuse and neglect were common. Those circumstances can lead to a cold, cynical heart. The sin inside each of us also tilts our hearts away from God and toward hardness. Willful sin accelerates the hardening process, especially when it is aided by rebellious behavior.

Are we willful, rebellious inmates reading these words right now? Are we wondering about the emptiness in our hearts?

There is a cure for hard hearts. It begins with getting real with our sin and then taking a hard look at the unconditional love and forgiveness of Jesus. Find a Christian sister or brother who can explain it to you, on the DL if necessary. We should never feel that it's too late. Seed in the hard soil can take root and prosper, as we'll see in the next meditation.

†

Making it personal: What does a tender heart feel like? How would your actions change if you had a softer heart?

Prayer: Lord Jesus, help me examine my heart. Give me the will and courage to let You make it tender. Amen.

Read Psalm 139:12-13 as a daily motto.

Hard Soil, Hard Heart

For nothing is impossible with God. Luke 1:37

When the farmer planted, "Some of the seed fell on a footpath, and the birds came and ate it" (Mark 4:4). The seed couldn't penetrate into the hard-packed soil, so the birds (the devil) could easily snatch it before it took root. Did the sower waste his time? The Bible says that he didn't. Although the harvest in this environment might be small, it could be significant.

Anthony was hard-packed soil clothed in the usual prison uniform. His tattoos were sleeved-out, showing lightning bolts and barbed wire. He had an "88" inked between his shoulder blades. Two small teardrop tattoos fell from the corner of his left eye. Anthony was known inside the walls, by both correctional officers and inmates, as a very tough dude. So it was a shock to the prison population when, after a prison ministry yard event, Anthony walked up to the stage during the altar call and surrendered his life to Jesus.

The seed planted that day bore fruit. Anthony stopped his illegal activities. He started attending the prison church, and after some time, he became the chaplain's clerk. He went back to school and earned an undergraduate degree and a master's degree. Today, after doing 30 years, Anthony is a leader of a prison ministry helping other cons when they are released.

The lesson here is for sowers of the Word inside tough prisons. The harvest potential may seem meager, but consider the results of the seed in Anthony's life. Jesus planted and then nurtured the seed at that yard event and began the transformation of Anthony's character.

When we scatter seed inside our prisons, we cannot prejudge a conclusion based on outward appearances. We must be fearless and sow the seed everywhere with the firm conviction that with God, nothing is impossible.

✝

Making it personal: Where will you sow seed in the hard soil? What would it mean to approach these hard cases?

Prayer: Lord, give me insight, wisdom, and protection when You call me to sow seed in the hard soil. Amen.

Read Acts 9:10-19 about the obedience of Ananias.

Shallow and Rocky Soil

Dear brothers and sisters, when troubles come your way, consider it an opportunity for great joy. For you know that when your faith is tested, your endurance has a chance to grow. So let it grow, for when your endurance is fully developed, you will be perfect and complete, needing nothing. James 1:2-4

In the Parable of the Soil Jesus calls attention to the condition of our hearts, which determines our receptivity to the Word of God. When seed falls on shallow and rocky soil, faith springs up with enthusiasm but then shrivels when threatened by challenges.

Challenges to our faith take many forms. One is if we view the Christian life as an enchanted potion that cures all our ills or a magic wand that produces a pardon, commute, or parole. If or when those things don't materialize, we are disappointed and disillusioned, and we sometimes throw our faith under the bus.

We may be tempted to abandon our faith when temptations increase in our lives. Instead of praising God for them, as today's passage instructs, we give up our commitment and consider it too tough.

Another threat may be persecution or ridicule. If our spouses or family members make fun of our newfound faith, we may fall away and cave in to the peer pressure. When our gang buddies intimidate us with potential harm, some of us may ditch Jesus. Laziness is also a reason we fall away. How many of us were raised in the faith as children only to get lazy and walk away as adults?

We must examine our hearts to determine what kind of soil lies there. What are the excuses we use to avoid church, Bible study, and a closer walk with God? These are serious questions with eternal consequences.

✝

Making it personal: What excuses keep you from a deeply rooted commitment to Jesus?

Prayer: Jesus, help me fully comprehend that You have overcome challenges and threats to my faith. Amen.

Read 1 John 4:4 for reassurance to grow deeper in the faith.

Shallow Soil, Shallow Roots

On the way, Jesus told them, "All of you will desert me. For the Scriptures say, 'God will strike the Shepherd, and the sheep will be scattered.' . . . Peter said to him, "Even if everyone else deserts you, I never will." Jesus replied, "I tell you the truth, Peter—this very night, before the rooster crows twice, you will deny three times that you even know me." Mark 14:27-30

In the Parable of the Soil, "Other seed fell on shallow soil with underlying rock. The seed sprouted quickly because the soil was shallow. But the plant soon wilted under the hot sun, and since it didn't have deep roots, it died" (Mark 4:5-6). The plant reminds us of people who hear the Word in an emotional setting, raise their hands in the air, and shout "Praise Jesus!" And then, when confronted in their living units, they give up Jesus without a whimper. The crowds greeting Jesus on Palm Sunday are a good example. On Sunday they love Jesus, but on Friday the same people call for His execution.

Today's passage suggests that Jesus' disciples are no different. Jesus predicts that when adversity and danger come, His followers will scatter like sheep. Peter will even deny that he knows Jesus (see Matthew 26:69-75). Seems hard to believe. For three years the disciples had a front-row seat to Jesus' miracles and teachings. Yet, they falter. The good news is that the disciples regroup after Pentecost and grow deep in the faith with the gift of the Holy Spirit.

When our faith is not deeply rooted, it withers and dies when non-Christians challenge us or when adversity threatens our self-satisfied spiritual life. This is a cautionary tale to all of us who are shallow, posturing, and giving off the appearance of a deep walk with God. God does not look at who spends many hours in church, in prayer, and in Bible study. God looks at our hearts. With our surrender and God's help, our faith can grow, strengthen, reach new depths, and bear much fruit.

✝

Making it personal: Search your hearts, and examine the depth of your faith in Jesus. How can you get it to go deeper?

Prayer: Lord, call out my posturing, and let me get real with You today. Amen.

Read Acts 5:1-11 to see how God treats insincere faith.

Good Soil with Thorns

Do not love this world nor the things it offers you, for when you love the world, you do not have the love of the Father in you. For the world offers only a craving for physical pleasure, a craving for everything we see, and pride in our achievements and possessions. 1 John 2:15-16

As Jesus calls attention to the condition of our hearts, He describes soil that is good, but it has many thorns and weeds. When seed falls on this soil, it takes root and begins to grow deep. However, thorns and weeds—the love of the world and our competing idols—choke it out, and the good seed dies.

A receptive heart contends with the attractions of this world like two competing heavyweight prizefighters. Both have appealing qualities. A heart that is responsive to the Word offers an abundant life and eternal security. The world proposes immediate gratification and sensual pleasures. Which side will win?

At the core of this fight is the question of what we will love. The first of the Ten Commandments says we are not to have any other gods or idols that take the place of God (see Exodus 20:3-4). The things of the world—money, sex, and power—were all created by God. In themselves, they are not sinful. Money fuels many good causes; sex binds husbands and wives; power can make good things happen. But when we love them more than we love God, they become idols. We push God off the thrones of our hearts. That is sin.

The tension between our love of this world and our love of God wraps its tentacles around the throat of our budding faith and starts to choke the life out of it. When we honor the cares and concerns of our daily life in place of trust and obedience to God, the God-centered spirit in us withers and begins to die.

†

Making it personal: What idols are doing battle in your heart? How are they choking out the seed planted there?

Prayer: Lord, the battle for my heart rages every day. Please enter my heart and give me victory in Jesus. Amen.

Read Psalm 119:34 as a daily prayer.

Choked by Thorns

Herod respected John; and knowing that he was a good and holy man, he protected him. Herod was greatly disturbed whenever he talked with John, but even so, he liked to listen to him. Mark 6:20

Good soil with thorns is the most dangerous kind of soil. It is dangerous because we feel safe being rooted in good soil. The seed, God's Word, takes root, but it is ultimately choked to death by thorns and weeds—the cares and attractions of this world.

When John the Baptist was in prison, King Herod feared him because John was popular with the people. Herod was living in sin with his brother's wife, Herodias, and when John confronted Herod with this sin, the king did not want to hear it. Herod wasn't willing to give up his pleasure.

How many of us in prison are like Herod? We love coming to church, singing the songs, and fellowshipping with the other sisters and brothers. It makes us feel good to be close to the living God. Yet, we have secret sins that we clutch to our souls. Our powerful reputations within the gang, our forbidden sexual relationship, or our status with the shot-callers compete with Jesus' call on our hearts. When we love these sins, they become thorns that choke out the seeds of God Word and kill our willingness and ability to bear fruit for God.

At the end of the day, the love of the world—our pet sins—will control our lives. Unless we can surrender them to Jesus and free ourselves, our faith will not survive. It would be better for us if we had never heard the Word and gotten close to it in the first place. For once we have heard the Word, and reject it, we are in a more dangerous place.

†

Making it personal: Conduct a ruthless, internal inventory of the pet sins in your life. Look at each one and ask, "Will I keep it or let it go?"

Prayer: Lord Jesus, I love these sins very much. Help me to know that I can survive and live without them. Amen.

Read Mark 10:17-22, the story of one man who cannot let his sin go—and misses Jesus completely.

Good Soil

Yes, just as you can identify a tree by its fruit, so you can identify people by their actions. Matthew 7:20

The Parable of the Soil (see Mark 4:3-9, 13-20) concludes with Jesus describing good soil where seeds take root and produce a very large harvest. Bearing fruit is the essential indicator of seed that has fallen on good soil!

What do we think about when contemplating good soil? For some of us, good soil was simply where we planted our marijuana seeds to maximize the harvest. Others of us remember our families as good soil where we played sports together, were encouraged to study hard, and felt the love of a good mother or father. Whatever our memories, there are specific characteristics of good soil that are key to our understanding of what good soil is for our hearts.

Good soil is *rich,* meaning seeds will be nourished when planted there. It is *easily tilled,* indicating a coachable, humble spirit ready to receive the seeds. Good soil *demands a lot of attention* to insure that the weeds are pulled up and discarded. Good soil needs to be *protected* against too much wind, sun, and rain that could deplete the soil's effectiveness by drying it out or eroding the topsoil. And, good soil needs to be *replenished* with a cover crop that is then plowed under to fertilize the soil for future plantings.

We maintain the richness and receptivity of good soil with time alone with God in prayer. Good soil is weeded by sharing the faith in community with other believers. And it is protected and replenished by avoiding obvious sin in our lives.

Are we good soil for the seed? Are we rich in His Word and ready to be cultivated? Have we watered the good soil with prayer and service to others? Have we laid down our cover crop? Are we ready to bear fruit?

†

Making it personal: If you gathered up a handful of your heart's soil, what would you find? What kind of fruit will it bear?

Prayer: Lord, cultivate the soil of my heart to make it ready to produce much fruit for Your glory. Amen.

Read Luke 8:15 as an assurance and blueprint for daily living.

Good Soil, Good Fruit

And the seeds that fell on the good soil represent honest, good-hearted people who hear God's word, cling to it, and patiently produce a huge harvest. Luke 8:15

As this passage reminds us, the seed that falls on good soil produces a large harvest. What fruit would demonstrate that our hearts are good soil? See the list in Galatians 5:22-23:

Love: This fruit encompasses them all. When we love because God first loved us (see 1 John 4:19), it shows that we understand grace and have accepted God's love for us.

Joy: When we know our names are written in the Book of Life, because of His grace, we will be joyful in the way we act and conduct ourselves around other inmates.

Peace: When we have "made peace with God," we will cease to be anxious. Our fruit will be a calm, untroubled spirit.

Patience: "Passive" love shows itself in a spirit of tolerance and endurance around any type of personality we meet.

Kindness: "Active" love is the most convincing evidence of God's love for us. When we are kind, people will be attracted to the Word and to us.

Goodness: Good people do the right thing, even when it hurts or pricks our pride.

Faithfulness: Integrity—doing what we say we are going to do—means we walk the talk.

Gentleness: This fruit makes the weak strong and the strong gentle.

Self-control: When we show this fruit to others, they will respect us and be convinced that we have changed.

If we bear this kind of fruit, we will live the abundant, fruitful life whether or not we are incarcerated.

✝

Making it personal: Examine each fruit listed. Is that fruit evident in your life? What impact does that fruit have on others?

Prayer: Cultivate Your fruit in my heart, Lord Jesus. Amen.

Read 1 Corinthians 13 to reinforce the supremacy of love.

Sowing and Serving

So, my dear brothers and sisters, be strong and immovable. Always work enthusiastically for the Lord, for you know that nothing you do for the Lord is ever useless. 1 Corinthians 15:58

Jailhouse lawyers are in great demand because they sow seeds of hope. They can bring a Rule 35 writ or a writ of habeas corpus in hopes of sowing a seed of doubt in a judge's mind, potentially resulting in our release or in reconsideration of our sentences. We rarely tire of submitting appeals or seeking a commute.

We must be as persevering and unrelenting in sowing the seeds of Jesus' love, forgiveness and grace, as we are in seeking a pardon. In the Parable of the Soil, the farmer worked tirelessly to sow his seed. That same level of tireless energy must be applied to our commitment to sowing seeds and serving others if we desire our lives inside prison to be meaningful and have an impact on others. Jesus' life was both. He never tired of sowing seeds and serving others.

As we sow seeds and serve others, we will plant seeds of meaning and happiness in our own hearts. And, the seeds lost to the birds and thorns will not discourage our hearts. Jesus did not measure the harvest. He served the people, but He did not count them. Heaven rejoices in one sinner saved.

In London's St. Paul's Cathedral, there is a memorial to Canon Samuel A. Barnett, who worked tirelessly with the poor in East London. On the bronze plaque is an image of a farmer, scattering seeds freely among the rows. The inscription reads, "Fear not to sow on account of the birds." With Jesus, we know, as Barnet did, that although birds eat some seed, it also falls on good soil and bears much fruit. Keep on serving and sowing!

†

Making it personal: How are you serving and sowing? If you are not, what is keeping you from serving God by serving others?

Prayer: Lord, give me a servant's heart to endure and to leave the results of the sowing to You. Amen.

Read Matthew 23:10-12 for Jesus' view on service.

Lessons from the Life of Jesus

These questions relate to the meditations found on pages 133-155:

Discuss together:

1. Discuss why "bending a knee" in surrender to God is so difficult. Why is taking a free gift so hard for proud people? In what ways are your actions and attitudes proud? Also, comment on the difference between *penitence* and *repentance*. What kind of behaviors inside the walls would announce to the facility that you are sorry and have turned toward a new life in Jesus?

2. When the devil whispers in your ear that your faith has let you down, what do you say to combat his attack? Discuss how often the devil assaults you and what it feels like when you are under attack. How do you feel about rejection? Discuss a time when you were rejected. What effects did it have on your life's direction? How is hope in Christ and the ability to look forward in Him for your future a remedy for rejection and despair?

3. Talk about why Jesus' forgiveness for our sins trumps our earthly prayer requests. Why do you think Jesus satisfies us and the world does not?

4. How has a relationship with Jesus labeled you a madman inside the prison or with your family? How is your "house" in order or divided today? What things, actions, or abuses were eliminated or are hindering your single-mindedness for Jesus?

5. What kind of soil are you inside prison? When you look around, what types of soil are most often inside? If your heart is hard, how will you go about trying to soften it? Are you in a position to sow seeds inside? Have you ever seen a hard-hearted person bear fruit? Share the story. Discuss the soil changes in your life. What were the thorns that choked the Word for so long?

Explore God's Word together:

1. **Matthew 11:28-30** shares the secret of how Jesus gives abundant life to anyone who is weary and weighed down with a heavy load. What do we learn about Jesus' character from this passage? What do you feel your life would be like if you were

"humble and gentle of heart"? What would that look like in real terms? Is Jesus' prescription for "peace and rest" crazy? Why, or why not?

2. **Hebrews 5:8** speaks of how Jesus learned obedience from the things that He suffered. How does suffering teach obedience? How have your sufferings taught you obedience, or are you still struggling to obey?

3. **Psalm 32:1-2** gives great comfort to us when we are disobedient and sinful. Read this passage, and share how it feels to truly understand that your disobedience and sins have been forgiven. Why is this a source of real joy, even inside prison?

Pray together:

1. Pray a prayer of thanksgiving to a God who loves us so extravagantly that our sins are covered and seen by Him no longer.

2. Pray that the Holy Spirit will lead you to imitate Jesus' life.

3. Pray hard for the facility in which you live—for peace, fairness, and protection.

Commit to **confidentiality** …

… **respect** each other

… **pray** for each other

… **encourage** one another

… **hold** each other **accountable**

Joy and Contentment

Not that I was ever in need, for I have learned how to be content with whatever I have. I know how to live on almost nothing or with everything. I have learned the secret of living in every situation, whether it is with a full stomach or empty, with plenty or little. Philippians 4:11-12

Marcia had a husband, two young daughters—and a lover. One day her husband was found dead from a gunshot wound. The police arrested Marcia and her boyfriend. Marcia didn't flip on her boyfriend because she was unaware of any murder plan. She was so confident he was innocent, she went on trial with him. The jury convicted them. They received LWOP—"life without parole." Too late, she realized her boyfriend had murdered her husband. When her two daughters went into foster care, Marcia fell into despair.

Several decades later, Marcia's joyful spirit radiates around thousands of women at her facility. What produced that joy and contentment? Drugs, power, sexual connections, or favor with the administration? No, it's Jesus—and Marcia's recognition that He gave His life for the forgiveness of her life's sins. Like the apostle Paul, Marcia figured out that joy is not dependent on circumstances but on relationship with a God who loves us so much that He gave up His only Son for our salvation (see John 3:16). That understanding supersedes all of our other challenges when we fully comprehend its impact on our lives.

Yes, Marcia suffered as she thought of her children and the circumstances that led her to prison. The apostle Paul had sleepless nights as he remembered his murderous actions. But, Marcia and Paul came to see that Jesus suffered an unjust trial and death sentence. Jesus, who was innocent, willingly went to the cross so that we, who are guilty, could live. When we really, *really* get this, our circumstances are not all that significant. The result will be joy!

†

Making it personal: Have you ever experienced joy in the midst of difficult circumstances? Tell a friend about it.

Prayer: Jesus, I desperately want joy in my life. My heart is open. Please make it happen. Amen.

Read Mark 15:16-32 to understand Jesus' suffering for us.

Joy behind Bars

Every time I think of you, I give thanks to my God. I always pray for you, and I make my requests with a heart full of joy. Philippians 1:3-4

Part of our purpose when God saves us is to live godly lives—lives that reflect the character of God. The apostle Paul gives us some of the best instructions for what it means to live a godly life. For the next few meditations we'll be looking at a letter Paul wrote to the believers who lived in the city of Philippi. Keep in mind that Paul is writing this letter from prison.

One of the many remarkable things about Paul is that even though he was unjustly imprisoned, even though he was stripped, beaten, and thrown into the inner dungeon of a Roman prison, he was full of joy. He had every right to complain, but he didn't. He kept his eyes on God's purposes for him. He chose joy!

Paul could have questioned God's plan. God had commissioned Paul to preach the Gospel in foreign lands, and he had just begun an aggressive missionary campaign. But two years in prison interrupted that plan. Again, instead of complaining, Paul kept right on serving God, choosing to see prison as his new mission field.

Like so many of us doing indeterminate sentences like "2-to-life" for sexual assault or "25-to-life" for second-degree murder, Paul is not sure he'll ever leave prison; he may even lose his life there. But listen to what he says about that: "But even . . . if I am to die [because I was preaching the Gospel], I will rejoice, and I want to share my joy with all of you. And you should be happy about this and rejoice with me" (Philippians 2:16-18). For a person in shackles, that is a pretty good response.

Paul is an inspiration to us. When we are tempted to complain, we can choose joy.

✝

Making it personal: In what part of your life do you need to choose joy? How will you do that?

Prayer: Lord, I want to reflect Your character. Help me to choose joy. Amen.

Read Acts 16:11-40 to learn about how the church in Philippi began and about one of the first times Paul was thrown into prison.

God: Long-term Investor

And I am sure that God, who began the good work within you, will continue his work until it is finally finished on that day when Christ Jesus comes back again. Philippians 1:6

When some of us read Marcia's story, we wonder if Jesus is some sort of magic salve that we neatly rub into our lives and instant joy is the result. That may be the result for some of us (after all, Paul's conversion was immediate and knocked him off his horse), but Marcia's decades-long story is compressed into three paragraphs and does not adequately reflect the time God invested in her to remold her into His character. God invested in Marcia and never gave up on her until His character shone through her to the other women. We can trust that God will be faithful to continue His work in us too.

People who buy shares of stock and then sell them quickly are not investors. They are speculators or gamblers. Wise investors, such as Warren Buffett, take a long view, knowing that companies like Amgen, Google, or Apple take time to mature and show a rise in their stock price. Companies that attract such knowledgeable investors take pride in the fact that they would invest with them and do all they can to justify the investment. God is a savvy, long-term investor in us. He knows our hidden qualities and value. He understands that the seeds of His Spirit may take a few years to produce a return on His investment. He never gives up on us.

From prison, Paul writes that very thing to the Philippian believers. He assures them that their lives have meaning because God has invested in them. His message is for us today as well. When God invests in us and works out His purposes through us, we are valuable and have worth.

✝

Making it personal: What "good work" has God begun in your life? How is He continuing that work?

Prayer: I am so honored that You would invest in me. Help me be all I can be for You, Lord. Amen.

Read Exodus 2:10–4:31 and Exodus 33:12-33, the story of God's long-term investment in Moses.

Purpose in Prison

And I want you to know, dear brothers and sisters, that everything that has happened to me here has helped to spread the Good News. . . . And because of my imprisonment, many of the Christians here have gained confidence and become more bold in telling others about Christ. Philippians 1:12-14

When we got locked up behind bars, many of us assumed life was over. We lost our jobs, our identities, our reputation, our families. What was left to live for except the dull routine of prison life? "Life without parole" felt like life without purpose.

So we locked up our hearts. We locked up our hopes and dreams. We steeled ourselves to endure the drudgery of the long months, the long years.

The apostle Paul, however, gives us a very different perspective. When he was locked up, he also lost his purpose, his identity, and his reputation. He had been bound for missionary work around the world.

But Paul did not see prison as an obstacle. He did not let jail stop him from having purpose. He saw that nothing is an accident, that his experience in prison actually *helped* him fulfill his purpose: to share the Good News about Christ. He understood that *because* of his imprisonment, others grew in their relationship to Jesus.

Can that be said of us? Can we say, *"Because* of my imprisonment, the people in my pod know Jesus"? Life doesn't end because we are behind bars. We can unlock our hearts and allow God to give us a purposeful life of sharing with others who He is and what He has done in our lives.

✝

Making it personal: What purpose can your imprisonment have in God's plan to bring others to Jesus?

Prayer: Lord, forgive me for locking up my heart and my dreams. Allow me to be part of Your plan to draw men and women into Your kingdom. Amen.

Read Philippians 1:20-26 to see the depth of Paul's commitment to Christ.

Put Yourself Aside

If you've gotten anything at all out of following Christ, if his love has made any difference in your life, . . . if you have a heart, if you care—then do me a favor: Agree with each other, love each other, be deep-spirited friends. Don't push your way to the front; don't sweet-talk your way to the top. Put yourself aside, and help others get ahead. Don't be obsessed with getting your own advantage. Forget yourselves long enough to lend a helping hand. Philippians 2:1-4, THE MESSAGE

Following Christ while in prison—doing *HIS* time—can be a challenge. As we have noted before, the convict code tells us "Look out for number one"; "Watch your own back"; "If you need to push others out of the way to get ahead, then do it"; "Use anyone you can to get what you want."

But Paul, who also lived in a prison with a convict code, called for a different attitude. He said, "If following Christ means anything to you, then do me a favor. Don't push yourself to the front. Put yourself aside. Help others instead." The New Living Translation puts it this way, "Be humble, thinking of others as better than yourself."

For the sake of Christ, we need to stop obsessing about our own needs and lend a helping hand. What does that look like? We know there are men and women in our living units that not only have *no hope*—they also have *no soap!* Being the face and hands of Jesus sometimes is as easy as simply walking over and placing a bar of Dial in someone's hand.

Remember that we can never love selflessly in our own strength. We can do it only when we surrender our self-centeredness to Jesus and ask the Holy Spirit to fill us.

†

Making it personal: Who needs a helping hand today? How will you help?

Prayer: Lord, I confess that I am obsessed with my own needs. I surrender my selfishness to You. Fill me with Your Spirit so that I can love others and think of them as better than myself. Amen.

Read Colossians 3:12-14 for the wardrobe God wants us to choose.

Give Up Entitlement

Think of yourselves the way Christ Jesus thought of himself. He had equal status with God but didn't think so much of himself that he had to cling to the advantages of that status no matter what. Not at all. When the time came, he set aside the privileges of deity and took on the status of a slave, became human! . . . He didn't claim special privileges. Instead, he lived a selfless, obedient life and then died a selfless, obedient death. Philippians 2:5-8, THE MESSAGE

One of the hardest things about coming to prison is giving up our rights as free men and women. We liked our rights: the right to make our own decisions, the right to meet with anyone we wanted, our right to travel anywhere we wanted. We rail against a system that denies us these rights. We smolder inside ourselves and would like to demand our rights. Aren't we entitled?

In today's passage Paul encourages us to think about ourselves as Christ Jesus thought about Himself. Even though He was God, He didn't demand and cling to His rights as God. Think about that. When Jesus was on earth and people got in His face, He could have said, "Look, man, do you know who you're talking to? I'm God. Give Me some respect." Or, when Jesus hung on the cross for our sin, He could have said, "Well, people, you can put Me on this cross, but I don't have to stay here. I'm God, after all. I'll just perform a little miracle here and come down."

But He didn't. Jesus gave up all His rights as God, and He made Himself nothing. He forced all of His divinity into the confining form of a human being. All because He loved us.

Jesus set an example for us. We need to give up our attitudes of entitlement and stop demanding our rights. In gratitude for what He has done for us, we can live in selfless obedience to Him.

†

Making it personal: Where are you clinging to your rights? How will you reflect Christ's attitude today?

Prayer: *Lord, forgive me for my attitude of entitlement, for thinking the world—and You—owe me. Help me take on the attitude of Christ Jesus. Amen.*

Read Philippians 2:6-11 to see how God rewarded His Son's obedience to His plan.

Stop Complaining and Arguing

In everything you do, stay away from complaining and arguing, so that no one can speak a word of blame against you. You are to live clean, innocent lives as children of God in a dark world full of crooked and perverse people. Let your lives shine brightly before them. Philippians 2:14-15

Like it or not, people watch us. They can tell who we are by how we act. If we have chosen to follow Christ, people can also tell who *He* is by how we act. We are a reflection of our Father.

What does that mean? Paul wants us to be pure reflections of God's character. He wants us to live clean, innocent lives so that when others look at us, they have a clear, unclouded picture of who God is.

Interestingly, the behavior that Paul focuses on here is complaining and arguing. He could have chosen any number of other negative behaviors, but he chose complaining and arguing. Why do you think he did that? After all, complaining and arguing aren't that bad.

But maybe that's the point. We don't see them as such destructive behaviors; in fact, if we were honest, we would admit that we indulge ourselves in them all the time. We whine about chow. We grumble that the chaplain is lazy. We find fault with the phone system and visiting hours.

But when we complain, when we argue, we smudge the reflection of God's character in us. We give Christ a bad name. Paul wants us to be blameless so that no one can reject Christ because they saw a poor picture of Him in our lives.

If that seems hard, that's because it is. But it is hard *only if* we think it's completely up to us to live clean, innocent lives. We need to remember that only when Christ lives in our hearts, when we have given Him full access to our hearts, can He live His life through us. When that happens, our lives are like lights that shine in a dark and perverse world.

†

Making it personal: Where do you need to stop complaining and arguing—today?

Prayer: Lord, You are pure and blameless. I want to reflect You accurately. Amen.

Read Titus 2:7-8 for more instructions about pure behavior.

Look Forward to What Lies Ahead

I keep working toward that day when I will finally be all that Christ Jesus saved me for and wants me to be. . . . I am still not all I should be, but I am focusing all my energies on this one thing: Forgetting the past and looking forward to what lies ahead, I strain to reach the end of the race and receive the prize for which God, through Christ Jesus, is calling us up to heaven. Philippians 3:12-14

For the first four years Jaleesha was behind bars, she struggled every day with the memories of the robbery gone bad and the video store owner who got shot. The images seared her brain—and her heart. Then, another woman in her facility introduced her to Jesus. Jaleesha was very resistant at first. On the outside she had known some men who claimed to know God but were abusive and foulmouthed. If that's what Christianity was about, she wanted no part of it.

But as Jaleesha sat in the back of the chapel on Sunday mornings, she heard about a Jesus who had compassion on outcasts and losers. She heard about a Jesus who forgave sinners, even gave His life for them. Eventually she surrendered her life to that Jesus.

And her life has never been the same. She has experienced hope for the first time in a decade. She occasionally feels real joy. And, most important, she has found forgiveness and has been able to put her crime behind her.

She is still not all that she knows Christ wants her to be, but she is putting the past behind her and is looking forward to what lies ahead. She knows she may never leave the prison, but she's made her peace with that. She is straining to run a good race and receive the prize of eternity with the Jesus who called her, forgave her, cleansed her, and gave her a future.

†

Making it personal: In what ways are you still weighed down by your past? How will you find forgiveness and embrace the future?

Prayer: Lord, I am a prisoner of my past, but You have set me free. Help me to leave my past behind and turn my face to my future with You. Amen.

Memorize Jeremiah 29:11 as God's promise for your future.

Be Full of Joy

Always be full of joy in the Lord. I say it again—rejoice! Let everyone see that you are considerate in all you do. Remember, the Lord is coming soon. Philippians 4:4-5

Some of us read today's passage and say, "What's there to be happy about? My spouse won't visit me. I can't see my kids. The parole board just rejected my appeal. Happy? Not me. Not today."

Why would the apostle Paul be so insistent that we be full of joy? He even repeats himself: "I say it again—rejoice!" These are commands, not suggestions. He doesn't say, "When the circumstances are right, be full of joy." He says *always* be full of joy.

Notice that Paul does not say, "Be happy." Instead, he says, "Be full of *joy*." What's the difference?

The difference is one of depth. *Happiness* is a feeling we have when everything is going well for us. Life is good, and we feel happy. *Joy* is something deeper. Joy is what we feel even when life is the pits, when everything that can go wrong does go wrong.

Remember that Paul is no stranger to things going wrong. In another one of his letters he wrote, "We patiently endure troubles and hardships and calamities of every kind. We have been beaten, been put in jail, faced angry mobs, worked to exhaustion, endured sleepless nights, and gone without food. . . . We have been beaten within an inch of our lives. Our hearts ache, but we always have joy" (2 Corinthians 6:5-10).

Did you see that? "Our hearts ache, but we always have joy." How is that possible? The secret to joy is that it is "joy in the Lord." Only when we understand that this life is not all there is, that the Holy Spirit's presence in our lives can lift us beyond the grayness of life in our cells, can we experience joy in the Lord. Because of Jesus, we can know a life that looks beyond circumstances and is joyful. Always.

✝

Making it personal: Do you know that joy? What can you do to increase the joy in your life?

Prayer: Lord, I long to experience the joy that Paul talks about. Fill me up with Your Spirit. Allow me to overflow with Your joy. Amen.

Read 1 Peter 1:6-9 for promises about joy.

Don't Worry!

Don't worry about anything; instead, pray about everything. Tell God what you need, and thank him for all he has done. If you do this, you will experience God's peace, which is far more wonderful than the human mind can understand. Philippians 4:6-7

For some of us, telling us not to worry is like telling us not to breathe. It's impossible. Our minds are full of worries. We worry about who's taking care of our kids. We worry about our safety. We worry about how we will endure years of incarceration.

Is Paul in touch with reality, telling us not to worry? He is not suggesting that the things we worry about are not real. Remember he suffered lots of abuses too. He is also not instructing us just to *pretend* that things don't bother us. No, he's telling us that when we are tempted to worry, we should pray instead. Again, these are not suggestions; these are commands. He doesn't say, "Maybe you should consider not worrying so much." He says, "Stop it! Don't worry about *anything*." Not one thing.

Instead—and that's a key word in this verse—pray. Not occasionally. Not when we feel like it. Pray about *everything*.

Why does Paul use such strong language? He knows that worry leads to evil and eats away at us—literally. It gives us ulcers. It gives us searing headaches. It robs us of sleep. So he suggests another way: Tell God what you need. Pray about everything. Picture God with His hands stretched out, waiting for you to place your worries in His hands. Then take each worry and give it to Him. Remember, He's strong. He can hold a heavy load.

Then after praying and giving your worries to God, thank Him for all He has done. All day long, thank Him. What will happen? Paul tells us that we will experience a peace that is beyond our imagining.

✝

Making it personal: What worries will you give to God today?

Prayer: Father God, today I want to stop worrying. Right now I give You [name your worries—all of them]. Thank You for carrying my worries. Amen.

Memorize Philippians 4:6-7, and repeat it throughout the day until praying is like breathing.

Paul's Words from Prison

These questions relate to the meditations found on pages 158-167:

Discuss together:

1. How can your life have purpose—a real meaning for existing—inside prison? How does faith in God's will for your life play a key part in your answer? Paul's purpose changed from missionary on the outside to minister inside a prison. How do you relate to his situation? How is his experience in prison like yours? In what ways could you be a minister inside your facility?

2. Inmates like to say, "Your walk has got to match your talk." How was Paul's (walk) behavior in prison a powerful witness for God's love in his life? Look back on your talk/walk over the past weeks, and reflect if they were a powerful witness for God—or something else. Share your thoughts.

3. After you accept Jesus and are saved (*justification*), your lives are still stained with sin. How can this fact perhaps confuse you and/or cause discouragement? *Sanctification* is "the long process of being set apart; made holy." Discuss the peace you discover when you see "your journey toward holiness" as a long-term progression. What road signs along the journey confirm that you are on the right path? Who among you can testify to this process? Describe your journey.

4. Discuss the difference between genuine concern and worry. Is Paul's command to not worry realistic? Contemplate what Paul means in Philippians 4:6-7 to give thanks to God before you know the answer to the prayer. Consider God's sovereignty, "His being in charge of all that happens." If you believe that God has your back, why is fretting unnecessary? According to Psalm 37:8, what does "fretting" lead to?

Explore God's Word together:

1. **In Isaiah 49:3-6**, the prophet wonders if his work has any purpose. In what ways do you combat this disheartening spirit as you face evil in prison? Have you been discouraged about lack of success in the growth of the prison church or your Bible study? How can you prevent this discouragement from becoming self-pity? What lessons can you take from Isaiah's conclusions?

2. **2 Corinthians 5:19-21** commissions you as an ambassador of Christ. With what attitude should you approach this weighty assignment? How can you find real purpose inside the walls, given this mission? How will sinful actions derail this purpose for your life in prison?

3. **Matthew 6:25-34** share the words of Jesus about worrying. In what ways do these verses address your fear and anxiety over life, your families, and your future? Share with your group how difficult it is to apply the message of Jesus to everyday life in prison. What concrete steps can you take, as a group, to reinforce each other day by day?

Pray together:

1. Pray for a large measure of faith and trust to shatter your anxiety and worry.

2. Pray that the Holy Spirit will lead you to find your specific purpose.

3. Pray specifically for those who are addicted to gambling, confused sexual attachments, anger, rage, unforgiveness, and bitterness..

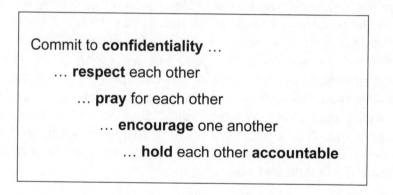

Commit to **confidentiality** ...

... **respect** each other

... **pray** for each other

... **encourage** one another

... **hold** each other **accountable**

The Wellspring of Life

Above all else, guard your heart, for it is the wellspring of life. Proverbs 4:23, NIV

A *wellspring* is the source of the water that flows into a well. It must be kept pure. If a factory dumps chemical waste into the ground and it seeps into the original source of water—the *wellspring*—it is contaminated. The waste will pollute the entire well and harm everyone who uses water from the well.

The same is true for our hearts. If our hearts—the source of all our thoughts, words, and actions—are poisoned, our whole lives are contaminated. Everyone will feel the effects of that poison.

So, how can we keep our hearts pure? In our gangs, we would never let someone near the gang leader if we thought he might harm our friend. It is the same with our hearts. The heart is the chief of our lives.

We must be on guard about what comes near that wellspring. Dirty talk about sex with men or women pollutes our spirits. Bragging about our crimes infects us. Don't indulge in that kind of action. If the longing for community and acceptance makes homosexuality attractive, we need to grab our Bibles to learn that God loves us so much He sent His only Son to die for us (see John 3:16). No other form of love is as pure and as satisfying as His love is for us.

Preventive actions help guard the wellspring of our hearts. While staying away from poison can help protect our hearts from contamination, being near sources of pure, life-giving water keeps our wellsprings clean. We must stay close to the purest source: Jesus Christ. We need to get into the faith pod, hang with other believers, and consider things that are wholesome and worthy of the persons God made us to be.

✝

Making it personal: What specific things will you do—or not do—to keep your heart pure today?

Prayer: Lord, I need help. Don't let my heart be drawn to what is evil. Keep me from taking part in depraved deeds with people who are evildoers. With Christ's help. Amen. (Adapted from Psalm 141:4)

Read Philippians 4:8 to learn how the apostle Paul kept his mind pure in his jail cell.

Guard Your Heart

Above all else, guard your heart, for it affects everything you do. Proverbs 4:23

Let's look at a different aspect of the previous meditation's verse. We are all familiar with guards. We see them everyday, walking the cellblock, poking their flashlights into our cells in the middle of the night, waking us up, saying, "I wanna see some skin!" But why does the Bible say our hearts need a guard?

The Bible tells us: "The human heart is most deceitful and desperately wicked. Who really knows how bad it is?" (Jeremiah 17:9). Not a pretty verdict is it. Yet, we know it's true. Today's culture uses the word *heart* to represent our emotions. When Solomon wrote Proverbs, the word *heart* referred to the center of a person's being— what really was most important. What we truly value in the core of ourselves (our hearts) is the most essential thing. Solomon knew that what we value most guides our thoughts, words, and actions.

What's in our hearts as we move around the yard and another inmate walks up and says, "Hey, dog, you straight?"? Our inner center (heart) may ache to score a blade and get high. The pain of our situation screams for an escape. In that position we may need a gut check to examine our core, our hearts.

We need to reflect on what lies at the center of our beings. For most of us, a war is going on between God's love and self-centered love. God's love brings forgiveness and peace; self-centered love breeds hatred, fighting, and depression. We can win that battle and guard our hearts from sin by seeking out those who walk their talk about Jesus. We can erect a fort around our hearts with daily Bible reading and memorization. Prayer constructs a perimeter fence with razor wire that protects our hearts from the enemy.

✝

Making it personal: What kinds of razor wire will you erect around your heart today? This week?

Prayer: Lord, create in me a new heart. Help me to guard my heart from hatred, anger, rebellion, and anything else that separates me from You. With the help of Jesus. Amen.

Read and memorize Ezekiel 36:26. Pray these words whenever your heart is threatened.

Take Time to Mature

[Enthusiasm] without knowledge is not good; a person who moves too quickly may go the wrong way. Proverbs 19:2

When we discover something for the first time and like what we've learned, we usually get excited about it. We can remember the excitement of skateboarding or putting on makeup for the first time. Similarly, many of us recall our excitement when we first came to Christ. We experienced His forgiveness and acceptance. We wanted to shout it from the rooftops.

Many new believers are on fire for evangelism and may impulsively walk out onto the yard and confront the shot-caller. As admirable as this enthusiasm is, the Bible teaches us that we need to mature, allowing older Christians to counsel us. Just as sixteen-year-olds need driver's training to go along with new driving privileges, newborn Christians need mentoring. Mature believers in the prison church have the responsibility to recognize that new Christians need help.

In their passion for Jesus, new Christians may be judgmental. They may rightly identify sin but could harshly condemn it in others, without the love and gentleness more mature men and women of faith might exercise. Baby Christians can be quite demanding in their desire to be fed. Just as newborn babies demand feeding, baby Christians insist on getting attention. Full-grown believers must teach and offer suggestions for contemplation, personal Bible study, prayer, and corporate worship. Allow new believers to mature before electing them to positions of leadership (see 1 Timothy 3:6).

The body of Christ in prison has many members, and each must nurture the other. New Christians must submit to the authority of the mature members, while the mature saints must not smother the ardor of the new ones. In unity, the work of Christ moves forward behind the walls.

✝

Making it personal: Where are you in your walk with Christ? How would being mentored or being a counselor strengthen your faith?

Prayer: Oh God, thank You for saving me. Help me to submit, and then guide me into a mature relationship with You. Amen.

Read 1 Corinthians 3:1-23 for the apostle Paul's discussion about Christian maturity.

Realistic Hope

Hope deferred makes the heart sick, but when dreams come true, there is life and joy. Proverbs 13:12

After serving seven years on manslaughter charges, Sara had high hopes at her second meeting with the board. Her jacket was clean. No write-ups. She was a chaplain's clerk and Bible study leader for four years. It looked good. But they gave her a two-year setback.

When hope and expectations are delayed or denied, it can send us into a tailspin of depression and hopelessness. Some of us deal with this possibility by abandoning all hope.

When our hopes are postponed, it's a good time to reexamine whether our hopes are realistic. Hoping our 1979 rape conviction will be overturned on DNA evidence (which will happen only if the rape kit is found in the storage room of the sheriff's office) may not be a valid hope. Hoping our husband or wife wins the lottery and hires the greatest defense attorney in the world isn't a reasonable hope.

We need *realistic* hope. Instead of the weight pile, which offers false hope in strength and power, we need to trust the power of God to resurrect our lives and give them purpose and meaning. Rather than placing our hope in the parole process or the court system, we need to look to the resurrected Christ as the source of realistic, true hope for the future.

A future with Christ at the center offers meaning. A life of service to others in Christ's name will fill our spirits instead of deflate them. We can embrace forgiveness and victory over sin in our lives. The freedom that comes when we submit to God's grace creates positive attitudes. And finally, as our time in prison wears on and on, we are assured of the richest hope for life everlasting with Christ in heaven. A real hope, worthy of our trust.

✝

Making it personal: List and examine three unrealistic hopes you are carrying around. Compare them to hope offered by Jesus.

Prayer: God, let me release these false hopes and put my trust in You and Your vision for my life. Amen.

Read Psalm 42:5-11, and learn of the psalmist's commitment to hope in God.

Making Peace

Together as one body, Christ reconciled both groups to God by means of his death, and our hostility toward each other was put to death. Ephesians 2:16

Remember those hot summer afternoons when all the relatives would come together, have a barbeque, and visit? But if two family groups were divided and angry at one another, the reunion could become hostile and unpleasant. The groups needed to be brought together for the family to live in harmony. Unfortunately, pride often kept fighting family members from admitting fault and making peace. It's pretty much the same situation with God and us.

God created a perfect world. Adam and Eve brought sin into the world through disobedience and pride (see Genesis 1–3). There was a disruption in the harmonious relationship between God and mankind, and that disruption still exists. It needs to be repaired because the deepest need all humans have is reconciliation with God. When we are at odds with God, we have no harmony in our lives. Our family relationships suffer. Our dealings with authority inside the walls deteriorate. We require peace with God. But, our pride, anger, and self-will keep us from making peace with Him.

The good news is that God pursues us, even when we ignore Him. He sends His Holy Spirit to follow us around, knocking at the door to our hearts.

When we respond to His call and make peace, our lives change. In place of stubborn arrogance, the Holy Spirit gives us loving spirits that are patient and kind. Rather than a cruel, heartless attitude toward the other people in the pod, we reach out with compassion, empathy, and a listening ear. When we are reconciled to God, we experience tranquility, perhaps for the first time in our lives. It is a major step on the road to becoming sons and daughters of God.

†

Making it personal: What needs to happen to your attitudes in order to make peace with God?

Prayer: Jesus, I am afraid of being hurt again if I reach out. Give me the strength to respond to Your call on my heart. Amen.

Read Luke 15:3-7, a parable Jesus tells to demonstrate how God brings us back into relationship with Him.

Peter Pan Christians?

I had to talk as though you belonged to this world or as though you were infants in the Christian life. I had to feed you with milk and not with solid food, because you couldn't handle anything stronger. 1 Corinthians 3:1-2

Many of us remember the story of Peter Pan, the boy who would not grow up. Peter, who lived in Neverland, loved playing games with his gang, the Lost Boys, and found meaning in his life by battling the wicked Captain Hook. Peter never wanted to assume the responsibilities of adult life. He liked being a child and was comfortable in his own juvenile behavior.

Many of us are Peter Pan Christians. We like being overgrown children. It allows us to avoid taking responsibility for our lives and actions. We like hanging out with our "lost boys." It is a very comfortable place to be. We use this childishness to excuse our sinful, rebellious behavior. We avoid the work of the prison church when we continually act out.

The trouble is, we cannot live like this forever if we desire to find real freedom and meaning in Jesus Christ. Sooner or later we must be fed a spiritual T-bone steak instead of milk.

Without solid food, we do not grow. If we don't grow, we can never be the kind of ambassadors that Jesus wants us to be for Him.

What solid food do we need? Bible study, prayer, time with other believers. So instead of skipping Bible study and playing cards, we must commit ourselves to study so that we can grow up. We must seek out old numbers in Christ who can mentor us into a deeper freedom with Jesus. Our goals must be to shed the skins of our old natures and move into a full-grown relationship with the One who gave His life for ours.

✝

Making it personal: Take a mental inventory of your attitude and behavior. How are you like Peter Pan, not wanting to grow up? In what ways are you maturing into an adult in Christ?

Prayer: Heavenly Father, I am afraid to grow up. I remember seeing the adults in my life abused. Help me trust You. Amen.

Read Hebrews 5:11–6:3 for directions for becoming mature.

Love Fulfills the Law

Love does no harm to its neighbor. Therefore love is the fulfillment of the law. Romans 13:10, NIV

Jesus commanded all of His followers then—and you and me today—to love God first and our neighbors as we love ourselves (see Matthew 22:37-39). That command, coupled with Paul's teaching, sums up the secret of the Christian life. If we love, we fulfill the law.

This is huge. When Jesus lived, Jews thought they would earn salvation by keeping the Ten Commandments and more than six hundred more laws that the Jewish leaders created out of the original ten. The burden was heavy. Jesus turned that belief on its head when He said that all those laws are satisfied by loving God and our neighbors. It's a simpler way.

How is this possible? Take any of the Ten Commandments, for example, "Do not take God's name in vain." Would we ever even consider using God's name as a swear word if we truly love Him? How about, "You shall not steal"? Who would knowingly steal from people they love? Or, "Keep the Sabbath day holy." If we love God, we would gladly give up one day of work to honor Him with our worship. Love satisfies each of these commandments. By loving, we fulfill God's law.

Why is this important? It is true that when we love God and our neighbor, we end up avoiding porn, gambling, drugs, and angry behavior. This new behavior is good and to be commended. But we must never think that our good behavior has any impact on our salvation. It doesn't. Avoiding all those things successfully does not *earn* God's love. Nothing is further from the truth. God does not love us because we have been good. We avoid porn, anger, gambling, and drugs because God *already* loves us! Trying to earn His love ourselves doesn't get it done. Loving God and our neighbors—because He loves us—does.

✝

Making it personal: How are you trying to earn God's love? How will you love God and your neighbor this week?

Prayer: Father God, I need Your Spirit's power to love You and my neighbor more. Amen.

Read Matthew 22:37-39, the summary of God's law.

People Are Watching

Be careful how you live among your unbelieving neighbors. Even if they accuse you of doing wrong, they will see your honorable behavior, and they will believe and give honor to God. 1 Peter 2:12

Our actions influence others. We have a responsibility to live in ways that reflect Jesus' love in our hearts. Why is that so important? Because we all know that other cons in our facility are watching us. Some are looking to accuse us if we act in a sinful way. Many times people who know they are doing wrong things try to avoid their own guilt by accusing others of wrongdoing. It gets their consciences off the hook.

This phenomenon is not new. The early Christians preached "loving one another" and the partaking of "the body and blood of Jesus" during communion services. Because of that, they were wrongly accused of incest and of being cannibals.

It is impossible to live perfect lives. We all are saved by God's grace, not our own good actions. But, when we act out in anger, we damage the Lord's work. We provide ammunition for the gun that wants to "shoot down" followers of Christ. We can never forget that more people have been turned off to Jesus because of the foolish, sometimes sinful actions of Christians than by the lack of persuasive arguments in favor of the Gospel. Some people in our cellblocks will never see the inside of a church sanctuary or prison chapel. But they see us.

So, when God finally comes to them through the action of the Holy Spirit, these cons will remember our kindness. They will be encouraged by our discipline and authentic witness for Christ. They will finally see how "really tough" a man or woman has to be to serve the risen Lord behind bars.

✝

Making it personal: What actions spoil your witness of God's love? How will you surrender those to Jesus this week? What kind, loving things can you do to attract people to Jesus?

Prayer: Lord, help me see clearly how my sinful actions harm Your cause, and give me the courage to bring them to an end. Amen.

Read Philippians 4:13 to rediscover our source of strength.

The Importance of Unity

May God, who gives this patience and encouragement, help you live in complete harmony with each other, as is fitting for followers of Christ Jesus. Then all of you can join together with one voice, giving praise and glory to God, the Father of our Lord Jesus Christ. Romans 15:5-6

Many prison choirs are very good. They're easy on the ears because there is a unified blending between the higher and lower voices. The choir members have a common goal, mixing their voices together to create harmony. Sports teams that win championships aren't always the ones with the most talented athletes. More often, they are the teams that have few superstars but really are united as a team. Ever wonder why that is so?

When people have common goals, like great harmony or winning a championship, they put aside their own agendas and work for that goal. However, if individual egos emerge, disunity destroys the harmony. This is why so many great teams fall apart after big wins. Too many egos want credit and demand bigger contracts. Without unity, the common goal is unreachable.

It is very much the same with the prison church. The most effective church is one that has the unified purpose of spreading the love of God. The goal is to preach the Good News and nurture those who hear and accept the Word.

When new believers accept Christ, they may think that that is enough. But seasoned Christians know that the devil is prowling around, waiting to cause believers to stumble. It is absolutely necessary for new Christians to have a safe and harmonious refuge where they can be nurtured and taught. Then they can grow in Christ.

We must commit ourselves to harmony in our prison churches so that each believer can be an effective servant of Christ.

✝

Making it personal: In what areas does your church body experience unity or discord? What can you do to promote unity and harmony?

Prayer: Jesus, help me put aside my agenda so that harmony and unity may reign in Your church every day. Amen.

Read Psalm 133, which celebrates the blessings of harmony.

No More Fear

There is no fear in love. But perfect love drives out fear. 1 John 4:18, NIV

The cycle of fear for those of us in prison began with our first arrest for a serious crime. The nakedness, the strip searches, and the delousing were designed to humiliate and debase us as human beings. It worked. We were processed to city or county jails. There the older cons filled our heads with disgusting and horrifying stories of homosexual pressure and physical beatings. Later, on the bus trip to our facility, the other cons tormented us with stories. We felt alone and afraid, not knowing who to trust as "new fish."

We fought our fears with our hopes for the hearings that would turn our case on its head and spring us. We tried to balance our fright with our high expectations for lawyers who would find a loophole to get us out. For many of us, our hopes ran dry, but the terror remained. Some of us chose the foggy, medicated road to deal with it. Others of us masked the fear with macho behavior or the protection of a predator. But we never really lost our fear.

Where can we find relief from these crippling fears? We find the antidote to fear in the perfect love of God shown through the life and work of Jesus Christ. His love says that we don't need to worry about our future (see Matthew 6:25-34). Christ's love offers us assurance of forgiveness and real peace and salvation (see John 14:27). Bad things can still happen to us behind prison walls. But Christ's love guarantees that nothing any person can do to us will destroy the spirit and soul that are made in God's image. When we live in that love, we have no need for fear, because "perfect love drives out fear."

†

Making it personal: How can you allow God's perfect love to fill your life and smother the fear that threatens to dominate you?

Prayer: Jesus, I give You all my fears. I can't control them. I surrender to Your love. Help me to feel Your peace today. Amen.

Read Matthew 10:28-31 to learn what Jesus said to His disciples about fear.

How Good Is Your Hearing?

The Lord came and stood there, calling as at the other times, "Samuel! Samuel!" Then Samuel said, "Speak for your servant is listening." 1 Samuel 3:10, NIV

Ever feel like God isn't talking to us? Ever wonder why?

To really understand something takes work. If we want to speak another language, we take language lessons and study it. We discipline ourselves to put in the hours to learn. Some of us are great piano players and jammed with groups before coming to prison. Did we wake up one day and play jazz piano? Not likely. It took years of practice to achieve excellence. So why don't we apply this same dedication and discipline to our relationship with God?

God called Samuel three times. Samuel was just a boy, but he knew something was up. Samuel heard God's voice because his ears were trained and open.

Why don't we hear the Lord's call for our lives? Is it because we take God for granted? Do we expect too much from God, thinking that He will get through to us somehow? Or, are we lazy, letting our ears fill up with the static of the world? To take our relationship with God as seriously as our relationship with our biker brethren, we must get the world's wax out of our ears. Then when God calls us, we will hear Him.

What are the Q-tips for cleaning out our ears? If we are involved in sin, we must repent and stop. We need to faithfully attend the prison church services. We may not always get something out of them, but we will never get anything if we don't attend. Besides, our presence in the church may feed someone else. Daily personal devotions are mandatory to keep our spiritual ears clean and tuned in to the voice of God in our lives.

With our ears cleaned out, we *will* hear God's voice calling us.

✝

Making it personal: What kinds of earwax are clogging up your hearing? What steps will you take to get serious about hearing God's call? Or are you just talking?

Prayer: Father God, give me the will to clean out my ears so that I can hear Your call. Amen.

Read 1 Samuel 3 for the full story of God's calling Samuel.

We Hear God—Now What?

Then I heard the Lord asking, "Whom should I send as a messenger to my people? Who will go for us?" And I said, "Lord, I'll go! Send me." Isaiah 6:8

Someone said the real disasters in life happen when we get what we want. We can relate to that. Some of us women wanted a man, but when we got one, he abused us and turned us out. We discovered we were better off without him.

Although that statement is true in some human circumstances, it's *not* true in our relationship to God. Sometimes the problem is that when God speaks to us, He says things we don't want to hear. Our idea of what we want God to say is different from what He says. Our plan may be for God to release us so we can mentor young men and women to help them avoid the mistakes that sent us to prison. A worthy and noble aspiration! But then God speaks to us and tells us to minister to the sexual offender community inside prison. Whoa! We immediately think, *God must be mistaken.* We turn it over in our minds, looking for a sign that we didn't hear correctly. This is wrong!

Oswald Chambers writes about trying to rationalize that we didn't hear God correctly. "When I have to weigh the *pros* and *cons,* and doubt and debate come in, I am bringing in an element that is not of God, and I come to the conclusion that the suggestion was not a right one."[11]

Our unwillingness to pay attention to what God says may very well lead to disobedience that disappoints God. But obedience leads to a richer and fuller faith. When we hear God's voice, we must move on it and begin to obey. Let God's hand be played out on His card table. When it's over, we may be privileged to witness the results of His work through our efforts. If so, we'll finally see that He was correct.

✝

Making it personal: What attitudes lead you to discard your ideas of what you *think* God has planned for your life and really *hear and accept* His leading?

Prayer: Lord Jesus, speak to me today, and help me act. Amen.

Read Matthew 14:22-33, and see real faith in action.

Keeping Good Company

**Do not be misled: "Bad company corrupts good character."
1 Corinthians 15:33, NIV**

As we were growing up, we always knew guys who could hotwire a car so we could take a joy ride. Those same guys were the ones who sold us a stolen piece or a hot Rolex. We were attracted to their power. But when we remember their evil impact on our lives, we can appreciate the role that bad character plays in our lives.

Have we learned our lessons from our experience with the losers in our lives? Or, are we still drawn to the cons who know how to manipulate the system? Do we admire the women who can flirt and get one over on the officers in the cellblock and influence events for their own benefit? Do we overlook the lies and the cover-ups it takes to operate in this fashion inside? If so, then our companions will lead us into sin.

The people we hang with will definitely have an effect on what we think about life. Friends who seem attractive to us and flatter us may not be the best influence on our attitudes. Our attitudes toward our families, other cons, the administration, and ultimately, our own sin and need for repentance determine how we act.

We must not be seduced into thinking we can keep bad company and still retain good character and a healthy relationship to God. Light and darkness do not go together; one chases the other away.

We need to evaluate our acquaintances and determine if they have a positive or negative effect on us. Do they promote sinful actions or encourage us to stay close to Christ? We need to find other believers who will have a godly influence on us. Good company promotes good character.

✝

Making it personal: Take a hard look at your friends. How many of them are "bad apples"? What steps will you take to distance yourself from them?

Prayer: *Lord, help me see those I hang with clearly, through Your eyes. Help me to surround myself with Your people. Amen.*

Read 1 Samuel 18:1-3; 19:1-6; 20:1-42, the story of the influence of a good friendship.

Many Kinds of Grace

Then he said, "Jesus, remember me when you come into your Kingdom." And Jesus replied, "I assure you, today you will be with me in paradise." Luke 23:42-43

Devotional writer Henry Drummond tells the story of two saints who argued about which of them was the "greatest monument of God's saving grace." The first man told of his wicked life of drugs, lies, and vicious behavior. God saved him on his deathbed. The second man was brought to Christ when he was a young boy. He'd led a quiet Christian life. He loved his wife and went to church regularly. He had anticipated going to heaven for a long time.

Who benefitted more from God's grace? Most would vote for the first saint, the lifetime sinner. But, no! The man who lived a long Christian life was granted the largest portion of God's special merit. God's grace saved him from reckless sins in his early years, steered him clear of the sins of adult life, and kept his feet on the right road as he grew old. This lifetime of God's favor was the greater portion of grace.[12]

It took a truckload of grace to pluck the first man out of sin and into heaven. Just like the thief on the cross next to Jesus, the first man was given *saving* grace and was freed from the guilt of his sin. The second man in the story was given *restraining* grace. The thief on the cross and the first saint were given *dying* grace; the second received *living* grace.

So it is with us. Without God's many graces on a daily basis, our lives resemble cars whose wheels need alignment. If we take God's hands off the steering wheel of our lives, our uneven tires run us into life's ditch every time. We rightly celebrate God's *saving grace*. It is a gift beyond measure. But never forget to appreciate and thank Him everyday for His *living* and *restraining* grace!

✝

Making it personal: Tune your heart to sense God's grace. Then for one week, count the number of times God's grace plays a part.

Prayer: Lord Jesus, open my eyes to all that Your grace does for me. Amen.

Read Luke 23:39-43, and see God's grace in action.

The Devil Smiles

For you are still controlled by your sinful nature. You are jealous of one another and quarrel with each other. Doesn't that prove you are controlled by your sinful nature? 1 Corinthians 3:3

The devil smiles when there's quarreling and arguing within the prison church. Nothing makes him happier than to hear one sister or brother in Christ trash another. The results of this behavior are conflict and hurt feelings. It's hard to demonstrate a loving attitude toward the inmates who are not Christians when the Christians themselves can't get along with each other. This type of fighting is sin! It must stop if the church is to be an effective witness to Christ's love.

But why do we divide the body of Christ? Today's verse tells us that we're controlled by our sinful natures. Almost every divisive argument in the body of Christ is rooted in selfish motivations that seek power over the direction of the church. We who yell the loudest sometimes use God's Word as a cover-up to hide our desire for power.

Our sinful natures want to control others. When we were on the street, some of us manipulated people with our charms. Others used guns and physical intimidation. Let's not use God's Word to bend people to our way of thinking. This is wrong and sinful.

The Bible offers us the blueprint for daily interactions. We must imitate the humility of Christ, considering others to be better than ourselves and loving others with patience and kindness (see Philippians 2 and 1 Corinthians 13). If these traits are part of our character, we can discuss differences of opinion without damaging our relationships. Humility and love will prevail. Disunity will fade away. We will unite and be a strong, integrated Christian front to the administration and the inmates on the yard. Only then will we get on with the battle against the enemy in prison.

✝

Making it personal: If you have differences with someone, sit down and discuss them. Avoid arrogance, and see the other person's side of the situation.

Prayer: Oh Lord, help me seek unity in Your example of loving-kindness. Amen.

Read Philippians 2 and **1 Corinthians 13** for thoughts about unity and love.

Compound Interest

We have no one to blame but the leering, seducing flare-up of our own lust. Lust gets pregnant, and has a baby: sin! Sin grows up to adulthood, and becomes a real killer. James 1:15, THE MESSAGE

Famous scientist Albert Einstein was asked what he believed was his greatest discovery. He replied, "Compound interest." Loan sharks know about compound interest and how it works. A person borrows $1,000 from a loan shark at 30% interest per week. After the first week, the person owes $1,300. Without a payment, after two weeks, the victim owes $1690. After three weeks, $2,197, and on and on.

Sin compounds too. C. S. Lewis wrote in *Mere Christianity*, "Good and evil both increase at compound interest. That is why the little decisions you and I make every day are of such infinite importance. The smallest good act today is the capture of a strategic point from which, a few months later, you may be able to go on to victories you never dreamed of. And apparently trivial indulgence in lust or anger today is the loss of a ridge or railway line or bridgehead from which the enemy may launch an attack otherwise impossible."[13]

Every day in the cellblock or at the weight pile, we make decisions. Swearing, bad-mouthing the administration, planning an escape or action against a rival gang are just a few bad loans we take from Satan, the ultimate loan shark. Macho trash talk sows a negative seed. That seed grows, and a plan emerges. Once the action plan is in place, it takes only a moment of madness for our world to blow up.

On the other hand, when we attempt to love people as Jesus commands, we find ourselves liking them more. As we practice good feelings toward people, we find ourselves liking more people, including those we could never imagine liking.

†

Making it personal: What seeds are you sowing for good or for evil? Where do you think they will lead?

Prayer: Father God, give me eyes to see the potential consequences of my actions. Amen.

Read Galatians 6:7-10 to understand the law of reaping what we sow.

How Do We Pray?

When you ask, you do not receive, because you ask with wrong motives, that you may spend what you get on your pleasures. James 4:3, NIV

We all have a need to feel connected to another human being. Good marriages thrive on communication. Without daily sharing, one partner feels disconnected and alone. Suicides occur when people lose all loving contact with another human being. In our prison friendships, we require connection to each other. The people with whom we walk to chow or lift weights offer us a sense of community that's vital to mental health and happiness.

But sometimes spouses or friends abuse that connection by using us for their own selfish, personal advantage. Some of us have been ripped off by a "friend" who stole from us to feed her habit. Perhaps we've done it to someone else. Any betrayal damages trust, but it also makes it less likely that we'll offer that gift of connection again.

Think about how we treat God and the connection He offers us through the intimacy of prayer. Don't we often bring our own selfish wish list to our prayers? Don't we often consider God a sort of Santa Claus and try to make deals with Him? And then we wonder why our prayers never seem to get an answer!

Prayer is not a way to get our wish list completed. Rather, and more important, prayer is a direct link to the Creator of the universe. He has a plan for our lives, but like most plans, He needs to share them with us. Without our willingness to put aside our selfish concerns and really be quiet and listen to God speaking to us, we'll never learn what He wants to say to us.

When we pray, let's connect to God by using our ears first and our mouths second. Let's keep our motives pure and ask God for the things we need so that we can serve Him.

†

Making it personal: Look at your wish list for your life. Then compare it to God's wish list for your life. Will you surrender to His list?

Prayer: Lord, purify my motives and align my desires with Your Word. Amen.

Read John 17, the prayer Jesus prayed for His disciples—and us.

Why Go to Church?

Come, let us worship and bow down. Let us kneel before the Lord our maker. Psalm 95:6

First, let's take a look at why we *don't* go to church. On the outside, we had choices about which denomination to join and what kind of service (traditional or contemporary) we wanted to attend. In prison, we don't have that many options, so one church service has to work for everyone. That can be a problem, but it doesn't have to be. If Christ is preached and He is raised up as the Savior of mankind, then the nonessentials and denominational differences (such as adult or infant baptism, whether or not to speak in tongues, welcoming women into leadership) don't matter. That's right, they don't matter! What matters is that we are in church—every Sunday—worshiping our almighty God.

Some of us use nonessentials as the reason to sleep late and not attend. What's really going down is that we don't want to be confronted with our own sin and our need to surrender our pride to God.

We are made by God, for God, and we cannot find any real joy in life until we are in relationship with Him. Our sinfulness blocks the path of God's love and plan for our lives. To unblock that flow of love and to experience God's plan for our lives, we must own our sin and turn away from it, receiving Jesus as the One sent to pay the penalty for our sin. When we receive Jesus, we are filled with gratitude and want to worship Him.

Worship reminds us that we belong in two worlds—one earthly and one eternal. Worship allows us to experience a place not only where we search for God but also where He is looking for us. Finally, we worship because our hearts desire to know God personally. When we meet Him, our lives change and we know true freedom, maybe for the first time.

✝

Making it personal: What is the evidence that you are committed to worshiping God in church? If you don't go, why not? Take responsibility for your excuses.

Prayer: Father God, I want to worship You with other believers. Help me to know real freedom in You. Amen.

Read Psalm 96, a psalm that celebrates worship.

God Knows Our Needs

I will answer them before they even call to me. While they are still talking to me about their needs, I will go ahead and answer their prayers! Isaiah 65:24

God is a God of divine anticipation and divine intervention. To *anticipate* means that we think beforehand what someone else needs. For example, we might know that another inmate is having a birthday without a visit or a card coming in. When we *think* about going to his or her cell and offering birthday greetings, we are *anticipating* the person's feelings of loneliness. When we actually *travel* to his or her cell and offer that word of encouragement, we are *intervening* in the person's life. God does the same thing.

Think about Joshua and the nation of Israel. Before entering the Promised Land, they didn't know how they were going to cross the Jordan River with hundreds of thousands of people and animals.

God intervened and provided the answer. When the priests who carried the Ark of the Covenant touched their feet in the Jordan River, it miraculously stopped flowing! The people and animals crossed the river on dry ground (see Joshua 3:15-17).

God *anticipated* His people's needs and *intervened* for them. He does the same for us. In the midst of our anxiety and helplessness, God demonstrates His merciful power.

God has already provided men and women who have a heart for our families and us. Every community has small prison ministries or chapters of national ministries (like Prison Fellowship) that are providing care, transportation, and help for us upon release. Many prison chaplains and administrations can provide information about all of these available services. We can ask the chaplain, a friend, or relative to do an Internet search for "prison ministries" to learn about organizations that can help us. God knows, He cares, and He provides. We are not alone!

†

Making it personal: Where has God intervened on your behalf? What is the evidence that you are not alone?

Prayer: Lord, thank You for anticipating my needs and intervening for me. You are so good. Amen.

Read 1 Kings 17:8-24, the story of the widow of Zarephath, to see how God anticipated her need and intervened.

Friendship with the World

You adulterous people, don't you know that friendship with the world is hatred toward God? Anyone who chooses to be a friend of the world becomes an enemy of God. James 4:4, NIV

This can be a confusing verse, even though it seems pretty straightforward. Does it mean that as followers of Jesus we must separate ourselves from all the pleasures and wonderful things that Creation offers? Are we denied permission to participate and enjoy the good things of earth? No! It doesn't mean that at all. This is not what James is talking about.

God created the heavens and the earth and pronounced them good (see Genesis 1). He is a very loving, creative God, and He desires that we, His children, enjoy what He has made for us. He feels the same way about giving pleasure to His children as we did when we took our kids to see a major league baseball game or baked chocolate brownies for them. God is delighted when we're happy.

What James means in today's passage by "the world" is everything that lies outside the community of God's people. A list of those things—including adultery, greed, pride, and anger—are listed in Galatians 5. When we indulge this worldly frame of mind, we are at odds with what God wants for us. The Bible instructs us to imitate the humble character of Jesus and to live unselfish lives of service to others. When we choose the way of the world, we lead self-centered lives that often abuse others. We indulge in drugs, sex, and booze, and don't give a rip about others. When we live by the world's standards, it's all about getting more money, more power to boss others around, greater status and prestige. Those things identify us and define us.

There is no accommodation of these two worldviews. There is no compromise available. We delude ourselves if we think we can have both. We cannot. It is our personal responsibility to make a choice between them.

✝

Making it personal: Decide today how you are going to live. Will it be world-centered or God-centered?

Prayer: God, give me the strength to make the right choices. Amen.

Read Galatians 5:16-26 to contrast the Spirit-filled life with the worldly life.

God's Seeing Eye

But the Lord said to Samuel, "Don't judge by his appearance or height, for I have rejected him. The Lord doesn't make decisions the way you do. People judge by outward appearance, but the Lord looks at a person's thoughts and intentions." 1 Samuel 16:7

An incident in the early life of David instructs us about how God sees people and how we should see them as well.

God was not happy with King Saul, so He told His prophet Samuel that He wanted to anoint another man to be king. God directed Samuel to travel to Bethlehem, to the house of Jesse. When Samuel arrived, Jesse did what any man in his community would have done: he brought his firstborn son to Samuel. Eliab was tall, handsome, and strong. Samuel looked at Eliab and said to himself, "Surely this is the Lord's anointed" (1 Samuel 16:6). But Samuel was wrong. There is an important lesson for us in his error.

We often make the same mistake Samuel did. We are attracted to things that are superficial. We look at other women in the cellblock and judge them according to their looks or crime. We honor the cons who are celebrities or have power. The weak are often ignored. We are blind to the things that God sees. Dr. Martin Luther King Jr. said in his famous speech, "I have a dream that my four children will one day live in a nation where they will not be judged by the color of their skin but by the content of their character."[14] Dr. King was talking about "kingly character." A kingly character looks to *serve* others, not to *use* them.

As we do our time, let's not make the blunder Samuel did. Let's evaluate men and women based on what is in their hearts, not on their looks or manners or popularity. Let's avoid the trap that sees only people's external qualities. Let's look at the *eternal* qualities and see value where none was visible before.

†

Making it personal: Identify five fellow inmates whom you've dismissed as weak and worthless. How would seeing them through God's eyes change your opinion?

Prayer: Lord, give me eyes to see the people around me. Help me to see through Your eyes. Amen.

Read Proverbs 20:12.

We Run, but We Can't Hide

For the word of God . . . judges the thoughts and attitudes of the heart. Nothing in all creation is hidden from God's sight. Everything is uncovered and laid bare before the eyes of him to whom we must give account. Hebrews 4:12b-13, NIV

We carry around secrets in prison. Those secrets are heavy burdens for us. We don't want anyone to know our crimes. We shudder at the thought of other cons being fully aware of our lives of violence, molestation, abuse, rape, and the other evils we have done. We fear what might happen to us if they found out the truth about us.

But God knows everything about us. We can't hide anything from Him. This is not a scary thought for us who love Him. It is a hopeful and comforting fact. In our hearts, we wish to be completely known and open and honest with Him. We long to lose our illusions, expose our deceptions, face the facts of our lives, confront our fears, and admit our failures. We crave to be loved by someone who knows us, accepts us for who we are, and forgives us for Christ's sake.

God's love and forgiveness come to us through Christ when we allow God's Word to penetrate our souls. Then we expose our hearts for the unclean things they are and uncover the sin that is in the deepest corners of our being.

To make this happen, we must confess our sin to God and turn away from it. We need to believe that God's Word will protect and sustain us. We can strengthen our faith by beginning each day with prayer and time in God's Word. We can meditate on (or sing) songs like "Jesus Loves Me" or "He Knows My Name." These disciplines will sustain us when we are tempted to flinch and turn away from God's presence.

✝

Making it personal: How will you open yourself up to the God who already knows you and is waiting for you to come to Him for full forgiveness?

Prayer: *Father God, You know everything about me. Thank You for loving me anyway. Amen.*

Read Hebrews 4:14-16, a description of the High Priest who paid for our sin.

The Power of Music

Shout with joy to the Lord, O earth! Worship the Lord with gladness. Come before him, singing with joy. Psalm 100:1-2

Music contains great power both to soothe us when we're anxious and to stir up our emotions. Dentists' offices play soft music. NBA pre-game music is loud and piercing. Advertising companies work overtime creating catchy jingles to remind us of their products.

Music plays an important role in our walk with God too. It can either help us combat evil, or it can lead us into evil. Like a rudder on a boat, music can set our frame of mind and steer our attitudes and actions toward something good or evil.

Music that degrades male or female dignity and glorifies drug use will poison our minds. Music and words create images in our brains. We visualize shameful stuff in our heads. And what we think is what we do. Bad stuff—wrong direction!

The opposite is also true. Rising from our bunks with the words to "Awesome God" running through our heads makes it easier to sidestep the devil's assault in the yard. Quietly singing "Amazing Grace" as we walk to chow focuses us on God's gift instead of the lousy food. Martin Luther, who wrote "A Mighty Fortress Is Our God," felt music was not our invention but rather a gift from God. He taught that the devil hates it because music drives evil out of us. Luther was right.

We must be extra careful about the music that goes into our ears and into our brains. We don't *eat* garbage, so why *feed* it into our heads through our ears? When we put wholesome spiritual food into our bodies, we can expect good spiritual health as a result. We need to discover the power of music and its effects for good or evil in our lives. After we start the day in prayer and in God's Word, let's add His music to our souls.

✝

Making it personal: What difference will it make in your life if you put aside trashy music that invades your soul, and try God's music for a month?

Prayer: Lord, fill my soul with Your music to drive away those demons from my soul. Amen.

Read Psalm 95 and Psalm 100, songs of praise.

Freedom from Ourselves

But he will pour out his anger and wrath on those who live for themselves, who refuse to obey the truth and instead live lives of wickedness. Romans 2:8

Ever thought about how we can be in another prison while we are already in prison? We are not talking about Ad-Seg or SHU, but a prison that surrounds us 24/7/365 until we are released from it through surrender to Jesus Christ. I am talking about the Prison of Self—selfishness, self-centeredness, living only for ourselves.

The Prison of Self is a dark, lonely place. We become obsessed with dreadful thoughts. When we are in the Prison of Self, thoughts of suicide increase, and we look to forms of escape—drugs, sexual encounters, and violence. The noise and frenzy of the living unit actually become a source of comfort, for they are quieter than the chaos running through our heads. We find ourselves impatient, angry, and more exhausted when we get up than when we went to bed.

Where can we find relief from this Prison of Self? Through God and the steady and sincere worship of His Son. The philosopher Blaise Pascal said that in the heart of every person is a God-shaped vacuum that only God the Creator can fill. We try unsuccessfully to fill that vacuum with thoughts about ourselves. When we worship God on Sunday and throughout the week in Bible studies, we replace our self-centeredness with the joy and hope of God's promises. His divine purpose for our lives kicks in, and we are set free from the Prison of Self. Worship takes our eyes off our own petty troubles and lifts them up in praise for what God has done for us and what He will do for us in the future. Let's break out of the cellblock of ourselves through worship. It's time to break free—escape to real freedom in God!

✝

Making it personal: How are you trapped in the Prison of Self? How will you throw off the comfortable but destructive habits of self-centeredness? Worship is the first step.

Prayer: Father, God, I ask Your Holy Spirit to free me from this Prison of Self. Amen.

Read Colossians 3:5-11 for a reminder of how to live for Christ.

Conflicted Spirits

I love God's law with all my heart. But there is another law at work within me that is at war with my mind. This law wins the fight and makes me a slave to the sin that is still within me. Romans 7:22-23

Some people get visibly ugly when they see others prepare to go to worship services. They want to pick a fight. Their hearts and their minds are at war with each other. They have conflicted spirits.

Inner conflict results from holding inside of us two opposing views that are equally strong. For example, perhaps we were brought up in a strict church environment but had a shocking experience with a minister or a priest. Or, maybe our mothers made us go to church as kids and then slapped us around when we got home for fidgeting during the service. These strong, clashing memories put us at odds with ourselves. On the one hand we see the hypocrisy and hurt, and we conclude that faith in God is bogus. But then our heart vibrates with some other rhythm. Our hearts say to us that God is real and that His Word and promises are true. We have conflicted spirits. What is true?

The apostle Paul was no stranger to conflicted spirits. He knew the war between good and evil in his heart (see Romans 7:7-25). He also knew where to find a Peacemaker. When our minds are denying what our hearts know to be true, the only source of a peaceful resolution is Jesus Christ. He suffered hurts greater than our own, yet He never gave up. Jesus resisted temptation and withstood torture, unfair trials, and the death penalty for us. With the help of God's power, we can let the hurts go, make peace with ourselves and with God.

✝

Making it personal: What spirits are at war in you? Even though your hurts have hurt you so much, let them go. Cut them loose, once and for all, today.

Prayer: Father God, help me get over wounds by understanding how much You took the hurt for me. Amen.

Read Romans 7:7-25, Paul's conflict with warring views.

Godly Living: Part 1

These questions relate to the meditations found on pages 170-194:

Discuss together:

1. Having your heart right is central to godly living. Why does Solomon suggest that the heart is the seat of the emotions, the intellect, personal motivation, and desire? How is this true? What sort of behavior indicates a heart that is off-center? What ideas, thoughts, and actions flow from a heart that is right with God?

2. In the prison movie *The Shawshank Redemption*, character "Red" Redding says, "Hope is a dangerous thing. Hope can drive a man insane." Contrast that statement with the words from a traditional hymn: "My hope is built on nothing less than Jesus' blood and righteousness" ("My Hope Is Built"). Red is speaking of what kind of hope? Compare Red's version with the godly hope expressed in the hymn. How and why are they clearly different? Which version will you bring into your facility? Why is hope so necessary for godly living?

3. Unity and harmony are powerful forces for godly living inside a prison. But unity can be a potent power for organized evil too! How can "Christian unity" combat the attractiveness of "gang unity"? In what ways does your church satisfy an inmate's hunger for fellowship, safety, common purpose, and acceptance? How unified is your prison's church? Where is unity found? What issues threaten to divide the congregation? Discuss how to repair any damage to the Gospel message by such divisions.

4. Grapes need the right climate in order to develop. "Killer frosts" can keep grapes from growing. So too, the fruit of the Spirit needs the right climate. What kinds of "killer frosts" kill the buds of the Holy Spirit in your life? Grapevines also need cultivation to mature. Discuss how private prayer, personal devotions, church attendance, and group Bible studies cultivate godly living. Why is obedience to God's call fundamental to harvesting the Spirit's fruits? Why and how is obedience the center of godly living?

Explore God's Word together:

1. **Ezekiel 36:26** brings hope to shattered lives. What is your response to the God who offers forgiveness, erases our past

sins, and gives us a "new heart"? Contrast a heart of stone and a heart of flesh. What does the prophet say here about a new life in Jesus?

2. **Galatians 2:20** highlights the death of Jesus and what it means for godly living. What does it mean to be "crucified with Christ"? The cross means death. What has died in your life? How is your new life different from your old life? Putting your faith in Christ means you have established a level of trust. What do you trust about Jesus? How is His death an act of love for you?

Pray together:

1. Pray for those who are deceived because they believe they will never have to answer for their actions.

2. Ask God for a special outpouring of His unifying Spirit and grace on your prison church.

3. Pray a special blessing on all the children represented by the parents who are in prison.

Commit to **confidentiality** …

… **respect** each other

… **pray** for each other

… **encourage** one another

… **hold** each other **accountable**

Abandoned by Family

When Joseph's brothers saw him coming, they . . . made plans to kill him. . . . When the traders came by, his brothers . . . sold him for twenty pieces of silver, and the Ishmaelite traders took him along to Egypt. Genesis 37:18, 28

The next few meditations will look at lessons from the life of Joseph. Not everyone knows the story, except we may have heard that Joseph had a "coat of many colors." Actually, Joseph's whole life was very colorful. The things he experienced were just like the stuff we experience: rejection, abandonment, abuse, setups, betrayal, disappointment, and imprisonment. But Joseph's story is also one of transformation: how a slave became a prime minister.

We wouldn't have liked Joseph if he'd been our brother. He probably was a spoiled brat, a liar, and a braggart. He was his father's favorite son and often ratted out his eleven brothers. He also had dreams in which his brothers bowed down to him, and he made the mistake of telling his brothers about them. They hated him for it because younger brothers were not supposed to be in charge.

One day the brothers were fed up and decided to kill Joseph. But they chose instead to strip off his coat of many colors and sell him to slave traders who took him to Egypt—where he was sold, again! Joseph had every right to feel depressed and angry. He felt betrayed and unloved.

How many of us remember those feelings? More than a few of us were abandoned by our families or betrayed by a friend for the reward money. We know the hurt.

Many of us came to the joint rejected, unloved, and unsaved. We are lost. But, just as God found Joseph, God finds us inside the walls and transforms us. Psalm 27:10 says that "Even if my father and mother abandon me, the Lord will hold me close." What a comfort in the face of rejection and abuse.

†

Making it personal: What will you do to see beyond your current circumstances and trust God's vision for your life?

Prayer: Father God, convince me of Your love for me so that I trust You in all things. Amen.

Read Genesis 37 for a fuller story of Joseph's early life.

Serving God Inside

Now when Joseph arrived in Egypt with the Ishmaelite traders, he was purchased by Potiphar, a member of the personal staff of Pharaoh, the king of Egypt. . . . The Lord was with Joseph and blessed him greatly. . . . From the day Joseph was put in charge, the Lord began to bless Potiphar for Joseph's sake. Genesis 39:1-5

Joseph was a slave—a prisoner—in Egypt. He was alone, without the comfort of family and friends. But the Lord was with Joseph. And that made all the difference.

No matter how cushy Joseph's surroundings, he was not free. But he didn't feel sorry for himself. The Lord blessed him—as well as the person he served: Potiphar. Joseph's positive attitude made a difference.

We can learn from Joseph's attitude. How do we face the prospect of long-term imprisonment? Do we throw up our hands and bail out of life and our responsibilities? Or, do we see that God is calling us to serve Him effectively wherever we find ourselves? Joseph shows us the answer.

We are God's agents and ambassadors inside the walls. He is with us and has work for us to do. Chapel services need choirs and setup teams for services. Chapels need to be cleaned up after services. Men and women who are clearly weak, vulnerable, and attractive to predators require a shield from harm's way. Chaplains need assistants and assistance. We must adopt a new *Joseph* attitude.

When we serve God with our whole hearts, as Joseph did, the Lord will bless not only us but also the people we serve. His presence will be very apparent to everyone around us. Think about it: Our positive attitude of service can transform an entire facility.

†

Making it personal: What is your attitude? Ask God for the kind of spirit He gave to Joseph.

Prayer: Father God, mold my spirit into the spirit of Joseph. Amen.

Read Acts 16:23-34, the story of how God blessed everyone in the prison because of the attitudes of Paul and Silas.

The Proper Use of Power

When [Joseph's] master saw that the Lord was with him and that the Lord gave him success in everything he did, Joseph found favor in his eyes and became his attendant. Potiphar put him in charge of his household, and he entrusted to his care everything he owned. Genesis 39:3-4, NIV

How do we define power inside prison? Obviously, the "badges" have power. They can write us up and revoke our visiting privileges. The administration can wake us up at midnight and tell us to throw our entire life's belongings into a garbage bag, then put us on a bus to a new facility or even a different state.

On the yard, the shot-callers and OGs are powerful. We are influential if we have good looks or money on our books, or if we are physically strong, notorious, or an old number. The chaplain's clerk has power. So do Bible-study leaders or inmates with an education. How should we use our power?

Joseph was a slave, but in his role as Potiphar's assistant, Joseph had enormous power and opportunity to enrich his own life. He could've coerced other servants for personal gain or used the authority to intimidate others to acquire more control. But Joseph did none of these things. He *used* power but was not *used by* power. Joseph may have been tempted by power, but he used it for good. His power blessed others.

If we are a chaplain's clerk, we have to be impartial to people of all faiths. If we're strong, we should protect the weak. If we have money, we can share our canteen. We must avoid the arrogance of power and must consider others as better than ourselves. If we adopt a servant's attitude, after the model of Joseph and Jesus Christ, we will bless others. Then they will praise God for His goodness because of our efforts in God's name.

✝

Making it personal: Take stock of how you are using your power. Is it for the good of others or for yourself?

Prayer: Jesus, You are all-powerful, but You used Your power for my salvation. Help me follow Your example. Amen.

Read Philippians 2:1-11 to discover how Jesus saw power.

Sexual Temptation

Now Joseph was a very handsome and well-built young man. Potiphar's wife began to desire him and invited him to sleep with her. But Joseph refused. "Look," he told her, "my master trusts me with everything in his entire household. . . . How could I ever do such a wicked thing? It would be a great sin against God." Genesis 39:6-9

As Joseph worked in Potiphar's house, the master's wife repeatedly demanded that he have sex with her. This was a tremendous temptation for Joseph. By seeing how Joseph handled it—what he did *not* do—we can conquer our own sexual temptation.

Joseph did *not* cave in to lust by deceiving himself into thinking it was the natural thing to do. He did *not* rationalize that she needed him because Potiphar was not "takin' care of business" at home. Joseph did *not* give in to self-pity. He could have fooled himself into believing he deserved a little comfort to compensate for the unjust treatment by his brothers. And, he did *not* give in to ambition. She was the powerful wife of a powerful man. Joseph could have powered up his career by having an influential woman whispering good things about him to her husband. Giving in to sexual temptation might have even helped Joseph gain his freedom!

Joseph found the strength to fight off this sexual temptation by having something stronger in his life—a more powerful attraction than sex: a relationship with God that transcended human pleasure. Joseph understood his sin would be a sin against God. Joseph's walk with God undoubtedly involved daily prayer and worship. He worked "God's free weights" to build up his spiritual strength. To defeat sexual sin, Joseph shows us we need to have a strong relationship with God in place—before sexual temptation strikes.

✝

Making it personal: Are you spiritually strong or flabby and soft? What can you do to strengthen yourself against sexual temptation?

Prayer: Lord Jesus, I commit to You to start working out with Your Word, so that I will be able to walk away from sexual sin. Amen.

Read 1 Corinthians 6:18-20 to learn about fighting any temptation.

Framed

"He tried to rape me, but I screamed. When he heard my loud cries, he ran and left his shirt behind with me." . . . When her husband came home that night, she told him her story. "That Hebrew slave you've had around here tried to make a fool of me," she said. "I was saved only by my screams." After hearing his wife's story, Potiphar was furious! He took Joseph and threw him into the prison. Genesis 39:14-20

In spite of Joseph's integrity, he ended up in prison. One day Potiphar's wife grabbed at his shirt, demanding, "Sleep with me!" Joseph got away, but in the process his shirt came off. Potiphar's wife was holding it as Joseph ran from the house.

Not happy that she had been refused, she began screaming. When the men around the house came running to see about the screams, she cried rape and blamed Joseph. Her husband believed her story and threw Joseph into prison.

Joseph did nothing to deserve prison. He had acted with complete integrity, constantly resisting the seductive woman's advances. He had done nothing wrong. Yet he was framed. He had no recourse. There was no justice system, no trial, no public defender to plead his case.

Some of us can identify with Joseph. Some of us were framed too. We thought the system would see through our ex-lover's lies when we were accused of rape, yet people believed that we had committed the crime. Injustice hurt us more than the lies did. How do we handle injustices in our lives? How do we treat people who have wronged us? In the apostle Paul's famous chapter about love, he says that love "keeps no record of when it has been wronged" (1 Corinthians 13:5). We need the Holy Spirit's power to do that.

✝

Making it personal: How are you handling the injustices in your life? What specific things did you learn from Joseph?

Prayer: Lord, help me to get past the hurt of the people who framed me or set me up. I need Your ability to forgive. Amen.

Read Isaiah 42:3 for a promise about how God will deal with injustice.

God's Free Weights

"My son, do not make light of the Lord's discipline, and do not lose heart when he rebukes you, because the Lord disciplines those he loves." Hebrews 12:5-6, NIV

Those of us convicted on false testimony know the extremely painful feelings of injustice. When they are coupled with the separation from our families, we wonder why a loving God allows such unfairness.

Joseph felt the same way. Sent to prison for doing the right thing, he must have cried out: "God, why did You allow such injustice?" Was Joseph being disciplined—or punished?

Today we think of discipline as punishment. Its original meaning was "tough love"—placing boundaries around our lives and those of our children, and allowing them to run into those barriers for their own good. God's discipline is His plan for making us weaker so that we'll become stronger. What does that mean?

Sometimes we must get weaker to become stronger. Think about lifting weights. We do multiple sets of curls and bench presses to gain strength. But the immediate effect of a session is that we feel weaker, not stronger. We have to break down the tissue to allow it to build itself back up into even greater strength.

Using our circumstances, God weakens us to make us stronger. He allows us to go to prison, knowing that He will use our experience for our salvation and His glory.

Notice the last part of today's verse: God disciplines those He loves. When we feel the Lord's discipline in our lives, we need to remember that it comes from the hand of a God who loves us enough to try to shape us for His purposes. What Joseph did not know was that while he was languishing in a dungeon, God would use his prison time as a stepping-stone to something so good that it would save an entire nation.

†

Making it personal: How will you let go of the resentment that clings to your soul like moss on a tree? What will you do to recognize God's hand on your life and trust His love?

Prayer: Father God, help me to trust that Your discipline comes from Your love for me. Amen.

Read Deuteronomy 8:5 and **Hebrews 12:10** for encouragement.

The Lord Is with Us

Before long, the jailer put Joseph in charge of all the other prisoners and over everything that happened in the prison. The chief jailer had no more worries after that, because Joseph took care of everything. The Lord was with him, making everything run smoothly and successfully. Genesis 39:22-23

Here was Joseph, in prison, in a hard place, a place he didn't deserve. We can only imagine what prisons of those days were like: dark dungeons, damp and cold, real hellholes.

But the Lord was with Joseph in the hellhole. Four times in the story of Joseph, the Bible tells us that "the Lord was with him." And the Lord is with us too. He has not left us in our "dungeons." He has not given up on us. Just when we think He's missing-in-action, God surprises us with a new plan and greater responsibility. Don't give in to despair. God is with us, working on our behalf.

Apparently Joseph did not spend his energy in rebellion or depression. If we read between the lines of the story, we discover that he did his best in every small task and responsibility he was given. His diligence and positive attitude caught the attention of the chief jailer, the warden, who promoted him and gave him administrative responsibilities.

Joseph's behavior in prison was godly. He understood that God was with him and that God would use his experience for His good purposes. Joseph was doing *HIS* time. How Joseph *responded* was more important than what happened to him.

Can the same be said of us? How are we responding to what happened to us? Is our behavior godly? Are we doing our time or *HIS* time? Do we work hard at tasks, showing diligence and reliability? Our godly behavior in the prison will have a positive effect on everyone around us.

✝

Making it personal: How are you doing *HIS* time? How is your life in prison part of God's good purposes?

Prayer: Lord, help me to look beyond the details of my circumstances to Your presence with me and Your purposes. Amen.

Read Psalm 118:6-7, the psalmist's assurance that God was with him.

Servant Leadership

When Joseph came to [the two new prisoners] the next morning, he saw that they were dejected. So he asked [them], . . . "Why are your faces so sad?" Genesis 40:6-7, NIV

As Christians, the way we conduct our lives must rise above our circumstances. Joseph's life points the way. When he was in prison, he didn't throw his human waste at the guards. He didn't curse all night long or feel sorry for himself. Joseph took his authentic relationship with God into the prison. As a result, the warden trusted Joseph and placed him in charge of the prison.

During this time, the king of Egypt threw two of his aides—his baker and his cup-bearer (his wine steward)—into prison. Because of Joseph's exemplary behavior, the captain of the guard (most likely Potiphar) asked Joseph to take care of the men, who were probably disoriented, confused, and needy. We see new fish like them every day, people new to the system or regressed inmates.

Joseph demonstrated servant leadership and provides an example of how we should serve others inside. He had developed a sensitivity to others. In the morning he observed the faces of the new fish and noticed that they looked dejected. He felt compassion for them. Compassion is more than just noticing that someone is in distress—it goes further. Compassion involves a desire to lessen that distress and help the other person through the hard times. These men were disgraced. So Joseph reached out to help them.

Isn't that what Jesus has done for all of us? Don't we have the same opportunities to show compassion as Joseph did? Every day we see men and women who are dejected, who need care. As we grow in Christ, we must throw off self-centeredness and ask others, "How can I help?" In this way we demonstrate Christ's love to them and open the way for them to receive Christ.

✝

Making it personal: Who needs your compassion today? How can you put aside your own hurts to serve the hurts of others?

Prayer: Holy Spirit, heal my hurts by allowing me to be Your healing hands to others. Amen.

Read Isaiah 53 to learn how Jesus served us.

Peaks and Valleys

Pharaoh's cup-bearer, however, promptly forgot all about Joseph, never giving him another thought. Genesis 40:23

The reason the two new fish were dejected was that they both had had troubling dreams they couldn't understand. With God's help, Joseph interpreted their dreams. The cup-bearer's dream meant that he would be released from prison in three days. Joseph asked the man, "Have some pity on me when you are back in [the king's] favor. Mention me to Pharaoh, and ask him to let me out of here" (Genesis 40:14). But when the cup-bearer was sent back to the king's court, he forgot about Joseph.

Joseph's hopes were dashed. He was once again in the valley. Our lives are like that too. We assemble letters of support, arrange a realistic parole plan, secure a positive parole board recommendation—only to have the governor disallow it. God's plan for our life includes peaks and valleys that bring us to our highest point with Him.

Mountain climbers know that in order to get to the very highest peak, they need to scale lots of smaller peaks and descend into many valleys. When we're on a spiritual peak and feel we're ready to fly into the outside world for Jesus, it may be only a smaller peak. God may have other, higher peaks for us to conquer behind the walls. We feel let down that our plans are frustrated, yet, as Joseph's life shows us, God may have something even better in store for our lives—and the lives of other inmates. Jesus gave up His peak for us. His valley included death on a cross before He reached the top.

Joseph's life helps us appreciate the valleys we cannot understand. Joseph's life shines a light on the hiking trails that may seem unfair and difficult to accept.

✝

Making it personal: How are you trusting God's wisdom for your life? Are you willing to allow Him to take you off the peaks and lead you down to the valley of greater service?

Prayer: Jesus, thank You for descending into the ultimate valley for my sake. Amen.

Read John 19 and John 20 to recount Jesus' climb for our sake.

Recognizing God's Power

Pharaoh told him . . . "I have heard that you can interpret dreams, and that is why I have called for you." "It is beyond my power to do this," Joseph replied. "But God will tell you what it means." Genesis 41:15-16

Two years later, King Pharaoh himself had two troubling dreams. He assembled all of his court magicians and asked them to interpret his dreams. But none of them could. The cup-bearer overheard the conversations and suddenly remembered Joseph and his ability to interpret dreams. So Pharaoh called for Joseph and asked him to tell him what the dreams meant.

Before Joseph interpreted the king's dream, he said to Pharaoh, "I don't have any power to do this, but God will tell you what it means."

Joseph could have said to Pharaoh, "You've asked the right man, Your Highness. Since I was a young boy, I've had the power to interpret dreams. I'm your man." That's what the young, cocky, self-confident Joseph would have said. But the mature, godly man—the man seasoned by his life in prison—recognized that his power to interpret dreams came from God. Joseph realized that he was God's servant, responsible to use gifts God had given him. Nothing more.

How do we respond when someone asks us to do something that we know we do well? Do we have confidence in ourselves, or do we realize that all of our gifts are God's and that He chooses to exercise some of them through us? Joseph is a model for us because he points Pharaoh to God. Joseph did not claim the power for himself and try to use it for his own gain. He humbly pointed to God. We must do the same.

†

Making it personal: When you are able to do something well, do you claim the power for yourself, or do you use it to point others to God?

Prayer: Lord, thank You for giving me gifts and abilities. Help me always to remember that these gifts come from You. I am merely Your servant. Amen.

Read 1 Chronicles 29:11 to see how the wisest and richest man who ever lived recognized the source of his power.

It Was God

"But don't be angry with yourselves that you did this to me, for God did it. He sent me here ahead of you to preserve your lives. . . . God has sent me here to keep you and your families alive so that you will become a great nation. Yes, it was God who sent me here, not you! And he has made me a counselor to Pharaoh—manager of his entire household and ruler over all Egypt." Genesis 45:5-8

Those who know Joseph's full story know that Pharaoh's dreams warned him of seven years of bumper crops followed by seven years of famine. Joseph advised the king to find the wisest man and let him stockpile grain so that when the famine hit, they would have enough food. Pharaoh appointed Joseph to be his prime minister—the second most powerful position in Egypt—and asked him to oversee the entire famine response.

In the course of the famine, Joseph's own family began to starve. Joseph's father sent his sons to Egypt to get some food. The drama about how Joseph recognized his brothers but they didn't recognize him is exciting. Read the whole story in Genesis 41–45. When Joseph finally told his brothers who he was, they were sure he would kill them because they had betrayed him when they were younger, selling him into slavery.

But look at Joseph's response. He didn't lash out at his brothers, although he had a right to do that. Instead, he again pointed to God: "It was God who sent me here." Joseph recognized that God was working out His plan, even when his brothers' evil motives and actions were involved. Joseph left revenge and punishment to God.

God allowed Joseph to be sold into slavery in Egypt, and He allowed Joseph to go to prison because He had a good plan for Joseph. As a result, God saved an entire nation through Joseph.

†

Making it personal: God is working out His good plan through your life. How is He doing it, and why is it so hard for you to believe it?

Prayer: Lord, help me to see Your larger plan. I give myself to You completely. I trust You with my life. All of it. Amen.

Read Genesis 41–48 for the exciting details of how God worked out His plan for Joseph's life—and his family's lives.

God Turns It into Good

Joseph's brothers became afraid. "Now Joseph will pay us back for all the evil we did to him," they said. . . . But Joseph told them, "Don't be afraid of me. Am I God, to judge and punish you? As far as I am concerned, God turned into good what you meant for evil. . . . I myself will take care of you and your families." And he spoke very kindly to them, reassuring them. Genesis 50:15-21

The climax to Joseph's story is told in today's verses. After their father died, Joseph's brothers were afraid Joseph would take revenge on them. Instead, Joseph forgave them and treated them kindly.

What allowed Joseph to forgive the very people who abused him, betrayed him, abandoned him, and sold him?

First, *Joseph left revenge in God's hands.* "Am I God, to judge and punish you?" Joseph had the spiritual maturity to know that it was not his place to retaliate and beat up on his brothers. Justice and punishment are God's business, not ours.

We can take some lessons from Joseph. Many of us have been abused, betrayed, and abandoned too. But we have also replayed our bitterness and revenge, focusing on—sometimes obsessing about—what was done to us. We need to stop playing God and release our bitterness, placing the entire situation in God's hands. Because Joseph made God responsible for revenge, he was able to show mercy to his brothers.

Second, *Joseph trusted God's goodness.* Joseph understood that God is sovereign, that He is in control of everything, and that He is good—even when we can't see anything good about our lives. God is a redemptive God, who takes even the bad things in our lives and turns them into good.

What about the people who have wronged us? Can we say, "You did evil things to me, but I trust God to turn it into good"?

✝

Making it personal: How will you leave revenge in God's hands? How will you trust His goodness, even in painful situations?

Prayer: Lord, I struggle with bitterness toward people who have done evil things to me. I release the situation to You, trusting Your goodness. Amen.

Memorize Romans 8:28 for a reminder of God's goodness and transforming power.

Lessons from the Life of Joseph

These questions relate to the meditations found on pages 197-208:

Discuss together:

1. Joseph was abandoned and sold by his brothers. How has rejection and abandonment by your "brothers" affected each of your lives? How have you fought off a spirit of bitterness at being flipped on or ratted out by someone you trusted? Compare your attitudes with Joseph's. What can you learn from Joseph's attitude and actions?

2. How would your life in prison be different if you were unfairly convicted, as Joseph was—and perhaps you were? How are your actions and attitudes different from or similar to those of Joseph? What gave Joseph the strength and power to get beyond his anger at unjust imprisonment?

3. Describe the feelings of getting a "setback" from the parole board. Compare your feelings with what Joseph must have felt when he was forgotten (set back)? Using Joseph's example, how will you navigate prison life's peaks and valleys? Describe some of each.

4. How often do you think about (or try) getting back at those who sold you out? What does that yearning feel like? Describe specific ways it shackles your walk with Jesus. How do you think Joseph overcame his desire for payback when his brothers appeared before him? Where does that grace and strength originate? Talk about how difficult it is to surrender to God's control as Joseph did.

Explore God's Word together:

1. **Hebrews 12:14-15** is a call to "work at" living in peace. What does that working involve? Do you have a desire to make peace? If not, why not? What happens when there is not peace? What are the obstacles to making peace? How is bitterness like contaminated water? What purifies it?

2. **Mark 14:66-72** tells the story of how Peter, one of Jesus' beloved followers, denies knowing Him. How many times did Peter deny his relationship with Jesus? How do you think Jesus must have felt when His friend lied about knowing Him? Share about a time when you were betrayed. How deep was the hurt?

3. **John 21:1-17** tells the story of how Jesus reconnected with Peter. Remember that shortly before Jesus' death, Peter had publically denied that he even knew Jesus. What is the question Jesus asks Peter? How many times does He ask Peter? What is Peter's response? And what is Jesus' response to Peter's profession of his love and loyalty to Jesus? When Jesus says, "Feed my sheep," He is expressing His renewed trust in Peter. Jesus does not hold Peter's betrayal against him. He welcomes Peter back into relationship. Each of the three times Jesus commissions Peter, He is wiping out the memory of the three denials. What can you learn from Jesus' actions?

4. **Galatians 6:7-8** describes what is known as "the law of the harvest." What kind of harvest do seeds of revenge produce? Why does Paul speak of not being deceived or misled? Comment on this statement: "We reveal the kind of God we trust by the method we use to handle life's tough problems." What are the world's methods? How have they been unproductive for you? What kind of God do you serve?

Pray together:

1. Pray for release from feelings of revenge and bitterness. Ask Jesus to substitute Himself for those emotions.

2. Pray for the power and courage to be peacemakers inside the walls.

3. Pray for the freedom and power to do what you *ought* to do and not simply *what* you want to do.

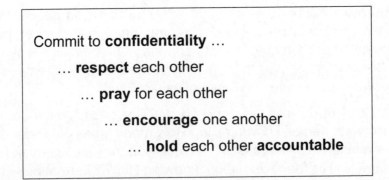

Commit to **confidentiality** …

… **respect** each other

… **pray** for each other

… **encourage** one another

… **hold** each other **accountable**

Resistance

Anyone who wants to live all out for Christ is in for a lot of trouble; there's no getting around it. Unscrupulous con men will continue to exploit the faith. They're as deceived as the people they lead astray. 2 Timothy 3:12-13, THE MESSAGE

When we run against the wind on the track around the yard, we feel the wind's resistance. We lift weights to gain strength. When we press more than the day before, it is the resistance of the weight that pumps us up.

So it is in our daily Christian lives. If we take a stand against a bully charging rent, we will face hostility. When we befriend the "short eyes" in the chow hall, we will meet opposition. Anytime we oppose the devil in his castle (prison), we make him angry. He will attempt to remove any opposition to his evil schemes. Jesus confronted the Jewish religious leaders and was mocked, beaten, and killed for His efforts. We can expect the same treatment (see John 15:20).

However, this is not cause for fear. Consider the attacks from Satan as confirmation that we are infuriating him. We should be concerned if we do *not* get hassled by the devil. If our lives are lukewarm, the devil won't even bother with us. He is angry only when we get in the way of his wicked plans.

We need to stand our ground in the face of wickedness, refusing to go along with the forces of evil inside the prison. We must avoid programs that promise early parole if it means denying the power of God. We must say no to false teachers who tell us to donate money to them instead of to God. When a new number is being pressured to join *La Nuestra Familia,* we can step into his life and introduce him to Christ's crew. We can make a difference for God. The attacks will come, but we can be ready.

✝

Making it personal: Shake off the halfhearted spirit, and be out there for God. Expect resistance, but count on God's strength.

Prayer: God, give me wisdom to recognize evil and strength to withstand the attacks of Satan and his followers. Amen.

Read John 16:33 to get peace and strength.

Wisdom from Others

Without good direction, people lose their way; the more wise counsel you follow, the better your chances. Proverbs 11:14, THE MESSAGE

When we come to prison as new numbers or repeat offenders, our goals are the same—survival. We increase our chances of survival if we acquire wisdom about how the prison system operates. Without it, we strut and swagger, inviting confrontation. We need someone who's "clued in" to share good judgment with us.

Wisdom most often comes from others, not from ourselves. Why? Our capacity for self-delusion is limitless. No one person can see all problems or issues from every angle. Young cons see situations in different ways from older inmates. Women see things very differently from men. Anger or emotional blind spots prevent us from making wise choices. Wise people consult with others before making decisions. As carpenters say, "Measure twice, cut once."

It is the same in our walk with Jesus. The Bible says that respect for God is the beginning of wisdom (see Proverbs 9:10). In addition, meeting with other believers every Sunday is taking a step toward wisdom. The opposite is also true. Choosing to separate ourselves from the body of Christ is egotistical. It leaves us vulnerable to the devil, who will pick us off. Community with other believers opens the faucet of wisdom into our daily problems. Other cons have already traveled the road we're on. Finding wise counselors who have "been there, done that" will decrease our feelings of isolation and despair.

Survival for us in prison is about choices. Even though most of life's decisions are taken away from us, we still have many open to us. When we find wisdom from God and others, the right choices become clearer. We no longer are easily misdirected or caught off guard by emotional appeals. Our lives take on a stability that only wisdom brings.

†

Making it personal: What situation in your life demands wisdom? Who will you go to for advice and wisdom?

Prayer: In You, Lord, is true wisdom. Direct me to Your disciples so that I will gain wisdom to serve You better. Amen.

Read Proverbs 1 and 2 to discover how to gain wisdom.

Worship Idols or God?

**After seeking advice, the king made two golden calves. He said to the people, "It is too much for you to go up to Jerusalem. Here are your gods, O Israel, who brought you up out of Egypt."
1 Kings 12:28, NIV**

Israel's evil King Jeroboam decided to erect golden calves for the people to worship because he didn't want them going to Jerusalem to worship the one, true God. The king was smart enough to know that his people needed to worship something. He knew their hearts demanded something greater than themselves.

We all end up worshiping something. We can choose to worship God or worship something else. If we don't worship God, we will find something else that captures our loyalty. We may not bow down to a statue of gold, but we might devote ourselves to the goal of getting rich—getting the gold! We may never have sex in a temple, but we'll be tempted to violate the temple of the Holy Spirit—our bodies—with sexual sin.

For us in prison, it's easy to worship idols instead of God. We worship our freedom, the appeals process, our friends, or even our jobs. We set ourselves up as our own god, loving ourselves and living a self-centered, self-important lifestyle. Worshiping ourselves and caring only for ourselves means we rarely consider the consequences or effects of our actions on others. That situation is the worst kind of prison, for it offers no hope.

Can we save ourselves? When we are wallowing in the slime of our own sin, do we have the power to pull ourselves out? Are we capable of offering ourselves forgiveness and a new start? Can we do that for ourselves? Of course we can't. Only God can rescue us, forgive us, and set us on the path to a life of freedom and service to others.

✝

Making it personal: Who or what do you worship? Who or what occupies your thoughts? Who will you choose as your God?

Prayer: God, I want to worship only You. Help me shed false gods here in prison. Amen.

Read Isaiah 42:8 and 17 to learn how God feels about our idols.

Becoming Light in the Darkness

Noah was a righteous man, the only blameless man living on earth at the time. He consistently followed God's will and enjoyed a close relationship with him. Genesis 6:9

The prisons where we live are wicked places, where cruelty is the norm and sin seems to be in control. How can we shine a light into these dark places? The story of Noah helps us with this question.

Noah lived in a place where sin was everywhere. While he was building the ark, he lived a clean and untarnished life in the wickedness around him. How did he do it? The answer is found in today's verse, "He consistently followed God's will and enjoyed a close relationship with him."

Events in our lives are rarely isolated occurrences. There is often a cause-and-effect sequence. None of us just happened, one day, to find ourselves smoking crack and turning tricks at age twelve in Pioneer Square in downtown Portland, Oregon. No, first came the sexual abuse from our stepfathers or brothers and our decision to run away. Needing a place to sleep introduced us to "friends" who offered sympathy and drugs to ease the pain of our shattered psyches. The drugs cost money. That need for money brought us into prostitution.

Being God's beacon of light inside the prison also follows a cause-and-effect sequence. It begins with obedience to what God wants us to do. That desire to obey God's teachings leads us to a closer relationship with Him. A closer relationship brings with it even greater perception of His will for our daily lives. Understanding and obeying His will inspires courage and nurtures our ability to become strong beacons of light in the darkness.

We can be like Noah, consistently obeying God's will, enjoying a close relationship with Him, and shining His light into a sin-darkened world.

✝

Making it personal: How will you draw closer to God? How will you shine a light in the darkness?

Prayer: Draw me closer to You, Lord God, so that I can be a light in the darkness of this prison. Amen.

Read Genesis 6:1–9:17 to learn of human wickedness, Noah's obedience, and God's love.

Do Not Conform—Be Transformed

Do not conform any longer to the pattern of this world, but be transformed by the renewing of your mind. Romans 12:2, NIV

Numerous TV shows portray virtuous police officers becoming exactly like the people they're trying to bust. This happens in real life too. We read about cops who steal the money from a drug bust and keep it for themselves.

This risk of becoming like the people around us is a persistent and dangerous threat to our Christian walk. When we are surrounded by people who scoff at God and practice sinful deeds, we are tempted to become like them. It's like swimming in a cesspool, and it's very difficult to avoid the stink.

The apostle Paul writes about this problem in today's verse. He uses the word *conform* to indicate the gradual process by which we take on and adopt the rules and standards of those around us. If we are not careful, we can slowly find ourselves becoming insensitive to God's leading and His grace.

Paul gives us the formula for resisting this temptation when he instructs us to be transformed by the renewing of our minds. As we've said before: How we think determines how we act. If our minds focus on negative things, we will behave in sinful ways. However, if we allow the Holy Spirit to renew our minds, our whole lives will be transformed.

To renew something often involves stripping off the old and replacing it with something better. As our lives have been stripped of drug addiction, guilt, and shame, we apply the finishing coat of Jesus over our new minds. Then to keep our minds fresh, we need to worship—not only individually through prayer and Bible study, but also with the prison church. This will help us keep our minds focused on the right things as we fight the pressures of prison life and the dangers of returning to the old life.

✝

Making it personal: How are you conforming to the old life? How can you be restoring your new life?

Prayer: God in heaven, stay close to me as I struggle with the old person inside me. Restore me every day. Amen.

Read Romans 8:5-6 for encouragement to allow the Spirit to shape your mind.

Releasing Hate

If anyone says, "I am living in the light," but hates a Christian brother or sister, that person is still living in darkness. 1 John 2:9

Jesus loved all people, not judging them for their gender, occupation, or race. When Jesus rose from the dead, He announced His resurrection to Mary. Jesus worked through a woman to bring Peter and John to Him. This was radical. Women had no status in first-century Jerusalem. Women couldn't offer testimony at a trial, and men rarely spoke to women in public.

Jesus also did not discriminate on the basis of occupation. He chose Matthew, a Jewish tax collector, to be His disciple. Tax collectors could charge whatever they wanted, as long as Rome got its share. As a result, tax collectors were considered traitors. The Jews hated them, yet Jesus chose a tax collector to be a disciple.

On another occasion Jesus went to Samaria and spoke to an adulterous Samaritan woman—an unthinkable gesture. Not only were Samarians considered to be trash, but He—a Jewish male—spoke to a woman who everyone in the town knew was sleeping around. His love reached beyond social barriers.

When we follow Jesus, we cannot hate others because of their skin color, gang affiliation, crime, chosen religion, or sexual preference. If we say we believe in Jesus, we give up any thoughts of revenge and feelings of contempt or disgust that we felt before we knew the Lord. Our unity with Christ through His sacrifice for our sins makes it unacceptable to hate others.

If these words irritate us, we have a problem. Are we mentally scrolling through the directory of inmates at SCI Cambridge Springs and naming those we hate because they are lesbian or child abusers? Then the love of Christ is not in us! We shouldn't be fooled or misled. We cannot hate those inmates and love God at the same time. To think otherwise is a delusion.

✝

Making it personal: Honestly examine your heart. Confess all hatred, contempt, or bigotry.

Prayer: Jesus, I have hated for so long, I am tired of it. Please, Holy Spirit, release me to love others fully. Amen.

Read 1 John 4:7-21, instructions for loving others.

Worship Unites Us

Always keep yourselves united in the Holy Spirit, and bind yourselves together with peace. Ephesians 4:3

To many people, the suggestion that worship and religion unite us is absurd. They point out that millions have been killed in the name of God through religious wars, the Crusades, and the Inquisition. They argue that religion has been a great source of division and suffering in the world—and in some ways they are correct.

Religion focusing on "do's and don'ts" kills the spirit. It is a set of rules and regulations that people use to show God that they are acceptable to Him. By keeping a set of rules and regulations, they mistakenly feel they have done something good—and God is *obligated* to accept them. They count on their performance to earn God's love.

Jesus had harsh words for rule-keepers—people like the Pharisees—because they missed the Gospel message: God loves and accepts us, even though we are sinners who offend Him. Jesus paid the penalty for our sin. *While we were still sinners*, Jesus came to die for us (see Romans 5:8). When we fully understand this undeserved gift, we respond by doing good things and avoiding sinful acts. *Religion* tied to regulations leads to arrogant self-righteousness. However, a *relationship* with Jesus leads to a life of service to others in love.

When we worship together, knowing that our sin has been covered, our worship unites us. It deepens our sense of brotherhood and sisterhood by pointing out our common needs. True worship reminds us that we are all sinners, making it difficult to point a finger of accusation at someone else. The fruit of the Spirit grows in each one of us, resulting in unity and loving attitudes.

Jesus came to abolish religion and replace it with a relationship with Him. We cannot earn His love; He gives it to us for free.

†

Making it personal: Examine yourself. Do you cling to religion or to a relationship? How can worship unite us?

Prayer: Jesus, thank You for coming into the world to free me from the rules and regulations of religion. Praise Your name for the free gift of love You offer. Amen.

Read Romans 5:1-11, a reminder of our freedom in Jesus.

The Law of Influence

We can be mirrors that brightly reflect the glory of the Lord. And as the Spirit of the Lord works within us, we become more and more like him and reflect his glory even more. 2 Corinthians 3:18

When we look back on our lives, we can point to people who influenced us—parents, other family members, teachers, friends, gang members. Who influenced us the most? Was the influence a positive or negative one?

We can only imagine how different our lives would be if we'd had a successful, law-abiding mentor while growing up. How would our lives have turned out if our mothers had not been addicted to crack? Today, if we admire cons with a fondness for trouble, we are soon in trouble. If we have a high regard for dope users, we will probably become dope users. Our lives are a collection of the people who influence us—for good or for evil. The more time we spend with certain people, the more we become like them. We become like mirrors that reflect the people's values and character. That's called the Law of Influence.

The apostle Paul experienced the Law of Influence when he met Christ on the road to Damascus. From then on Paul hung out with Jesus, and his life changed. He went from being a murderer to being a missionary, from being the hunter to being the hunted. He learned the truth of what he wrote in today's verse.

When we hang out with Jesus, His presence influences us, and we become more like Him. With extended exposure to the Savior, our hearts will produce kindness and tenderness toward people. Our words will soften. Our manners will be more gentle, our conduct more unselfish.

When we spend time with Jesus, we become like a mirror that reflects the character of God. When other people look at us, they don't see us—they see Jesus.

†

Making it personal: Who are your friends? How are they influencing you for good or evil? If evil, what will you do to change friends?

Prayer: Lord, I want to be like You and reflect Your character so that others can see You in my life. Amen.

Read 3 John 1:11 for words to live by.

God Won't Forget

But God remembered Noah. Genesis 8:1

Sometimes the agony of loneliness feels like a switchblade penetrating our souls as it slices up the last bit of hope in the secret places of our hearts. Sometimes the craving for the taste of our mamma's burritos makes us cry. We wonder if God has forgotten us. We cry out to God like the psalmist who wrote, "Has God forgotten to be kind? Has he slammed the door on his compassion?" (Psalm 77:9).

When these feelings and thoughts overwhelm us, we can remember Noah during the Flood. Noah felt alone. All he saw was water. God promised him safety, but He never told him the timetable. Noah's days of waiting were long and excruciating. He must have cried out, as we do, for God to reappear and remember him. Then, the dove returned to the ark with an olive branch in its beak as the sign that God had not forgotten Noah. It was proof God can be trusted (see Genesis 8:6-11).

This story of Noah offers hope because the floodwaters receded and the mountaintops reappeared. God did not forget Noah, and God does not forget us when we are overwhelmed by the floodwaters of loneliness. God may seem to have vanished, but He is only in the background, working on our behalf. Just because we don't hear Him doesn't mean He is not there. And, just because God's actions don't fit our plan does not mean that He does not have a plan for us.

During the darkest moments in our ark of hopelessness, God gives signals that He is faithful. Is it the unexpected gift of a new study Bible? Is it perhaps an unanticipated letter or a crayon drawing from a four-year-old daughter? Is it a cellie who finds Christ? The signs will be there. God remembers us. He will not forget.

✝

Making it personal: How will you place your discouragement and loneliness in God's hands, trusting Him to care for you?

Prayer: Lord, thank You that You remember me, that You care about everything that happens to me. I will trust You even when I can't see You. Amen.

Read Matthew 10:29-31 as a reminder of how much God deeply cares for you.

Take Control of Anger

Don't sin by letting anger gain control over you. Psalm 4:4a

Most of us are angry 24/7. We're angry at our families, ourselves, other cons, the administration, and the courts—to name just a few.

But what is anger? Why do we choose to get angry? How do we contribute to our anger? Are we born with it? Are we slaves to it? Can we ever hope to control it? Can we ever be free of our anger? The next few meditations will look at what the Bible says about anger.

Anger is different things. Anger can be a mask we wear to hide our fear of others or our hatred of ourselves. Anger can communicate displeasure. Anger can be a strategy for control. If we get angry over our cellie's behavior and that behavior changes, we might use anger again to control behavior. Anger is a great excuse to do things we already decided to do but needed a reason. If we disrespect somebody when we're angry, we duck personal responsibility, hiding behind the excuse that we "said it in anger." Anger is a strong indicator that something is wrong in our lives.

But is anger itself wrong? Not always. Anger is a God-given emotion. The Bible does not outlaw anger, but it does teach us not to sin by letting anger *control* us. Anger can be used for good or for evil. Jesus got angry when He went to the temple and chased out the moneychangers (see Mark 11:15-17). But Jesus' anger was a righteous anger. It was not self-centered or self-serving. In His anger, Jesus did not sin.

We almost always sin when we are angry. Rather than indulge anger because it feels good to go off on someone, we have to admit our powerlessness over it and surrender it to God's will for our lives.

✝

Making it personal: Look at times when you were angry. Where did you sin while under anger's power?

Prayer: Lord, teach me how to control my anger so that I do not use it to hurt You or others. I need Your help. Amen.

Read Psalm 37:7-8, and use it as a motto for today.

Look behind the Anger

Your anger can never make things right in God's sight.
James 1:20

Why do we choose to get angry? Anger makes people pay attention to us. It is like a snake's *hiss-s-s.* Some of us felt rejection by our parents when we were growing up. We wanted them to notice us and tell us they loved us. When they were too busy or pushed us away in favor of our brothers or drugs or their friends, we acted out. We fought with other kids, joined a gang, got a tongue stud, or violated curfew. We knew our parents would be angry, but at least when they yelled at us, they noticed us.

Anger also masks our fears. We adopt an angry exterior because we are afraid of the other cons who victimize some of the weaker inmates. We walk around with a surly attitude, communicating to other cons that we are not to be messed with. We take on the rude attitude, slouched posture, and bored facial expressions to preserve the image that we acquired on the street.

But what does the anger really accomplish? If the anger is truly about needing someone to pay attention to us or about protecting ourselves from fear, then we should opt to trust God and put down the mask. Listen to these comforting words: "You are precious to me. You are honored, and I love you. Do not be afraid, for I am with you" (Isaiah 43:4-5). Or: "I will lie down in peace and sleep, for you alone, O Lord will keep me safe" (Psalm 4:8). God notices us. He loves us and will protect us.

We can put away our anger. It will never make things right. It will never accomplish what God wants for us.

✝

Making it personal: Examine your anger, and see it for what it really is. How can you let it go in favor of real safety and peace?

Prayer: Lord, I use anger to cover up my fear. Help me to trust Your love. Take care of me and keep me safe. I want Your will for my life. Amen.

Read Psalm 145:8-9, verses about God and anger.

Anger and Expectations

Oh, the joys of those who trust the Lord, who have no confidence in the proud, or in those who worship idols. Psalm 40:4

As children, when our birthdays and Christmas came around, our heads were filled with expectations of gifts we would get. We wished for a new bicycle or doll. When they did not appear, when our expectations were not met, we sulked, pouted, or got angry at our parents for letting us down. For some of us the disappointments still linger and hinder our daily lives. As they say in Al-Anon, "Expectations are premeditated resentments."

Unmet expectations are another cause of anger. We expect things to happen in a certain way at a certain time. When they don't happen, we get fearful or angry. For example, when our spouses don't call us at the expected time, we worry and suspect they are cheating on us. We expect that another con will walk with us to dinner, but when he or she fails to appear or chooses to walk with someone else, we feel betrayed and get heated. Why?

Anger brought on by misguided expectations is wrapped up with fear, self-centeredness, and pride. When we are afraid or angry when our expectations are not met, pride says, "You can't do that to me." Fear whispers, "My wife [husband] is taking the kids to another state; that's why she [he] missed the visit." Self-centeredness screams, "That is *my* friend, and we always walk together to chow."

At the root of this anger is a lack of trust in God and His plan for our lives. If we list those things that make us afraid or angry, we will often recognize that they are areas where our faith is weakest. We can go to God with these fears. Let's not allow these concerns to become idols that we worship in place of the living God. Experience the joy of those who trust in God.

†

Making it personal: What expectations are really idols in your life? Make a list, and release them to God.

Prayer: Lord Jesus, help me to trust You and feel the joy that You bring to my existence in this place. Amen.

Read 2 Samuel 12:13-25 to learn how King David responded when his expectations were not met.

Think about Your Thoughts

Don't sin by letting anger gain control over you. Think about it overnight and remain silent. Psalm 4:4

We choose to be angry by how we think about things. The ancient Greek philosopher Epictetus said, "Men are not troubled by things themselves, but by their thoughts about them." He meant that how we think about an event is often the problem, not the event itself. Many of us who attend AA know this as "Stinking thinking."

An inmate was given a banana (a true story) in the chow line. It was smaller than the banana given to the man ahead of him. The first man got so angry over the difference in bananas that he hit the other con and did thirty days in Ad-Seg. The banana was not the problem. The angry inmate interpreted his receiving a smaller banana as an insult. His perception of the event, not the event itself, contributed to his choosing anger.

At times we perceive an event in our lives as a gross injustice. Our partner in crime "narcs" us out and receives a slap on the wrist while we do fifteen years hard time. We turn that over in our heads, letting it fester like an infected tooth. The apparent unfairness simmers within us and causes great pain when it boils over at the smallest provocation.

When we walk around angry, we tend to use harsh, hostile language. A small annoyance over which TV channel to watch becomes a serious confrontation. Tempers flare, and obscenities follow. We say and do things that we regret.

How would Christ react to receiving a smaller banana? Did Jesus ever use obscenities with people who beat and crucified Him? No. As the character of Christ takes root in us, we gain control over our anger. As we mature in Him, we acquire the discipline to think about things before flying off the handle.

†

Making it personal: What thoughts do you need to control so that you can control your anger? What first step will you take?

Prayer: My temper controls me too often, Lord. I want to change, but I'll need Your help. Fill me with Your Holy Spirit. Amen.

Read Proverbs 14:29 to learn the advantage of controlling anger.

See with God's Eyes

The Lord does not look at the things people look at. People look at the outward appearance, but the Lord looks at the heart. 1 Samuel 16:7, NIV

The way we talk to ourselves contributes to our anger. In our minds we indulge silent conversations that shape our emotions. For example: "That guard is a jerk just waiting to write me up." Or, "The guy in the next cell is a child molester." Or, "I hate Short-eyes." Or, "My boyfriend hasn't written me in months. I know he's cheating on me." These statements fuel our anger to a point of irrationality. We operate with very little information yet make judgments that seem absolute. This is called destructive labeling.

We call officers, watch commanders, and other convicts SOBs— or worse. But labeling casts them in a totally negative light. We oversimplify. That makes it impossible for us to see *any* good in them. If we can make the other person look totally bad, we convince ourselves that we are totally right.

When we label in this destructive way, we do not allow ourselves to appreciate another person's good qualities. We disable our minds from seeing that other person through Christ's eyes. We look at the outer person and judge.

God doesn't act that way. He sees the inner person, loves him or her, and knows what good still lies within. Just as Christ has forgiven us and sees the best that we can be, so must we see others as Christ views them. When we do, our anger will have less power over us.

The more we are aware of our destructive labeling, the more we can choose to see with God's eyes. This is another step on the path that leads toward freedom from anger.

✝

Making it personal: What destructive labels have you used in the past week? How did they distort your thinking? How have they led to anger?

Prayer: Lord, I'm so quick to judge others with destructive labels. Thank You that You don't do that with me. Let me see others through Your eyes. Amen.

Read Ephesians 4:31-32 to discover the right attitude to have.

Godly Living: Part 2

These questions relate to the meditations found on pages 211-224:

Discuss together:

1. An old proverb says, "Tall trees catch much wind." What does this mean for you if you take a stand for God's truth? What actions get a person labeled a "tall tree"? What danger is there in doing these things? What types of wind might blow against you if you stand tall for Jesus?

2. Why is wisdom found in a community of believers? Which of your choices increase or decrease wisdom? What does the phrase "decision of character" mean? (Hint: Does sweet water flow from a bitter stream?)

3. Choices affect your life's direction. What are some "good choices" and some "bad choices" available in prison? Discuss where each choice might ultimately lead. Then, share your thoughts about your friends. How did your choices of friends influence where you ended up in life? What can you do to surround yourself with friends who will influence you in positive ways?

4. It has been said, "Holding onto anger is like drinking poison and expecting the other person to die." What does this statement mean? Why is anger so corrosive? Discuss the role anger played in your life and eventual imprisonment. What type of anger is not a sin? What does anger reveal about a person? Are you angry right now? What is the cure for anger?

Explore God's Word together:

1. **Proverbs 29:9-11** speaks of wisdom and foolishness. List and discuss the traits of a fool and contrast them with the traits of a wise person. What is the difference in how wise people and foolish people handle anger? Why do you think wicked people hate men and women of integrity?

2. **Luke 15:11-32** tells the story of a father and his two sons. Which son is the "prodigal" son? Why is he called that? Which son is more distant from God? What is the sin of the older brother? How did anger and self-righteousness play a role in his life? To which of the sons do you relate?

3. **Psalm 103:8-9** shares some insight into God's anger. How is this a comfort to you? Why is God "slow to anger"? How is that a positive example for our lives? Discuss personal situations where anger is hurting your walk with Jesus. What is it going to take to free yourself from this prison of anger?

Pray together:

1. Pray for the strength to be a person of integrity and wisdom.

2. Ask the Holy Spirit to lead you to worthy companions and true friends.

3. Pray for God to reveal your anger and free you from it.

Commit to **confidentiality** …

... **respect** each other

... **pray** for each other

... **encourage** one another

... **hold** each other **accountable**

Prayer for Godly Living

Lord God, inside the walls of this prison
I am surrounded on every side by temptation
and enticements to do what I know is wrong and
hurtful to You and to my spirit.

Let Your Word and Spirit surround me rather than
the gambling, drugs, and power-tripping.
Help me, Lord, to see that all that is gold
does not glitter and that the way up is down.
Help me see that to really see You,
I have to be on my knees!

Lord, burn away all the pride and
garbage that pollutes my walk with You.
Keep me from wanting to sin.
Help me not to crave the foolishness of the world.
Pour Your restraining grace into my life.
Keep me from blowing up my life
with things that do not satisfy.
Amen.

✝

A Cup of Cold Water

And if anyone gives even a cup of cold water to one of these little ones because he is my disciple, I tell you the truth, he will certainly not lose his reward. Matthew 10:42, NIV

Ron is doing "life + 1." He is so dangerous that visitors can see him only behind Plexiglas. The "badges" move Ron around the facility only when he is in leg shackles with his arms cuffed behind his back. He's Native American and has no use for "the white man's God."

The first time Ron encountered a prison ministry volunteer, he screamed, "Jesus died for His crime, and I intend to die for mine!" He told the volunteer that he was praying to his witch-doctor gods for harm to come to the volunteer and his family. The meeting lasted only a short while.

The volunteer wrote Ron a letter thanking him for spending time with him and reminding Ron that Jesus loved him. He told Ron how Jesus died for all men and women. He restated that Jesus wanted to capture his beautiful Native American heart for the Kingdom. He informed Ron that forgiveness was available along with a new start. He could have a purposeful life.

At the next visit the volunteer brought his wife along. They asked to meet with Ron. After Ron shuffled in and sat, he said in a quiet voice, "You wrote me a letter." He explained that he had never received any mail. He apologized for being rude and mean during the previous visit. The man was softened by a letter. A letter that is as simple to write as it is to get a cup of cold water from the faucet.

The husband and wife asked for permission to pray with Ron. His eyes filled with tears as He gave his life to Christ at that moment. A small act of love changed this man's destiny.

✝

Making it personal: Who needs a cup of cold water in the cellblock today? What will you do about it?

Prayer: Lord, give me ears to hear the pain and eyes to see the needs of those thirsting for the living water. Give me courage to be Your faucet to these men and women. Amen.

Read John 4:1-42, the story of how Jesus gave living water to the Samaritan woman.

You Are an Ambassador

We are Christ's ambassadors, and God is using us to speak to you. We urge you, as though Christ himself were here pleading with you, "Be reconciled to God!" 2 Corinthians 5:20

When a message needs to be delivered, sometimes a messenger does it. When a family member on the outside is seriously ill or dies, the chaplain comes by and delivers the emergency notification to us. On the yard, the person in charge sends a torpedo (messenger) to deliver the messages. In much the same way, countries have messengers in every capital of the world to deliver messages between leaders. These people are ambassadors.

God calls us to be His ambassadors. When we truly appreciate how much God has done for us in Christ, we want to tell others. Unfortunately, some Christians accept God's forgiveness, but they shy away from delivering His message of salvation to others. It's comfortable to sit back and enjoy our salvation, but we can't stay in comfort. Love is a verb, and it demands action. As the recipients of God's love, we are called into His service as messengers. Just as our lawyers were advocates in our criminal cases, so we are God's mouthpieces to a fallen world. (Let's be better than some public defenders.) This is a necessary outgrowth of our love and gratitude toward God, but it's not an easy task. It takes courage.

The first time our witness and lifestyle conflict with our cellie's drug use or violent behavior, we might receive a hostile response. The conflict that God's message brings is the war between darkness and the light (see John 3:19-21). Our job as Christ's ambassadors is to announce the freedom and joy that come from the miracle of God's love. That is God's message. Our responsibility is to insure that it is delivered with love and in the spirit of reconciliation, not arrogance or judgment.

✝

Making it personal: How will you be Christ's ambassador today? Who needs to hear His message?

Prayer: Lord, thank You that You sent Your ambassadors to tell me about You. Help me to do the same to the people here. Amen.

Read Acts 8:5-40, about how God chose Philip as His ambassador to an Ethiopian man.

Living Sacrifices

Dear brothers and sisters, I plead with you to give your bodies to God. Let them be a living and holy sacrifice—the kind he will accept. When you think of what he has done for you, is this too much to ask? Romans 12:1

Some people loved God so much that they were killed for their beliefs. The first martyr, Stephen, spoke out against the Jewish leadership and was stoned to death. Ironically, the future apostle Paul was a member of the killing party (see Acts 7:54-60).

Jim Elliot, a missionary, gave his life in Christ's service. Jim, along with four other missionaries, was killed by the very people God called him to serve in Ecuador. He wrote these memorable words in his journal, "He is no fool who gives up what he cannot keep to gain that which he cannot lose." These words have inspired many people to become missionaries.

Does God require us to become martyrs? Must we die for the sake of His kingdom? Usually not. But He does ask something much more difficult and daring of us—that we *live* for the sake of His Kingdom.

Living as faithful witnesses to the love of God takes more courage on a daily basis than making one split-second decision to give our lives for His sake. In one quick moment, we might decide to die for Jesus, but what about waking up every day in a depressing prison and deciding to be a "living sacrifice" for Him? The reality of talking and acting our faith inside the walls of prison is a dangerous and difficult thing to do. Yet that is what Jesus calls us to. We are challenged to heal the suffering with a listening ear. We are commissioned to banish the fear in someone else's heart with a kind word and encouraging friendship. We are commanded to get into other people's business—something quite risky in prison.

Die for Jesus? Yes—if He asks us to. Live for Jesus? We already have those orders.

✝

Making it personal: What small, courageous step will you take to live for Christ in the living unit today?

Prayer: Lord God, give me the courage to be a living sacrifice for You every day. Amen.

Read Acts 6:8–7:60, the story of the martyr Stephen.

The Power of One

**I am the only one left, and now they are trying to kill me too.
1 Kings 19:10, NIV**

Elijah had a bad day and threw a massive pity party. He thought he was the only follower of God left in Israel. How could Israel be reclaimed for God if he was the only good guy left?

We look around at the hundreds of people locked up with us at Valdosta State Prison or York Correctional Institution and wonder the same thing. How can a small minority of ragtag Christians ever hope to have any positive influence on facilities with this many inmates? Is there realistic hope for changing the general population with so few followers of Christ?

Look back on other small groups that accomplished great things. After the Israelites left Egypt and wandered around the desert for forty years, only a small group of people remained to conquer the Promised Land. Esther and her uncle Mordecai, the only two godly people in a powerful but corrupt king's household, saved the Jewish population from destruction (see Esther 1–10). Later on, twelve uneducated men were entrusted with bringing the Gospel of Christ to the world. Each of these groups was small, but each had a powerful impact.

Take courage from these men and women who influenced their world for good. They were not hindered by the enormity of the task. Instead they trusted the One who could give them the supernatural strength to overcome the odds. We can take strength from each other. Together, we can resolve to continue the struggle, knowing that other prison churches are fighting next to us. Always remember that salvation for all of us came from only *one* person: Jesus Christ (see 1 Timothy 2:5-6). One person can make an incredible difference. Stay strong in that knowledge, and trust God for strength.

✝

Making it personal: How can you and just a few other believers influence your cell, your pod, your prison for Christ?

Prayer: Lord, I want to accomplish great things for You. I may be only one person, but use me as You used Elijah and Esther. Amen.

Read Daniel chapters 1–2 to discover how just four godly young men influenced a corrupt empire for God.

But, Lord, Who Am I?

"But who am I to appear before Pharaoh?" Moses asked God. "How can you expect me to lead the Israelites out of Egypt?" Then God told him, "I will be with you." Exodus 3:11-12

Has God ever asked you to do something? Maybe He's asked you to befriend a sexual offender or to confront someone about a sin. What was your response? Did you say yes? Or did you brush off God's call?

Many of us are like Moses. When we sense God calling us to do something for Him, we respond with a long list of excuses. When God spoke to Moses at the burning bush in the wilderness and asked him to lead the Israelites out of slavery, Moses did not eagerly answer "Yes, Lord." Instead, he argued with God: "But, Lord, who am I?" "But, Lord, they won't believe me." "But, Lord, I am not a very good speaker."

How did God respond to these "buts"? He said to Moses, "I will be with you." That is enough.

Are we at burning bushes in our lives? Is God calling us to do something for Him? It's natural for us to be aware of our inadequacies and our lack of experience. Like Moses, we may ask, "Who am I?" God will be patient to hear our reservations. But in the end, He will ask us to trust Him. When Moses reminded God that he was not a very good speaker, God asked him, "Who made your mouth?"

When God gives us a task, He promises two things: "I will be with you. I will give you what you need to do the task."

In the face of those two strong promises, our only response should be, "Yes, Lord. I will do what You want me to do. I trust you to be with me."

✝

Making it personal: Is God calling you? What is your response? How will you trust Him and take the first step?

Prayer: Lord, I am not confident in my abilities to do what You call me to do. I choose to trust that You will be with me. Amen.

Read Exodus 3:1–4:17, the full story of God's call to Moses at the burning bush.

Who Am I, O Lord?

"Who am I, O Sovereign Lord, . . . that you have brought me this far? . . . For the sake of your promise and according to your will, you have done all these great things and have shown them to me. How great you are, O Sovereign Lord! There is no one like you." 2 Samuel 7:18-22

At first glance, the question King David asks in today's passage is identical to the one Moses asked in the previous meditation. But if we look closely, we'll see a world of difference in the attitudes of the two men.

Today's verses come from a conversation King David had with Nathan the prophet. Nathan came to the king with good news in two parts. First, God wanted to have a temple where His people could worship Him. Second, God promised He would establish David's "throne" (his kingdom) forever. David's response was a prayer of overwhelming gratitude and humility.

Moses asked "Who am I?" in reaction, in defiance. He focused on himself: "I'm not this" and "I can't do that." Moses was looking to duck responsibility. David asked "Who am I?" in humility, awed by God's greatness. The question here is similar to the one David expressed in another psalm: "When I look at the night sky and see the work of your fingers—the moon and the stars you have set in place—what are mortals that you should think of us, mere humans that you should care for us?" (Psalm 8:3-4).

Unlike Moses, David didn't look at his own inadequacies; he focused instead on God's greatness, His almighty power, His awesome miracles, His faithfulness to redeem His people, His promises. In that context, David had confidence and willingly accepted God's plan. The key difference is that David placed his confidence in who God is, not in his own human abilities.

✝

Making it personal: What is God calling you to do for Him? How will you trust in His character to help you fulfill that plan?

Prayer: *O Lord, I choose to trust in who You are rather than who I am. Amen.*

Read 2 Samuel 7:1-29 for the full story of David's response to God's plan for his life.

Practical Service to Others

Worry weighs a person down; an encouraging word cheers a person up. Proverbs 12:25

When we discover and accept God's love for us in Jesus, our fears are banished, allowing us to live with more freedom. Our existence inside the walls takes on a new excitement and purpose as we understand what God has done for us. Our outlook on our life's purpose changes like a compass whose needle was facing south but now points north. We migrate from a life of self-centered fear to a life of service. As a result, fears evaporate. Our lives become a mirror of Christ's as we forget ourselves and begin to pour out our life's energy into others who have yet to discover the Savior's love and its power over fear.

But what does that new life look like? What are the practical ways to show Christ's love to others in prison?

How many inmates around us cannot read or write? Do they need a stamp? Or paper? Can we write to their children for them?

If we are in a women's facility, how can we offer a word of encouragement to the new numbers who arrive daily? Do they need simple things like shampoo, deodorant, or toothpaste? Offering to braid a woman's hair makes her feel a little more human. Each time we share our lives with others, we not only cheer up a person but also show Christ's love. We become Christ's face and hands and voice to that person. As we pour our lives into others, we will experience joy and a sense of meaning that may have never existed before prison. But, more important, we help these men and women accept forgiveness for their past, make peace with their present, and discover hope for the future. Jesus' life was spent showing kindness and mercy to others. We can do it too.

✝

Making it personal: Who needs an encouraging word in your pod today? Who needs a kind touch? What will you do about it?

Prayer: Lord, because You first loved me, I can love others in Your name. Show me who needs to see You through my practical service today. Amen.

Read and memorize Ephesians 4:32, using it as a motto for your service this week.

The Most Unlikely People

In the same way, was not even Rahab the prostitute considered righteous for what she did when she gave lodging to the spies and sent them off in a different direction? James 2:25, NIV

Think back on how we all felt the day we realized we had committed a crime that would send us to prison. The feelings of failure and shame that followed us into prison sometimes make us quietly cry into our pillows after our cellie is asleep. We wonder, *Can God give a person like me worth and value?*

The book of Joshua tells the story of how Joshua sent spies into the city of Jericho to check out the enemies the Israelites would face when they attacked the city. The spies dressed like the people of Jericho and stayed with a woman named Rahab, a prostitute. More than likely, the spies picked up lots of gossip as customers waited at the brothel. But when the king found out the spies were in the city, their lives were in danger. Sensing that the spies were men sent from God, Rahab risked her life and hid the men, asking in return that the Israelites would protect her and her family. When Jericho was later attacked, only Rahab and her family were saved.

Rahab lived with the Israelites and married. She ultimately bore a son named Salmon, who was in the lineage of Jesus Himself. Think about that—a hooker in Jesus' family tree! The point of this story is not to sensationalize or condone prostitution but to show that God includes the most unlikely people in His plans. God gives purpose to people the world has forgotten. Know anyone like that?

As we experience the consequences of what we have done, we can look to the story of Rahab for encouragement. God loves us and will take our lives, however broken, and use them for His purposes. Nothing is impossible with God.

†

Making it personal: How can you offer yourself to God, asking Him to include you in His plans?

Prayer: Thanks, God, that You use unlikely people for Your good purposes. Take my life, and make it count. Amen.

Read Joshua 2:1-21 for the exciting story of how Rahab risked her life for God's people.

Only God Can Save

There is salvation in no one else! There is no other name in all of heaven for people to call on to save them. Acts 4:12

Burnout—feeling drained and exhausted—is a common problem among Christians who work inside prisons and among inmate believers.

Society craves results. We want to see the results of our efforts immediately. Instant gratification isn't fast enough! When we give our lives to Christ and are His face and hands to the inmate population, we get anxious for results too. We have experienced the joy that forgiveness brings and long to share that news with others. We demonstrate the happiness we experience, but we often feel as if we are watering a rock—nothing ever grows out of our efforts. So we struggle on, sharing and witnessing, only to get discouraged when not one of the people we talk to comes to chapel or Bible study. We become weary when we see people begin to get the message but then fall down and go back to their old ways. We beat ourselves up. We imagine that if we had just gone to their cells one more time, they would not have fallen. We are self-centered, missing the mark and beginning to burn out.

We are self-centered in that we take too much ownership of the salvation process. Only God's Spirit can draw someone to Christ. We must never forget that "those who take the blame when God fails to act in a person's life are likely to take the credit when He does."[15] Our job is to be faithful to Jesus. We are never going to hear God say to us, "Welcome good and *successful* servant." God wants to say, "Welcome good and *faithful* servant."

So, move through the crowds of men and women on the yard with a light heart. Our responsibility is not to save anyone, only to be God's messenger. Only God can save.

✝

Making it personal: Are you approaching burnout by taking too much responsibility for saving people? What step will you take today to change that?

Prayer: Lord, let me rest easy in Your arms, knowing You are the One who saves. Amen.

Read 1 Corinthians 3:6-9 to see who is really responsible for making the seed grow for a person's salvation.

Pay It Forward

You were [God's] enemies, separated from him by your evil thoughts and actions, yet now he has brought you back as his friends. He has done this through his death on the cross in his own human body. Colossians 1:21-22

A popular phrase that has found its way onto bumper stickers encourages people to "Practice random acts of kindness and senseless acts of beauty." Many people have taken this to heart. Sometimes people pay the toll for the car behind them at a tollbooth. Others anonymously pay the restaurant check for a table of people they don't know. This type of kindness creates a sudden burst of joy and unanticipated pleasure. It's been documented that those who receive this surprising kindness often go on to offer kindness and thoughtfulness to others in response. They cannot pay back their debt to the giver, so they shower someone else with unexpected generosity—they "pay it forward."

Have we ever considered that God did exactly this for us when He sent Jesus to die for our sins? We were God's enemies, but He made us to be His friends through Christ's death on the cross. Christ paid the debt for our failings. He paid our toll. He picked up our check.

How do we respond? When we understand the enormous gift that God "paid forward" for us, our eyes are opened to the massive sacrifice of God's grace and we experience transformation in our hearts. We clean up our personal lives, not because we are being restrained by legalistic rules and regulations, but because we are so grateful. We start to perceive others as needy and ourselves as God's ambassadors to them. Our actions change as our hearts transform in recognition of God's gift, and we begin to "pay it forward" ourselves. We define our lives in terms of helping others who are hurting. We respond to God's love with love. We pay it forward, in Jesus' name.

✝

Making it personal: How can you gratefully respond to God's gift of salvation by paying it forward? Who needs your love and care?

Prayer: Lord God, help me love others as You love me. Amen.

Read 1 Corinthians 13, the classic chapter about love.

Become a Barnabas

Then Barnabas took [Saul] under his wing. He introduced him to the apostles and stood up for him, told them how Saul had seen and spoken to the Master on the Damascus Road and how in Damascus itself he had laid his life on the line with his bold preaching in Jesus' name. Acts 9:27, THE MESSAGE

Barnabas was one of the most admirable characters in the Bible. His name means "Son of Encouragement." He was generous to those in need (see Acts 4:36-37). He was open-minded, gladly taking a chance on Saul. Barnabas brought Saul to the other disciples, giving him "street cred" with them. Later, Barnabas came to the defense of John Mark, a young disciple whom Paul didn't trust. Barnabas even interrupted his travels with Paul to stand with this young man who needed someone (see Acts 15:36-41). Barnabas always thought good thoughts about people.

Some of us have experienced the encouragement of a Barnabas when we felt the world was caving in. We understand the wonderful feeling of having someone speak up for us when we needed it. If we haven't, we certainly long for someone like that in our lives. When we arrive at a new facility or transfer into a new living unit, having somebody to stand with us can make the transition smoother.

How can we be a Barnabas inside the facility? New numbers come into the reception unit every day. The gangs are immediately trying to recruit them as new members. New fish need a trusted inmate to step forward and offer them a hand of friendship that does not involve bondage to someone who will use them. We can be the encouragers in our facilities. We can be the people who make a difference in others' lives. By being the hands and face of Christ to those in need of an encouraging word, we serve Christ in a huge and significant way.

†

Making it personal: Adopt the Barnabas attitude. Find and encourage a needy con today.

Prayer: Jesus, show me the needy people in the pod today. Give me courage to speak to them. Amen.

Read Acts 4:36-37 and Acts 15:36-41 for the story about Barnabas.

God's Amazing Grace

God put His love on the line for us by offering his Son in sacrificial death while we were of no use whatever to him. Romans 5:8, THE MESSAGE

In a few Midwest prisons, a handful of cons in each facility practice something called James Ministry, named after the apostle James, who says in his letter: "Suppose you see a brother or sister who has no food or clothing, and you say, 'Good-bye and have a good day; stay warm and eat well'—but then you don't give that person any food or clothing. What good does that do?" (James 2:15-16). A volunteer provides the funds that allow Christian inmates to give a bag of hygiene items to new numbers or regressed inmates who arrive in the facility without anything. The inmates demand nothing in return. Later, the new fish come by, wondering why the cons would give to them, without strings attached. The Christians are then able to share the wonderful message of God's grace. When the new inmates hear and understand the Christian inmates did it because God did it for them, the new fish are often open to God's grace and salvation.

Grace is God's "undeserved kindness" given to us. God sent Jesus to pay the debt for our sin. We don't deserve this kindness; we can do nothing to earn it. Other religions require people to do something to earn their gods' favor. This creates an atmosphere of guilt, breeding a counterfeit lifestyle based on behavior and leads to frustration when people's recurring sins continue to haunt them.

God's free gift to us is not based on what we do. Grace produces a life of trust and security. Salvation based on grace allows us to come to God in humble repentance, without fear of rejection. When we receive God's grace, we are motivated to dedicate our lives in service to God—by choice, not by obligation.

†

Making it personal: How can you be like the people in the James Ministry, passing on God's grace and kindness to others?

Prayer: Father God, I would like to be an instrument of Your grace in my facility. Show me who needs Your love. Amen.

Read Romans 6:1-17 to discover more about God's incredible gift to you.

Work That Refreshes

The generous prosper and are satisfied; those who refresh others will themselves be refreshed. Proverbs 11:25

True freedom and purpose in prison are found in the truth in today's verse. As we're generous toward others with our time, we will be refreshed in ways we never thought possible. This may seem like a foolish thought because serving others in prison goes against the convict code. Most of us have lived self-centered lives, wanting others to serve us. However, as we grow in wisdom, we learn that our self-centeredness leaves us dissatisfied, unhappy, and lonely.

Jesus showed us another way. He lived only for others. His life was and is dedicated to serving others—the forgotten ones, the weak ones, the discarded ones. He invites us to do the same.

Today's verse reminds us that when we are generous with ourselves and serve others, we are refreshed by our work, not depleted.

When we look around the unit, we see men or women who are struggling. On the way to chow, we can walk alongside them and ask them if they would like to join us. They may be suspicious at first, but deep down, they will be grateful. When we invest in the lives of others, we discover that we have something valuable inside that they need. When we pour ourselves into other people, the power of the Holy Spirit will flow through us. We will not suffer exhaustion; the incredible power of God will strengthen us. We will move smoothly back to our houses as if we are flying on the wings of God's love.

This secret is reserved for those who acquire godly wisdom. Understanding that the work of God is a source of change, purpose, and incredible energy is a gift more precious than any contraband.

✝

Making it personal: Who is God calling you to serve? In what specific way will you serve that person this week?

Prayer: Lord, I want to serve You, but I need Your grace. This is dangerous stuff. I need Your strength and courage to be generous with others. Amen.

Read Joshua 24:14-24, and choose to serve the Lord.

Old Numbers—Take Heart!

Even when I am old and gray, do not forsake me, O God, till I declare your power to the next generation, your might to all who are to come. Psalm 71:18, NIV

Many of us are growing old in prison. Some of us came to prison when we were already over fifty. Some were sentenced to life without parole. The years march forward, and we discover what life without parole means—life and death in prison. There's a real danger to our souls when we realize this fact.

Depression often accompanies advancing years. We realize we've missed weddings, baptisms, ball games, funerals, and other events that make life so rich. We see our childbearing years evaporate with time. We suffer the anguish of our actions along with the fears, insecurity, loneliness, and worries as we age.

The writer of today's passage realized what was important: even though we age, God isn't finished with us yet. The psalmist wanted to live long enough to declare God to the younger generations.

Instead of thinking that we are washed up because we are older, we need to realize that our years have given us valuable insights and experience we can share with the next generation. We are valuable *because* of our age, not in spite of it.

How can we have an influence on the next generation? Many of us want to tell our stories to young men and women to help them avoid prison. Why not look around at the younger cons who feel helpless but are afraid to show it. We can mentor them and speak wisdom into their lives.

What about our own families? Even though we're behind bars, our new gentleness and humility will have a positive influence on our children, nieces and nephews, and grandchildren. We can write them, sharing God's activity in our lives, encouraging them to give their lives to Christ.

✝

Making it personal: How will you reach out to share about God's power to the next generation?

Prayer: God, help me even in my advanced years to build Your kingdom. Show me the work You have for me to do. Amen.

Read Psalm 103 for encouragement.

Old-Number Power

Command [those who are rich] to do good, to be rich in good deeds, and to be generous and willing to share. 1 Timothy 6:18, NIV

Our culture tells us that money is power. Rich people can do almost anything they choose. They can choose to use their wealth for themselves or for others, for good or for evil.

But we aren't wealthy. We aren't rich. In the world's eyes. We're the world's garbage, the empty beer can to be tossed away. Does today's verse have meaning or application to us in prison? What lessons can we take from this passage?

Wealth doesn't always take the form of money. In prison, riches have many different forms. Strength and celebrity are types of currency. Being an old number is another. For when we are old numbers, we have the respect of the new fish and younger cons. If our old numbers are associated with a capital crime, our prestige and status inside the joint actually increases. What will we do with this wealth?

Just as persons of means on the outside have to choose what they will do with what they have, we also have to decide how to use the power of being an old number. We have the influence to manipulate weaker, younger inmates into doing whatever we want them to do. That might be sexual favors or other violent or risky things. Or, we can use our stature to show these men and women a better way to live. We can instruct them how to do *HIS* time, to do life that leads to life with God forever. When we choose to spend our currency on God's things, we are putting away treasure in the Bank of God. When we help others, we help ourselves (see Proverbs 11:25). We must use our riches for God's glory and His work. We must avoid the temptations to do otherwise.

✝

Making it personal: What riches do you have? How are you spending those riches inside the walls?

Prayer: Father God, show us how can we best use our rich gifts for the people around us and Your work. Amen.

Read Jeremiah 9:23-24 and **1 Timothy 6:17-19** for thoughts about wealth and what to do with it.

Be Willing to Serve

While Peter was still thinking about the vision, the Spirit said to him, "Simon, three men are looking for you. So get up and go downstairs. Do not hesitate to go with them, for I have sent them." Acts 10:19-20, NIV

In prison, feelings of inadequacy are as common as losing gamblers in Las Vegas. We have hurt those who loved, trusted, and depended on us. Serving Christ by serving others sounds good to us, but we doubt if we have the substance to do it. We observe other better-educated inmates and church leaders and feel insufficient when we compare ourselves to them. We are not sure we have the godly wisdom needed to serve. How do we go about getting it?

The first step is to stop comparing ourselves with others. God is not concerned with our *ability*, but with our *availability*. Our duty is to be on hand for Him to work through us. God knows who needs our help. He will direct them to us.

Peter didn't know the three men who were at his front door, but God had plans for them, and He needed Peter's help. Peter greeted the men and made them feel at home. He treated them like guests. He poured himself into them. God directed these men to Peter. Peter did not have to go out searching for them. He only had to be obedient when God sent them to him.

God works the same way today. Our willingness to serve our fellow inmates is what God requires. If we *will* to do *His will*, we find out what God wants us to do. He will lead His hurting sheep right to our cells. Prepare by cultivating a soft heart and a sensitive spirit that feels God's touch when He gently points out men or women in need. We can welcome them, share canteen, make them feel at home, and listen to them. Our kindness will demonstrate the gentleness of Jesus. God will lend a hand with the rest.

†

Making it personal: In what specific ways are you willing to serve others? Trust God to lead you to the right people.

Prayer: Father God, send Your sheep to me, and give me eyes to see them and a heart to help them. Amen.

Read Acts 10 for the full story of God's plans for Peter.

Does Jesus' Life Make a Difference?

"Lord, when did we ever see you hungry or thirsty or a stranger or naked or sick or in prison, and not help you?" And he will answer, "I assure you, when you refused to help the least of these my brothers and sisters, you were refusing to help me." Matthew 25:44-45

Today's passage is very clear. When Jesus comes to judge us, He will use a simple test. It will consist of how we treated His people who were hungry, thirsty, sick, in need of shelter and clothing, or in prison. Note: Jesus doesn't mention how many times we were in church, the amount of money we contributed, or whether we believed all the correct doctrines. What He says matters most is how we loved—or didn't love—the least of these, His brothers and sisters.

Henry Drummond, in his great essay on 1 Corinthians 13, states that the final test of our religion will be love. The evidence will demonstrate how we fulfilled the simplest charities of life. Nowhere are sins of pride mentioned or the achievements of wonderful evangelical endeavors. What matters most to Jesus is how we loved our fellow human beings.

Why is this so crucial? Drummond points out that "the withholding of love is the negation of the spirit of Christ, the proof that we never knew Him, that for us He lived in vain."[16] If we truly know Jesus, we're transformed into His likeness. We'll feel compassion for the sick, the hungry, the stranger, the thirsty, and those in prison. Without that compassion welling up inside of us and translating into concrete action toward these specific people, the Spirit of Jesus is not in us.

> I lived for myself, I thought for myself,
> For myself, and none beside—
> Just as if Jesus had never lived,
> As if He had never died.[17]

✝

Making it personal: Take a look at your life. Are you living as if Jesus never died? What will you do to change?

Prayer: Jesus, I am selfish, living for myself. Help me live as You did—for others. Amen.

Read 1 Corinthians 13, again and again—and yet again.

The Weak and Forgotten

Each time [the Lord] said, "My gracious favor is all you need. My power works best in your weakness." So now I am glad to boast about my weakness, so that the power of Christ may work through me. 2 Corinthians 12:9

When God selected David to be the king of Israel, He broke the rules of society. In Israel, the eldest son was the heir apparent of the family. David was son number eight and so irrelevant that David's father hadn't even brought him to Samuel when he was looking for a new king.

But David mattered to God. God loves to give value to the things that the world throws away to demonstrate His power and to work His will. Many times in the Bible we see that God chose the people who didn't matter much in society. God chooses people in spite of their weaknesses.

Sometimes we think that we cannot possibly matter to God. How could He find us valuable? Thoughts of worthlessness are everywhere in prison, as common as lousy food, bad haircuts, and hard beds. These feelings seemed to be handed out along with the prison clothes issued at Evans Correctional Institution or Arizona State Prison Complex in Yuma. But that way of thinking is not accurate. God can transform us. He can redeem our weakness for His work.

Inmates are always watching other inmates. When a con with a long stretch walks her talk and lives a life that is outwardly sincere, other inmates notice. First impressions die, and a reputation for integrity builds. What better counselor to speak to another woman who is feeling worthless than one who has *felt* worthless? Worthless, until she found significance in Christ! Who better to encourage a woman or man who is struggling with sexual sin than someone who found freedom from the same temptation?

When other cons see our real joy, backed up with our real walk, they will be attracted to the God who gives us worth.

✝

Making it personal: Self-pity sometimes feels pretty good. Are you willing to let it go and serve God? What will it take for you to begin?

Prayer: Lord, I want to serve You and be Your representative to hurting people in prison. Give me Your grace. Amen.

Read Hebrews 11, how God chose people in spite of weaknesses.

Taking on the Leadership Role

Now that my servant Moses is dead, you [Joshua] must lead my people across the Jordan River into the land I am giving them. Joshua 1:2

Leaders are very important. They plan activities and keep organizations focused. When leaders die or retire, they leave an empty space unless new leaders are ready to take over. Think about how the prison church would function if the chaplain retired or moved to another facility. How would the church body operate if the strong Christian inmate leaders were paroled or shipped out to Virginia or Texas? Does the Lord want to train us for new leadership? Are we prepared for that role? Our lives must demonstrate several character qualities if we want to consider moving into a leadership role.

First, we must have humble spirits and be willing to be trained. Second, we must love God and all His children. This would be evident to everyone through our actions toward others, inside and outside of the church body. Third, we need a powerful prayer life. God's servant-leaders depend on Him for strength and guidance, especially when times get tough. God will guide us when we listen and talk with Him through prayer. Fourth, it is critical for us to spend consistent and lengthy time in the Word of God. In the Bible we discover His course for our leadership.

Finally, we must feel God's call. God's call is the sense in our hearts that God is demanding our obedience to His request to shoulder the burden of leadership. Although God's call is specific and clear, it must be confirmed by other Christians through prayer (see Matthew 18:19; 1 John 4:1). If we feel that God may be calling us, we should talk with mature believers about our potential for leadership. Then, if we sense the call and others confirm it, we need to obey the call and take up responsibilities as leaders.

†

Making it personal: How does your character stack up against the checklist above? How might God be calling you to a leadership role?

Prayer: Lord, what do You want me to do? If You call, I am willing to be trained and to serve. Make Your will clear. Amen.

Read Joshua 1:1-5 about God's promise to Joshua; use verse 5 as a daily reminder.

Marching Orders

Be strong and very courageous. Obey all the laws Moses gave you. Do not turn away from them, and you will be successful in everything you do. Joshua 1:7

We can learn what God says about leadership by looking at Joshua. After Moses died, God gave marching orders to Joshua, the new leader.

God told Joshua *to be strong and very courageous.* This command demanded action. As partners with God in accomplishing His goals, we must do our part, especially as leaders. The prison church cannot simply leave it up to God and sit back and expect things to get done. And, we must anticipate opposition. God told Joshua then—and He tells us now—that times will get tough. We will need courage and strength. Even so, we have to share in the work of God's divine purposes.

God told Joshua *to obey all His laws.* God gives us wisdom in His Word, in passages such as the Ten Commandments, the Beatitudes, and the other teachings of Christ. For God to work through us, we need to stand for His guidelines. Then, we need to teach and encourage others to follow God's path and faithfully obey those instructions.

God told Joshua *not to turn away from His teachings.* God instructs us to be unwavering and committed to the right path. One essential role of church leaders is keeping God's people on the straight and narrow road. Accomplishments achieved by empty, trendy preaching or gimmicks never bring about God's divine purposes. For example, if leaders promised to distribute crack cocaine at every service, the chapel would be packed. But that gimmick would seriously damage the purpose of true worship. Holy purposes are never accomplished by ungodly methods. Leaders must show integrity not only in their intentions but also in their methods and their personal walk.

✝

Making it personal: As a potential leader, how will you accept and live with God's marching orders?

Prayer: God, I want to be strong and courageous for You. Help me to love Your wisdom and not fall away from Your guidelines—under any circumstances. In Your strength, amen.

Read Joshua chapter 1 to discover God's formula for success.

Godly Service

These questions relate to the meditations found on pages 228-247:

Discuss together:

1. Remember the Firestone advertising catchphrase "Where the rubber meets the road"? Today, that phrase means where your *walk* meets your *talk*. How should accepting God's grace translate into godly service in prison? Describe a few examples of what a "cup of cold water" might look like in your prison.

2. What are the enemies of godly service? What excuses do inmates commonly use to avoid serving others? How often do self-centeredness and fear influence you in dodging service to others? Give some illustrations of where anxiety or prejudice might hinder God's effort to work through you. What will defeat those excuses?

3. Growing old in prison can be a gift from God. What are the advantages of being an older con? Describe three circumstances in which age could be used for God's glory. Why is authenticity so respected in prison? How do age and authenticity often go hand in hand? How could fear of rejection fade as you grow older?

4. Actions have consequences. Share a story of when someone's positive or negative actions affected your life. How have you learned from that event? What does the term "ripple effects" mean as you reflect on your life? Consider what "ripple effects" God could work through your godly service, both immediately and in the future. What comes to mind as you contemplate this?

Explore God's Word together:

1. **Job 12:12** is a true statement about wisdom and age. Why are age and wisdom linked here? Why does wisdom come with age and experience? From what things does age free you so that you might better perform godly service? What specific groups in prison might benefit from this freedom to serve?

2. In **Romans 12:3** Paul warns about arrogance while serving. How can pride tarnish godly service? What steps can you take to guard against an outbreak of self-importance? What would you consider to be the indicators of humble service to God?

3. **1 Chronicles 29:6-14** describes a scene in which the leaders of Israel gave freely and generously. What was the effect on the ordinary citizens of Israel? What was King David's reaction to this outpouring of generosity? How does this passage speak to your willingness to serve? How will it influence your service in the future?

Pray together:

1. Pray for the willingness to serve with grace and humility.

2. Pray that the Holy Spirit will fill you with courage and clarity about what needs to be done.

3. Pray that God's love will flow through you as you represent Him to the searching souls in your facility.

Commit to **confidentiality** …

… **respect** each other

… **pray** for each other

… **encourage** one another

… **hold** each other **accountable**

Prayer for Godly Service

*As I contemplate Your sacrifice on the
cross for my sin, I want to serve You inside
this prison. But my fear overwhelms me as
I watch the gangs take revenge on those
who break ranks and declare a new life for You.
I am scared, Lord, and need Your power to
step out in boldness for my newfound life.*

*Help me, Lord, not to fear those who will
remind me of my old life of turning tricks
and selling myself when I was a lost soul.
Father God, give me the strength to
really believe that I am a new creature
and not the dirty, smelly one that You found
and hosed off with Your blood on that cross.*

*Father God, as I walk around the yard,
give me eyes to see hurting people and
ears to hear their cries.
Lord, give me the will and courage to step up,
as You did for me,
and help them with their hurts.*

*Give me the words to say, the ability to listen
and not judge as I move into areas that are
not permitted by the convict code. Lord, I trust You
to empower me and to protect me.*

Amen.

✝

Notes

1. Bill Bright, "The Four Spiritual Laws" (Orlando, Fla.: NewLife Publications, 1994).

2. Helen Wodehouse, quoted in *The Choice Is Always Ours,* Dorothy Berkeley Phillips, ed. (New York: Richard R. Smith, 1948), 44, emphasis added.

3. Henry Drummond, "The Three Facts of Sin," *The Ideal Life* (London: Collins, 1970), 196.

4. C. S. Lewis, *Mere Christianity* (New York: Touchstone, 1943), 110.

5. *The Interpreter's Bible*, vol. 9 (Nashville: Abingdon Press, 1950), 402.

6. Lewis, *Mere Christianity*, 58.

7. Henry Drummond, "The Programme of Christianity," *The Greatest Thing in the World and 21 Other Essays* (London: Collins, 1970), 75.

8. *Jubilee*, Prison Fellowship Ministries, 2001

9. Illustration from Dr. Timothy Keller, Redeemer Presbyterian Church, New York City, New York, January 2005.

10. Lewis, *Mere Christianity*, 56.

11. Oswald Chambers, *My Utmost for His Highest* (New York: Dodd, Mead & Company, 1935), March 28.

12. "Strife in Heaven," a story told in Henry Drummond, *The Greatest Thing in the World*, 150.

13. Lewis, *Mere Christianity*, 117.

14. Martin Luther King Jr., "I Have a Dream," speech delivered on August 28, 1963.

15. Bishop Frank Costantino, Good News Jail & Prison Ministry Annual Conference Keynote Speech, June 2003.

16. Henry Drummond, *The Greatest Thing in the World*, 64.

17. Ibid.

Index of Scripture Passages in Meditations

With Gratitude

Writing a book is a daunting undertaking, as any author will admit. When someone begins writing a book without any experience, it is less intimidating because "ignorance is bliss." It is a bit like marriage or raising children. God blesses us with little foreknowledge about these activities, so we move into them with high hopes and enthusiasm born of being completely unaware of the enormous challenges and reality of our endeavors.

This is the mind-set that I brought to the writing of *Doing HIS Time* in June of 1999. Having a firm conviction that the Holy Spirit called me to write a devotional that spoke uniquely to men and women who are incarcerated, I launched ahead but soon was surprised by the enormity of the task.

How the Holy Spirit would use this book for His Kingdom after it was published in March 2008 was also astonishing. Since that date, the Holy Spirit has led us to give away more than 300,000 copies, in more than 35 countries, and in eight languages. This 2014 revised edition, with added meditations and study guides, is dedicated to the Holy Spirit. We anticipate His leading again to give away thousands of copies anywhere He asks us to send them.

So, considering all of this, I extend humble gratitude to the people and the written works that influenced my writing and contributed so much to the book's form, clarity, substance, and completion.

T*he Interpreter's Bible* shed light on many meditations in this book. Now out of print, these volumes were written in 1950 by the theological "Wise Men" of their day. C. S. Lewis' *Mere Christianity* and Henry Drummond's essays also influenced this devotional.

Dr. Timothy J. Keller, senior pastor of Redeemer Presbyterian Church in New York City, contributed to this devotional through his many sermons and insights that I absorbed while attending the church and by listening to podcasts. For any thoughts, spiritual insights, or examples that seem familiar to those who listen regularly to Dr. Keller but are not attributed directly to him, I apologize. I also thank Dr. Tremper Longman III and Dr. Dan Allender, who were available when I needed a colorful phrase to make a point.

Much love to Chaplain June Hendricks of the Limon Correctional Facility. Chaplain June is a prayer warrior and spiritual mother. Thanks also to Howard and Connie Waller of Set Free Ministries and Bear Valley Church. They have been friends, supporters, and trusted confidants for the entire span of my prison ministry experience.

I am grateful for my inmate friends who read and reread the draft copy for accuracy in the depiction of the prison culture. Richard Duran spent hours giving me invaluable insights and corrections. Thanks also to Monir Wood, the man with the anointed smile; to John E. Lopez, the "Paul behind Walls"; to Wilson Lopez; to Adam Thompson, the quiet, persistent "James minister." A special thanks to Tim Callis, a longtime Christian brother who has gone over and over the manuscript with me by phone and through the mail. His help has been invaluable as he consulted with many others in his living unit to make the devotional authentic. In addition, Tim Callis recruited Michael Stillwell, Jason Burkholder, and William Paxton to read and contribute their authentic insights, edits, and affirmations to the devotional. Without these "insiders," we would be guessing as to how the meditations would be received.

Thanks to Chris Mays and his wife, Suzy Rader Mays, two warriors for Christ. They edited the book while Chris was inside, and now, upon his release, they operate Doing HIS Time Prison Ministry in Denver, Colorado. Our lives have been intertwined by the Holy Spirit for purposes we could never have imagined.

Many thanks to Robert Baillie, Ricky Servine, Carlos Marquez, Arthur Urrutia, Robert Wilner, and "Paco" Castillo for your encouraging words and for helping me keep the book real. Also, the feedback, insights, and encouragement from former inmates Cynthia Feagin, Marta Ulen, Lisa Cotter, and Caroline Taito were enormously helpful to make the book relate to women inside the walls. Joanne Neidiffer, and Candace Pete of Central California Women's Facility also gave many honest and invaluable insights.

I want to be sure to thank Mel Goebel, president of Daughters of Destiny, my friend and prison mentor. Mel's love for Jesus and passion for those in prison is infectious. He has been my prison brother since 1988. Also, Harry Greene, former president of Good News Jail & Prison Ministry, influenced the book with his experiential insights. Thanks to Clint Pollard, who was very helpful in sharing his real-life prison experiences that found their way into this book. The late Chuck Colson's advice, counsel, tough words, and friendship were akin to a father's. I am grateful to him for writing Born Again, the book that started my walk toward prison ministry in 1987.

Most important, deep thanks to Lynn Vanderzalm, editor and trusted friend. We came together through the hand of the Holy Spirit. Several years into the writing, I felt the need for direction and guidance to make this book better. So I began to pray. I asked the Holy Spirit to send an experienced editor. For eight months there was no answer. Then someone gave me a copy of Josh McDowell's book *Beyond Belief to Convictions*. As I read the acknowledgments in that fine book, the name of his editor, Lynn Vanderzalm, popped out. It was as if the Holy Spirit had pushed me physically. I heard the Spirit say, "There she is. That is your editor."

I wrote to Lynn, asking her to consider taking on this project, independent of her duties as a senior editor at Tyndale House Publishers. About a month later, Lynn called to say that she could help me strengthen the book. When we began to talk about our personal lives, Lynn mentioned that she was from Holland, Michigan, and that she had attended Holland Christian High School and Calvin College in Grand Rapids, Michigan.

We knew we were meant to collaborate when I informed her that I also had been born in Holland, Michigan and that I had graduated from the same two schools. From that time, Lynn took artistic control of the book and has made incalculable improvements to the book's form, substance, and style. She also wrote nearly 40 of the meditations. If the Holy Spirit had not put us together, I doubt that this devotional would have been published.

Thanks to Anna Piro for her design skill, which has enriched this edition of the book. I am grateful also to Carol Teegarden for her invaluable skill in copyediting and proofreading this book.

Thanks most of all to the Holy Spirit for the intimate promptings and faithful guidance throughout the long process of writing this book. Thank You for teaching everyone involved so much during this time together.

And finally, thanks to Mary Beth, my wife since 1972. Thank you for the feminine touch you have brought to my life, for your loyalty, spiritual insights, faithfulness, and love—through good times and bad. Thanks, too, for allowing me the quiet time to finish this book without a deadline. I love you dearly!

Our prayers are that this book will be a blessing to everyone who reads it. All the praise belongs to God. All mistakes are mine.

In HIS Service,
James C. Vogelzang
Doing HIS Time Prison Ministry
2014

About the Authors

James C. Vogelzang spent thirty years in the investment-management marketing business before being led to start Doing HIS Time Prison Ministry in 1999. The ministry serves inmates and their families through the reintegration ministry of **72-Hour Fund** and the transportation program called **Barn-A-Bus.** Jim and his wife, Mary Beth, live in California and have two grown daughters.

Lynn Vanderzalm was first involved with prison ministry when her husband worked as a pre-release counselor in a maximum-security prison. Since that time she has worked as an educator, editor, and writer and has published two books, one of them a devotional. She currently shares in her husband's ministry to the poor around the world. Lynn and her husband, Bas, live in Oregon and have two married children.

The authors welcome your feedback, letters, and testimonies. Please understand, however, that due to the volume of mail, a personal response is not possible. Please do not be offended if we cannot answer your personal letters, but know we enjoy them and value them greatly!

Additional Copies of *Doing HIS Time*

Inmates and chaplains: Doing HIS Time Prison Ministry welcomes individual requests for additional copies of this book. Inmates are encouraged to talk with their chaplains, who can order cases of books at www.doinghistime.org at no charge.

Others can order individual copies at www.amazon.com.

Doing HIS Time Available in Other Languages

Doing HIS Time is currently translated into several languages. In addition to the Spanish version, *Cumpliendo SU tiempo, Meditaciones y Oraciones para Hombres y Mujeres en la Prision,* the devotional has been translated into Thai, Bantu (for Uganda, Burundi, and Rwanda), Telugu (for India), Cebuano and Tagalog (for the Philippines), and Mandarin (for Hong Kong, Macau, and Singapore).

In Memoriam

William Vogelzang

1921–2013

"A Life Well Lived"

"How excellent is thy lovingkindness, O God!
The children of men put their trust under the shadow of thy wings."
Psalm 36:7, KJV

My father, Bill, lived a life that followed Jesus. It was a life highlighted by a warm personality, ready smile, and gracious spirit. He taught me the power of prayer, hard work, and reliance on God, although it took a few years to sink in. He visited prisons with me and distributed this devotional to all of his friends. His hard work left a significant inheritance, which is dedicated to paying for the printing, translation, and distribution of the 2014 revised, study guide edition of this book.

Thank you, Dad. You are missed!

About Doing HIS Time
Prison Ministry
"Kneeling With Those Who've Stumbled"™

Doing HIS Time Prison Ministry, founded in 1999 by James C. Vogelzang, is a Christ-centered ministry that is "the face and hands of Jesus" to inmates, ex-offenders, and their families. Three ministries facilitate this mission:

72-Hour Fund: This ministry assists ex-offenders in Colorado with reintegration by providing, free of charge: clothes, bus tokens, hygiene items, backpacks, and help securing identification documents. Appointments upon release are recommended. Call 303-292-2304. People from all faiths are welcome.

Barn-A-Bus: This transportation ministry offers low-cost round trips to most prisons in Colorado for families on visiting days. There is a regular schedule, and appointments are necessary. Please see the website (www.doinghistime.org) for exact scheduling information, or call 303-300-3670.

Doing HIS Time: Meditations and Prayers for Men and Women in Prison: This prison devotional is available free of charge to prisoners and chaplains worldwide. More than 300,000 copies have been given away in more than 35 countries, and the book has been translated into eight languages. Please view the book at www. amazon.com or www.doinghistime.org.

Doing HIS Time Prison Ministry
4045 Wadsworth Blvd., #310
Wheat Ridge, CO 80033

PO Box 1508
Wheat Ridge, CO 80034
303-292-2304

Doing HIS Time Ministry Headquarters
PO Box 91509
Santa Barbara, CA 93190
805-730-1700

www.doinghistime.org
info@doinghistime.org

Words of Blessing for You

*And I pray that Christ will be more and more
at home in your hearts as you trust in him.
May your roots go down deep into the
soil of God's marvelous love.
And may you have the power to understand,
as all God's people should,
how wide, how long, how high, and
how deep his love really is.*
Ephesians 3:17-18

✝

*May God give you peace, dear brothers and sisters,…
from God the Father and the Lord Jesus Christ.
May God's grace be upon
all who love our Lord Jesus Christ
with an undying love.*
Ephesians 6:23-24

✝

*And now, may the God of peace,
who brought again from the dead our Lord Jesus,
equip you with all you need for doing his will.
May he produce in you,
through the power of Jesus Christ,
all that is pleasing to him.…
To him be glory forever and ever. Amen.*
Hebrews 13:20-21